MANAGING TOURISM ENTERPRISES: START-UP, GROWTH AND RESILIENCE

MANAGING TOURISM ENTERPRISES: START-UP, GROWTH AND RESILIENCE

Rob Hallak and Craig Lee

CABI

CABI is a trading name of CAB International

CABI
Nosworthy Way
Wallingford
Oxfordshire OX10 8DE
UK

CABI
200 Portland Street
Boston
MA 02114
USA

Tel: +44 (0)1491 832111
E-mail: info@cabi.org
Website: www.cabi.org

Tel: +1 (617)682-9015
E-mail: cabi-nao@cabi.org

The views expressed in this publication are those of the author(s) and do not necessarily represent those of, and should not be attributed to, CAB International (CABI). Any images, figures and tables not otherwise attributed are the author(s)' own. References to internet websites (URLs) were accurate at the time of writing.
CAB International and, where different, the copyright owner shall not be liable for technical or other errors or omissions contained herein. The information is supplied without obligation and on the understanding that any person who acts upon it, or otherwise changes their position in reliance thereon, does so entirely at their own risk. Information supplied is neither intended nor implied to be a substitute for professional advice. The reader/user accepts all risks and responsibility for losses, damages, costs and other consequences resulting directly or indirectly from using this information.

CABI's Terms and Conditions, including its full disclaimer, may be found at https://www.cabi.org/terms-and-conditions/.

A catalogue record for this book is available from the British Library, London, UK.

ISBN-13: 9781789249422 (paperback)
         9781789249439 (ePDF)
         9781789249446 (ePub)

DOI: 10.1079/9781789249446.0000

Commissioning Editor: Claire Parfitt
Editorial Assistant: Lauren Davies
Production Editor: Marta Patiño

Typeset by SPi, Pondicherry, India

Contents

Supplementary materials for this book can be accessed via the QR code below.

1 Conceptual Foundations of Tourism Enterprises

> Small and medium tourism and hospitality businesses are the foundation of the tourism industry. They play a critical role in the supply of tourism and hospitality products and services, creating jobs in the tourism industry, building the experience and image of tourism destinations. (Fu *et al.*, 2019)

Introduction

This chapter provides an introduction to the concepts around small and medium tourism enterprises, presenting insights into business characteristics, owner motivations, and the broader context around global tourism and the role of independently owned businesses that represent the industry and play a critical role in tourism destinations. Despite the devastation of COVID-19, tourism is in revival and the performance of tourism businesses, along with the determination of the entrepreneurs who run them, is integral to a thriving and resilient industry.

Learning Outcomes

After completing this chapter, you should:

- Understand the importance of tourism firms in the success of tourism destinations
- Recognize the role of the entrepreneur in driving the performance of tourism enterprises
- Have learnt the definition and unique characteristics of tourism enterprises
- Understand the challenges experienced by tourism enterprises
- Recognize the opportunities for business success by building key capabilities in organizational operations and strategies.

© Rob Hallak and Craig Lee 2023. *Managing Tourism Enterprises: Start-up, Growth and Resilience* (R. Hallak and C. Lee)
DOI: 10.1079/9781789249446.0001

Tourism in a Post-COVID Environment

The idea of writing this book first came about before the COVID-19 pandemic of 2020. Globally, the number of international tourists had reached a record 1.46 billion in 2019 (UNWTO, 2020), with UNWTO forecasting an increase to 1.8 billion by 2030, driven by significant growth in Asia and the Pacific regions (UNWTO, 2017). Travel and tourism were among the world's largest industries generating US$9.2 trillion (Figures 1.1 and 1.2). Moreover, from 2014 to 2019 almost 25% of all global new jobs were created by travel and tourism with 54% of these jobs being occupied by women. Entrepreneurship was also flourishing with small and medium enterprises (SMEs) representing 80% of all businesses in the tourism industry (WTTC, 2021). Tourism was also leading the way in the implementation of new innovations and digital technologies. For example, wine tourism destinations began adopting AR and VR technology for branding, and experiential marketing, blockchain and cryptocurrency had become integrated in the tourism ecosystem with certain regional destinations accepting cryptocurrencies – via an innovative cryptocurrency point of sale (POS) system – as payment for tourism goods and services (Hallak *et al.*, 2019).

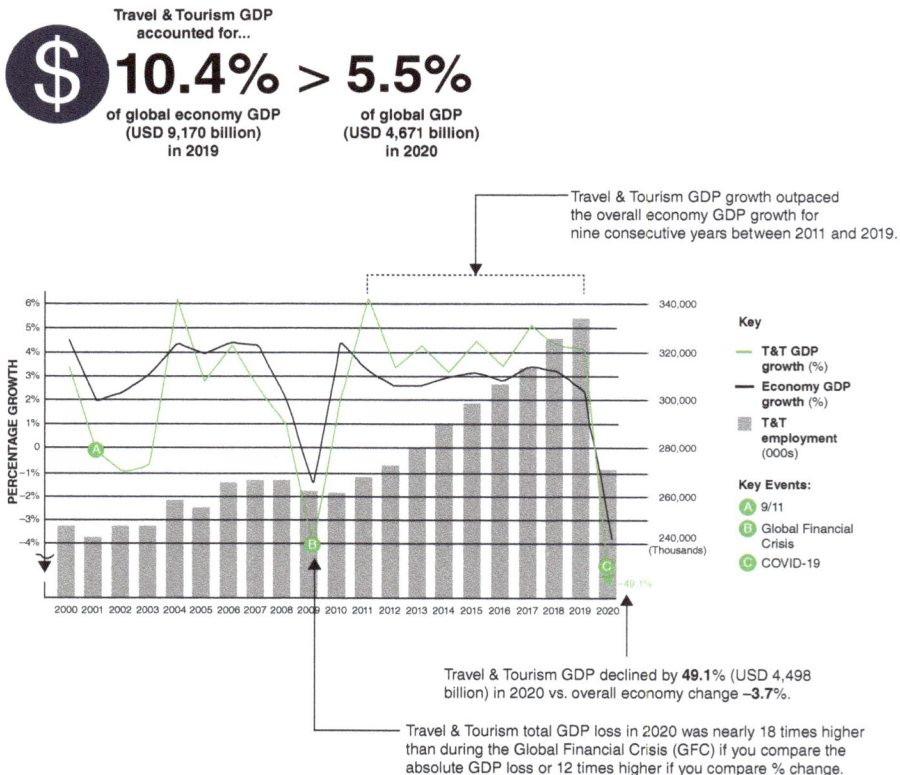

Figure 1.1 Travel and tourism GDP 2000–2020. (Source: WTTC, 2021, Licensed under the Attribution, Non-Commercial 4.0 International Creative Commons Licence.)

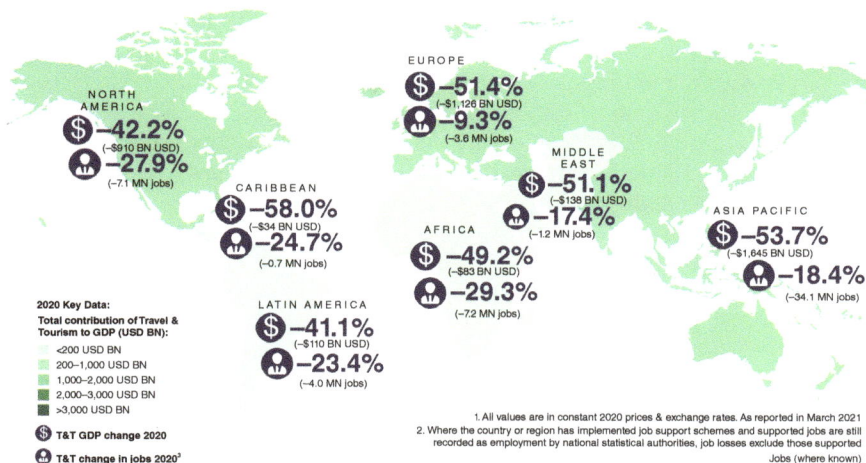

Figure 1.2. Regional performance 2020. (Source: WTTC, 2021, Licensed under the Attribution, Non-Commercial 4.0 International Creative Commons Licence.)

The pandemic of 2020 created a different landscape that put the brakes on the tourism juggernaut. Border closures, travel restrictions, event cancellations, lock-downs, social distancing measures, venue capacity limits, etc. caused an unprecedented impact on the tourism sector with small and medium enterprise bearing the full brunt. International travel declined by over 90% from the previous year with the sector incurring a US$4.5 trillion loss globally. In 2020, over 62 million tourism-related jobs were lost, although this number would have been much higher if it were not for government relief packages keeping businesses on life-support. From the period of January 2020 to October 2020, the US is estimated to have incurred a US$147 billion loss in tourism revenues, with many other European destinations, including Spain (US$47 billion loss) and France (US$42 billion loss), as well as Asia and Pacific nations such as Thailand (US$37 billion loss) and Australia (US$27 billion loss) experiencing significant losses (Statista, 2020).

The World Travel & Tourism Council (WTTC, 2021) has stated that the recovery of global tourism is dependent on both public and private sector initiatives; government policies aimed at supporting the return of travel also require the creation (and re-creation) of tourism enterprises (WTTC, 2021). The next section expands on the definition and unique characteristics of tourism enterprises.

Defining Tourism Enterprises

Tourism businesses play a vital role in the tourism industry and destinations. They provide the essential services of tourism including accommodation, transport, attractions, experiences, food and beverages. Tourism businesses also play a key role in visitor realization, visitor satisfaction, return visits and loyalty.

They are pivotal in supporting tourism in regional and rural destinations, as is the case in Australia where tourism in regional areas accounted for 44% of all visitor spending between 2018 and 2019 (Tourism Research Australia, 2019). Tourism enterprises act as 'economic engines' in tourism destinations by boosting growth and prosperity in declining and impoverished communities (Getz et al., 2004). Revenues generated from tourism investments create a large multiplier effect that stimulates local economies (Cole, 2007).

Research focused on tourism and hospitality enterprises has expanded over the past two decades with specific interest on the characteristics of tourism entrepreneurs, their motivations and lifestyle objectives. Definitions of which businesses are categorized as tourism enterprises vary across countries, and these businesses cater for both tourists and non-tourists alike. However, a common approach is to categorize businesses as tourism enterprises if their *predominant source of revenue comes from tourism-related activities*. These can include:

- Accommodation
- Visitor attractions (e.g., wineries)
- Cafés/restaurants
- Pubs/taverns
- Transport – air/water/taxi
- Motor vehicle hire
- Travel agents and tour operators
- Arts and recreation
- Retail trade.

Tourism destinations require the creation and development of tourism enterprises in order for the tourism industry to thrive. These enterprises play a crucial role in providing tourism services, ensuring tourist satisfaction, as well as creating a positive destination image (Kozak and Rimmington, 1998). Their performance is critical to the success of the tourism sector and for the livelihood of tourism destinations (Hallak et al., 2012). Without the existence of tourism enterprises a community's objectives of attracting tourists cannot be accomplished (Koh, 2000). However, the tourism industry remains fragmented and disjointed as businesses operate in diverse sectors of the tourism industry including adventure tourism, ecotours, nature-based tourism, indigenous tourism, sport tourism, wine tourism, gastronomic tourism, cultural tourism, festivals and events, etc. (McKercher, 2016). Different countries categorize and evaluate tourism businesses differently; for example the UK in their Tourism Business Monitor focuses on accommodations and attractions, with accommodations sub-categorized into 'hotels, guesthouse/B&B, self-catering, caravan camping (VisitBritain, 2018).

Definitions of tourism enterprises encompass a focus on 'small and medium-sized enterprises'. Wang et al. (2019) define a small tourism and hospitality firm as 'a firm in the tourism and hospitality industry employing less than 10 persons' (p. 78). Breen et al. (2005) posited that 'Small and medium tourism enterprises comprise all businesses, which by their own definition, operate in the tourism industry and employ up to 100 employees and include sole operators not employing any staff' (p. vi). However, just as definitions of tourism businesses can vary across countries, so does the categorization of small businesses. The OECD provides a definition that

Small and medium-sized enterprises (SMEs) are non-subsidiary, independent firms which employ fewer than a given number of employees. This number varies across countries. The most frequent upper limit designating an SME is 250 employees, as in the European Union. However, some countries set the limit at 200 employees, while the United States considers SMEs to include firms with fewer than 500 employees. [Moreover] Small firms are generally those with fewer than 50 employees, while micro-enterprises have at most 10, or in some cases 5, workers. (OECD, 2019, 2021).

Despite different perspectives on categorizing businesses as small, medium or large depending on number of employees, a common agreement is that small businesses are independently owned private companies, which is an important distinction from publicly listed corporations. Thus, in this book we adopt the definition presented by Hallak (2010), which specifies small and medium tourism businesses as those being independently owned and visible within tourism and hospitality (Box 1.1).

Box 1.1. Definition of small and medium tourism enterprises.

'Independently owned and operated businesses operating within sectors of the tourism and hospitality industry – these include restaurants/cafés, pubs, accommodations (hotel/motel/b&b), tour operators, visitor attractions, travel agencies, souvenir shops' (Hallak, 2010)

Box 1.2. Characteristics of tourism enterprises – the role of the entrepreneur. (Source: developed by the authors, drawing from Getz *et al.* (2004); Wang *et al.* (2019); Verreyne *et al.* (2019).)

Despite the dominance of small firms in tourism, research on understanding the characteristics of tourism enterprises has only recently expanded. Characteristics of tourism enterprises include:

- Tourism enterprises operate in an industry that is dominated by small firms, including micro-enterprises.
- Businesses are normally independently owned and financed by the owner(s).
- Tourism enterprises operate in an industry with high competition and relatively low barriers to entry – i.e. low skill requirements and start-up costs.
- Tourism businesses are often created by individuals with lifestyle objectives, rather than profit-oriented.
- Tourism offers diverse opportunities for starting up various types of business, which appeals to both sole proprietors and families.
- Tourism enterprises being small in size are more nimble and agile and can adapt quickly, especially in niche tourism markets.
- Tourism enterprises may be exposed to a range of uncertainties originating in other parts of the supply chain or in other countries that negatively affect demand and revenue.
- Tourism enterprises operate simultaneously in local and international markets, and therefore face a highly competitive and dynamic environment.

An industry that is dominated by independently owned small and medium enterprises, created and managed by 'entrepreneurs', is subject to the motivations, goals, experience and capabilities of the business founder(s). The performance of tourism firms is driven by both internal and external factors. The internal factors include entrepreneurial behaviour and financial resource of the business. External factors include the market, competition and network among stakeholders (Kallmuenzer *et al.*, 2019). However, there is a sound argument that entrepreneurs can shape or manage the internal and external factors facing the enterprise, and that the tourism entrepreneurs and the tourism enterprise are so closely intertwined that success (or failure) of the business comes down to the entrepreneur (Sanchez-Medina *et al.*, 2020). Definitions of a 'tourism entrepreneur' are also contentious as not all businesses are considered to be entrepreneurial and not all business owners are categorized as entrepreneurs. A more detailed discussion on the definitions of 'entrepreneur' is presented in Chapter 2; for now, we consider a tourism entrepreneur as 'a creator of a touristic enterprise motivated by monetary and/or non-monetary reasons to pursue a perceived market opportunity' (Koh and Hatten, 2002, p. 25). The entrepreneurs create the essential products, services and experiences and therefore play a critical role in the success of the industry and the sustainability of destinations (Hallak, 2010).

There are several key differences between tourism entrepreneurs and entrepreneurs from other industries:

1. Tourism entrepreneurs create 'touristic' enterprises.
2. Tourism products are mostly 'intangible', which creates greater complexity of testing of products. This also affects the ability to attract investors and/or lenders.
3. Tourism enterprises deliver service-based experiences; therefore business operators need to adopt service-oriented management and marketing practices.
4. Tourism entrepreneurs must deal with seasonality and frequent sales (and profitability) fluctuations.
5. In the tourism industry, the buyers/visitors are required to come to the destination, as opposed to product manufacturers that can deliver products to the customer. This means that tourism business owners are susceptible to external disruptions affecting the buyers.
6. Many major tourism attractions are government owned (e.g., national parks) and this restricts the ability of tourism businesses to operate in a relatively free market system. (Source: Koh and Hatten, 2002.)

Challenges Facing Tourism Enterprises

Although there are advantages to tourism businesses being small in size, such as the ability to innovate and adapt quickly, and to provide a personalized service experience, SMEs in tourism will experience a wide range of challenges. These challenges include aspects related to accessing finance, human resource management, staff training, digital marketing, etc. Thus, tourism business owners are considered to be 'generalists', operating across all functions of the organization from finance to marketing to HR, while simultaneously operating in a fragmented, dynamic and fluctuating environment that is susceptible to global events such as terrorism, economic recession, fuel price hikes, digital disruptions, etc.

Tourism SMEs are not small versions of large companies. Decision making in these organizations is usually *ad hoc* and with a short-term focus. They are price takers (rather than price makers) and compete directly against other small firms, as well as larger organizations.

Challenges facing small tourism businesses can be grouped into four major categories (Figure 1.3):

1. Financial challenges
2. Managerial challenges
3. Marketing challenges
4. External challenges.

Managerial challenges

Short-run decision making and planning: Strategic and long-term planning seem out of reach for tourism enterprises, coupled with uncertainty about

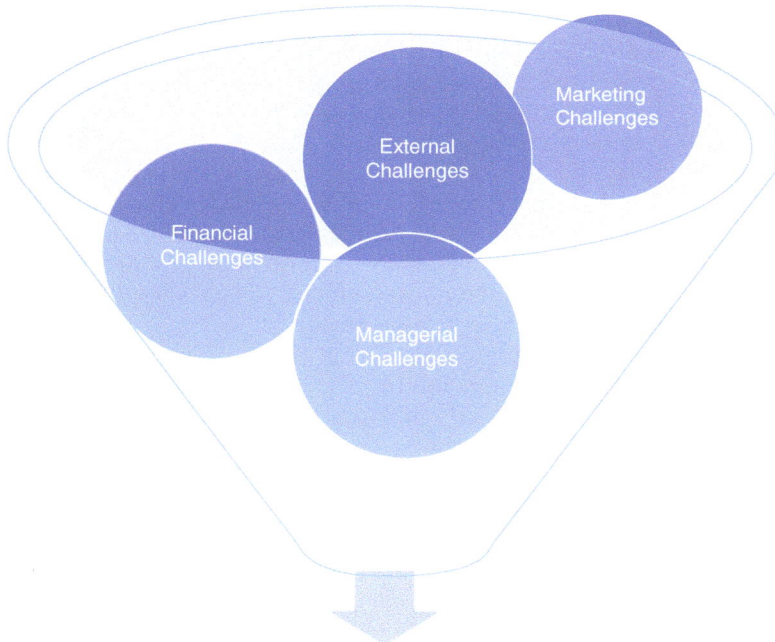

Challenges for Tourism SMEs

Figure 1.3. Challenges for Tourism SMEs. (Source: author created, drawing from Cole *et al.* (2017); Kim and Shim (2018); Lee *et al.* (2019); Perkins and Khoo-Lattimore (2020).)

future business performance; management tend to focus on short-term and reactive decision making rather than future-foresight planning. A longer vision and strategy are overshadowed by day-to-day operations and short-term revenue targets.

Challenges in establishing organizational structures: Owner/operated firms in tourism and hospitality are influenced by the attitudes and behaviours of the business owner. Organizational structures are often not made explicit, and delegation of responsibilities tend to be improvised.

Shortfalls in human capital: Human capital of the entrepreneurs and the organization has a significant impact on business performance. Tourism SMEs are typically owner-managed leading to shortcomings in human capital through the limited capabilities of the owner/manager, or the inability to build sufficient human capital in the organization. Owner/managers may also have limited entrepreneurial experience (see Chapter 6).

Less experienced in 'managerial' decision making: Business owners in tourism may have greater experience in the development and delivery of tourism products and services, but have less expertise in managerial decision making and organizational strategies.

Slow to adopt innovations and technology: Tourism owner/managers are often tied up with day-to-day operations of running the tourism business, and as a consequence, the business is slow and reactive in the development of new innovations and adoption of new technology. Business owners may not have the time, expertise or resources to innovate and adopt technologies.

Staff resistant to implementation of new innovations: Tourism businesses need to innovate in product development and service delivery. The challenges for business owners are staff resistance to implementation of innovations (see Chapter 3).

Staff training and retention: A major challenge for tourism SMEs is regarding leadership and human resources management (see Chapter 7). A lack of professional development and training opportunities for staff results in key personnel leaving the organization, often moving to larger businesses where there is greater potential for career development.

Owner/managers not experts in HRM practices: Similar to the challenges to staff training and retention, tourism SME operators may not have the appropriate expertise in HRM and employee performance. This can result in an underperforming workforce, putting more pressure on the business operator to carry more responsibility rather than delegating duties. Tourism SMEs do not have specialist HRM departments or experts in HR to handle matters around staff performance, absenteeism, harassment complaints and work culture.

Marketing challenges

Shortfalls in marketing expertise: Tourism business operators are generalists rather than specialists. Small firms seldom have dedicated marketing departments or experts; thus, marketing becomes the responsibility of the business operator, in addition to day-to-operations.

Smaller customer base and fewer repeat purchases: As compared to larger organizations, tourism SMEs are limited in the number of customers they are able to service. In addition, depending on the type and location of the business they may often become reliant on new customers, as repeat purchase from certain customers (e.g., international visitors) may be insufficient to support the revenues of the business. A constant need to attract new customers/tourists represents a high cost and marketing challenges for the business

Limited knowledge of the external market environment and trends: Tourism business operators dealing with day-to-day operations of the business may struggle to look externally and obtain foresight on market opportunities and customer trends. Businesses may become reactive rather proactive, often slow in innovating their marketing mix (product, price, place, promotion) and losing out to larger competitors.

Smaller marketing budgets and resources: Unlike larger organizations with dedicated marketing budgets, small tourism firms have restricted resources and must be prudent about spending on advertising and promotion. Small marketing budgets also restrict the ability to build brand recognition. The amount invested in advertising is influenced by the business's resources, but also by an owner's attitudes toward advertising spending and the perceived return on investment. Marketing may be considered an expense, rather than a strategic investment.

Capabilities in digital marketing and social media: While SMEs can reach local and global audiences through digital marketing, search engine optimization, social media and effective digital marketing requires resources and expertise that may be lacking in smaller firms.

External challenges

High business failure rate: Tourism businesses operate with a certain degree of risk and uncertainty. The failure rate of tourism businesses is high compared to other industries as businesses are susceptible to the volatility of the tourism industry.

Seasonality and revenue fluctuations: Many tourism businesses operate in environments influenced by seasonality. As a result, businesses need to manage fluctuating revenues while balancing fixed operating costs. Problems with managing irregular cashflows can see businesses struggle to meet their short-term financial obligations, resulting in business collapse.

High competition due to low barriers to entry: The tourism industry attracts entrepreneurship due to its low start-up costs and restrictive barriers. However, a consequence of low entry barriers is a high volume of competition, making it more difficult for businesses to survive.

Susceptible to external shocks: Tourism is vulnerable to external events such as wildfires, floods, terrorism, natural disasters, pandemics, oil/fuel price increases, economic downturn, etc. While small tourism businesses may operate with an internal focus on service delivery of the customer experience, the external environment has a profound effect on business revenue sources. This was clearly evidenced throughout COVID-19 as the tourism industry was among the hardest hit.

Destination management and government policy: Tourism businesses are closely intertwined with tourism destinations. The performance of the destination and the impacts of government policy and regulations on supporting tourism activity will have flow-on effects on the sustainability of the tourism enterprise. This is especially the case for tourism businesses in regional/rural and remote locations that rely on tourists making the effort required to visit the destination.

Remoteness of regional destinations: Tourism businesses operating in remote destinations with small residential populations experience major challenges in attracting and retaining a skilled workforce. Creating incentives for attracting employees may be beyond the capacity of small firms.

Digital disruptions and technology: Most businesses, especially small businesses, are affected to some extent by changes in technology and digitalization. For tourism businesses, this becomes impacted when changes in technology impact on the viability of existing business models. Evidence of this is the impact of online travel agencies (OTAs) such as Expedia and Booking.com on the traditional bricks-and-mortar travel agencies.

Financial challenges

Inability to influence price: The tourism industry is highly fragmented and predominantly comprised of small operators. As such, individual small firms have limited market share and a limited ability to influence price in the market. They are price takers as opposed to price makers. Products and services in the tourism industry are difficult to patent or to prevent from imitation; thus, economic advantage gained through innovation is replicated by other organizations, therefore restricting price premiums and profitability.

R&D investment: As highlighted earlier, tourism businesses, being small in size, are restricted by financial constraints. These constraints affect the firm's ability to invest in R&D.

Access to finance: A major financial challenge for tourism firms, and especially tourism SMEs, is the ability to access financing. The volatility of the tourism industry and the high failure rate of tourism enterprises mean banks perceive these firms as high-risk and are therefore conservative in their lending. The banks may assess small tourism businesses as having a weak asset base and less established credit reliability.

Limited cashflow: Irregular revenues brought about by seasonality and the need to attract new customers create a tight cashflow position for the enterprise. This limits the ability of the business to invest or expand, as it struggles to cover its expenses from its cash inflows.

Opportunities for Business Success

Despite the challenges facing tourism SMEs, these businesses have several advantages, including a diverse range of business opportunities, fewer restrictions, fewer organizational layers, and greater flexibility. This enables businesses to be entrepreneurial, creative and adaptable. Tourism SMEs are on the front line with customer engagement and can use this to their advantage in regard to product and service development.

The objective of this book is to present empirical insights into the strategies for business success in the tourism industry. It is inevitable that tourism businesses will encounter challenges; however, the industry also provides immense opportunities, and business owners can build capabilities in innovation, marketing, leadership, risk management, etc., to increase their chance of success. Each chapter in the book focuses on an important area of business success and outlines strategies for supporting performance. Tourism business operators can build capabilities in the following functions of business:

- Entrepreneurship and opportunity recognition (Chapter 2)
- Creativity and innovation (Chapter 3)
- Marketing and delivering service quality (Chapter 4)
- Business strategy and growth (Chapter 5)
- Human resources management and building human capital (Chapter 6)
- Leadership strategies for tourism enterprises (Chapter 7)
- Accessing sources of finance (Chapter 8)
- Financial management for business performance (Chapter 9)
- Building networks and social capital (Chapter 10)
- Crisis management and resilience (Chapter 11)
- Digital disruptions and business models (Chapter 12).

In addition, the book provides working templates for businesses to support their preparation of:

- Marketing planning and strategy (Chapter 13)
- Business feasibility analysis (Chapter 14)

Summary

This chapter provided the context of tourism businesses and their role in the global tourism industry. It presented insights into the definitions of tourism enterprises and their characteristics, with investigation into how these firms are different to businesses in other industries. The important role of the entrepreneur in a tourism enterprise was illustrated and will feature throughout the chapters in this book. The chapter also described four types of challenges for tourism business success including managerial challenges, marketing challenges, external challenges and financial challenges. While it may seem that tourism businesses face an uphill battle, this book will present empirical insights on how tourism enterprises can overcome these challenges as there are immense opportunities for business success that can be achieved through building capabilities in key organizational functions around innovation, creativity, service quality, leadership, resilience, etc.

Review Questions

1. Describe the characteristics of tourism enterprises and how they are different from organizations from other industries.
2. Identify and provide examples of three key managerial challenges facing tourism SMEs.
3. The tourism industry is synonymous with low barriers to entry; explain how this can be both a challenge and an opportunity for business success.
4. Out of the four categories of challenges facing tourism SMEs (managerial, marketing, external and financial), which do you think presents the greatest challenge to the success of tourism enterprises and why?

References

Breen, J.P., Bergin-Seers, S., Jago, L.K. and Carlsen, J. (2005) Small and medium tourism enterprises: the identification of good practice. Technical Report. Cooperative Research Centre for Sustainable Tourism, Queensland, Australia.
Cole, H.S., DeNardin, T. and Clow, K.E. (2017) Small service businesses: advertising attitudes and the use of digital and social media marketing. *Services Marketing Quarterly* 38(4), 203–212.
Cole, S. (2007) Entrepreneurship and empowerment: considering the barriers – a case study from Indonesia. *Tourism: An International Interdisciplinary Journal* 55(4), 461–473.
Fu, H., Okumus, F., Wu, K. and Köseoglu, M.A. (2019) The entrepreneurship research in hospitality and tourism. *International Journal of Hospitality Management* 78, 1–12.
Getz, D., Carlsen, J. and Morrison, A. (2004) *The Family Business in Tourism and Hospitality.* CAB International, Wallingford.
Hallak, R. (2010) Examining the place identity–performance relationship among tourism entrepreneurs. PhD thesis, University of South Australia, Adelaide, Australia.
Hallak, R., Brown, G. and Lindsay, N.J. (2012) The place identity–performance relationship among tourism entrepreneurs: a structural equation modelling analysis. *Tourism Management* 33(1), 143–154.
Hallak, R., Corsi, A., Akbar, S., O'Connor, A., Onur, I. and Ludwichowska, G. (2019) *Impacts of Technology Investment on Tourism Growth and Employment.* Regional Australia Institute, Barton, Australia.
Kallmuenzer, A., Kraus, S., Peters, M., Steiner, J. and Cheng, C.F. (2019) Entrepreneurship in tourism firms: a mixed-methods analysis of performance driver configurations. *Tourism Management* 74, 319–330.
Kim, N. and Shim, C. (2018) Social capital, knowledge sharing and innovation of small and medium-sized enterprises in a tourism cluster. *International Journal of Contemporary Hospitality Management* 30(5).
Koh, K.Y. (2000) Understanding community tourism entrepreneurism: some evidence from Texas. In: D. Hall and G. Richards (eds) *Tourism and Sustainable Community Development.* Routledge, London, pp. 223–236.
Koh, K.Y. and Hatten, T.S. (2002) The tourism entrepreneur: the overlooked player in tourism development studies. *International Journal of Hospitality & Tourism Administration* 3(1), 21–48.
Kozak and Rimmington (1998) Benchmarking: destination attractiveness and small hospitality business performance. *International Journal of Contemporary Hospitality Management* 10(5), 184–188.

Lee, C., Hallak, R. and Sardeshmukh, S.R. (2019) Creativity and innovation in the restaurant sector: supply-side processes and barriers to implementation. *Tourism Management Perspectives* 31, 54–62.

McKercher, B. (2016) Towards a taxonomy of tourism products. *Tourism Management* 54, 196–208.

OECD (2019) *OECD SME and Entrepreneurship Outlook 2019*, OECD Publishing, Paris, Available at: https://www.oecd.org/industry/smes/SME-Outlook-Highlights-FINAL.pdf (accessed 8 November 2022).

OECD (2021) *OECD SME and Entrepreneurship Outlook 2021*, OECD Publishing, Paris, Available at: https://doi.org/10.1787/97a5bbfe-en (accessed 8 November 2022).

Perkins, R. and Khoo-Lattimore, C. (2020) Friend or foe: challenges to collaboration success at different lifecycle stages for regional small tourism firms in Australia. *Tourism and Hospitality Research* 20(2), 184–197.

Sánchez-Medina, A.J., Arteaga-Ortiz, J., Naumchik, R.M. and Pellejero, M. (2020) The intention to quit entrepreneurship in tourism SMEs: the effect of work addiction. *International Journal of Hospitality Management* 89, 102400.

Statista (2020) Countries with the highest tourism revenue loss due to the coronavirus (COVID-19) pandemic from January to October 2020. Available at: https://www.statista.com/statistics/1221255/countries-with-the-highest-tourism-revenue-loss-due-to-covid-19/ (accessed 8 November 2022).

Tourism Research Australia (2019) Tourism business in Australia: June 2014–2019. Available at: https://www.tra.gov.au/data-and-research/reports/tourism-businesses-in-australia-june-2014-to-2019 (accessed 8 November 2022).

UNWTO (2017) *UNWTO Tourism Highlights, 2017 Edition*. Available at: https://www.unwto.org/archive/global/publication/unwto-tourism-highlights-2017 (accessed 8 November 2022).

UNWTO (2020) *UNWTO World Tourism Barometer and Statistical Annex, January 2020*. Available at: https://www.e-unwto.org/doi/abs/10.18111/wtobarometereng.2020.18.1.1 (accessed 8 November 2022).

Verreynne, M.L., Williams, A.M., Ritchie, B.W., Gronum, S. and Betts, K.S. (2019) Innovation diversity and uncertainty in small and medium sized tourism firms. *Tourism Management* 72, 257–269.

VisitBritain (2018) Tourism business monitor. Available at: https://www.visitbritain.org/business-confidence-and-performance-monitor (accessed 8 November 2022).

Wang, S., Hung, K. and Huang, W.J. (2019) Motivations for entrepreneurship in the tourism and hospitality sector: a social cognitive theory perspective. *International Journal of Hospitality Management* 78, 78–88.

WTTC (World Travel & Tourism Council) (2021) *Global Economic Impacts & Trends 2021; Travel and Tourism Economic Impacts 2021. June 2021*. Available at: https://wttc.org/Research/Economic-Impact (accessed 8 November 2022).

2 Entrepreneurship and New Ventures

When you have seen the birth of a great many business ideas, it becomes clear that there is no simple explanation of how they arise or why some are successful while others fail. The spectrum is wide and its diversity overwhelming. (Hougaard, 2005, p. 23)

Introduction

This chapter presents an overview of entrepreneurship and new venture creation. In doing so, the chapter defines entrepreneurship, and discusses three main types of entrepreneurial attributes – innate, acquired and undesirable. This is followed by an explanation of 'pull' and 'push' motivational factors for entrepreneurship. The chapter will also focus on the characteristics of entrepreneurial organizations, and the different paths to entry for entrepreneurship (start-up, purchase existing business, franchising, bootstrapping). The chapter concludes with an illustration of bootstrapping a new venture creation.

Learning Outcomes

After completing this chapter, you should:

* Understand the definitions of entrepreneurship and the attributes of high-impact entrepreneurs
* Recognize the criteria that investors look for in supporting entrepreneurs
* Be able to differentiate between 'entrepreneurial' organizations and 'solid-state' businesses, understanding key differences
* Understand the different paths to entry in tourism entrepreneurship.

© Rob Hallak and Craig Lee 2023. *Managing Tourism Enterprises: Start-up, Growth and Resilience* (R. Hallak and C. Lee)
DOI: 10.1079/9781789249446.0002

Why Focus on Entrepreneurship?

The past two decades have witnessed a growing interest in research on tourism entrepreneurship, recognizing the contribution toward innovation and creating value to a destination (Solvoll *et al.*, 2015). An early focus on tourism entrepreneurship emerged in the late 1970s and early 1980s (see Kibedi, 1979; Simms, 1981). For example, Kibedi (1979) was among the first to reference 'tourism entrepreneurship' when reporting the actions of the Ministry of Industry and Tourism in Ontario to train and educate tourism business owners. The need to understand entrepreneurship in a tourism context was raised by Simms (1981) and by Shaw and Williams (1998) who observed that many tourism entrepreneurs play a key role, not only in the tourism industry, but in the community where they become embedded.

Entrepreneurship is a driving force for economic growth, development, job creation and productivity. Entrepreneurship, at its core, is described as a 'dynamic process of creating value to society, business and environment' (Frederick *et al.*, 2019, p.10). The process involves individuals that identify opportunities for innovative utilization of resources, and then pursue the actions needed for creation and implementation. Entrepreneurs see gaps, problems or inefficiencies, and are driven to find creative solutions to these complex problems. The pursuit of opportunities to create value is manifested through business creation and market disruption through new or improved technologies, products, services, processes and business models. Thus, where others see constraints or problems in a market, industry or society, an entrepreneur takes the risk and coordinates resources – including building teams and raising capital – to address these challenges and create positive change.

As outlined in Chapter 1, the tourism industry is predominantly comprised of independently owned small and medium-sized enterprises, and the creation of these businesses 'is not an act of nature but an act of the tourism entrepreneur' (Koh and Hatten 2002, p. 22). In this respect, both entrepreneurship and tourism share a common focus on small firms and their creators (Walmsley 2019). They are active in the essential services of tourism including accommodations, transport, food and beverages, and for design experiences that create demand for tourism destinations, visitor realization, satisfaction and loyalty. Entrepreneurship and innovation are recognized by the United Nations' World Tourism Organization (UNWTO) as the catalyst for the recovery of tourism post-COVID-19. The tourism industry provides broad economic benefits such as the fostering of regional development, diversification of the economy, increasing public revenue, and the balance of payments (Lerner and Haber, 2001). Tourism entrepreneurship contributes to the creation of social and economic exchange among a network of stakeholders including consumers, employees, suppliers, community and businesses. The industry is synonymous with low barriers to entry, both in terms of funding or skill requirements, which consequently provide opportunities for low-income or minority groups, migrants or refugees to enter into entrepreneurship and create a better life for their families and community, as well as supporting their financial independence and well-being (Altinay, 2010; Alrawadieh *et al.*, 2021).

Definitions of Entrepreneurship

There remains no concrete definition of 'entrepreneurship 'or 'entrepreneurs', or consensus on what distinguishes entrepreneurs from a business owner. 'Entrepreneurship' implies many different things and is used in diverse contexts referring to innovation, ideas, creativity, new venture development, business start-up, etc. (Audretsch *et al.*, 2015). Moreover, the field of 'entrepreneurship' is 'multifaceted' and studied from different angles, including the 'individual' (entrepreneur) – in regard to personality traits, behaviours, motivations, etc., and the 'organization' – business start-up, innovation, entrepreneurial orientation, social entrepreneurship, etc. (Audretsch *et al.*, 2015). However, a common view is that entrepreneurship is the process of recognition and exploitation of opportunities that lead to the creation of new ventures (Hisrich *et al.*, 2013). This is best summarized by Timmons and Spinelli (2009, p.101):

> Entrepreneurship is a way of thinking, reasoning, and acting that is opportunity obsessed, holistic in approach, and leadership balanced for the purpose of value creation and capture...at the heart of the process is the creation and/or recognition of opportunities, followed by the will and initiative to seize these opportunities. It requires a willingness to take risks – both personal and financial – but in a very calculated fashion in order to constantly shift the odds of success, balancing the risk with the personal reward.

Although the term 'entrepreneur' is often loosely used to describe all business owners, the reality is that most business owners are not entrepreneurs, and their businesses are not entrepreneurial organizations. The discussion on entrepreneurship attempts to differentiate 'entrepreneurs' from 'small-business owners', as well as 'entrepreneurial organizations' being distinct types of businesses. For example, Schaper and Volery (2007, p.100) argue that:

> Entrepreneurs discover, evaluate and exploit new business opportunities...in contrast, a small business owner-manager is a person who runs an existing small business; there may be little innovation, idea-generation or risk involved in such a project.

The majority of small businesses remain small in scale and market impact; they offer undifferentiated products and services and rely primarily on a domestic market that is often limited to regional proximity (Australian Government Office of the Chief Scientist, 2015). On the other hand, entrepreneurship is a 'high-impact' activity that generates:

1) Innovation;
2) Job creation;
3) Wealth creation; and
4) Societal impact. (World Economic Forum, 2014)

So what explains these differences between entrepreneurs and small-business owners? And, are entrepreneurs born with innate characteristics or can these be nurtured and developed through interventions? These questions have sparked much debate in the entrepreneurship literature.

Entrepreneurial Attributes

The literature over the past 30 years has sought to examine what differentiates entrepreneurs as unique individuals who create wealth in society. In the 1990s there was much focus on understanding entrepreneurial traits and innate characteristics. For example, are certain individuals born to be entrepreneurs, as opposed to learning certain behaviours? Research has also sought to uncover a 'profile' of an entrepreneur, to identify personality or psychological traits that discriminate between entrepreneurs and non-entrepreneurs (Frederick *et al.*, 2019). However, the evidence suggests that entrepreneurs come in all shapes and sizes, with different cultures, religions, backgrounds, etc., and that high-impact entrepreneurs are a product of multiple internal and external factors.

In the report *Boosting High Impact Entrepreneurship in Australia: A Role for Universities*, by the Australian Government Office of the Chief Scientist (2015), there are several internal and external factors that positively influence whether an individual becomes an entrepreneur (Table 2.1). Although not all are required, the presence of most of these factors increases the likelihood that an individual will pursue an entrepreneurial pathway.

In regard to entrepreneurial attributes and characteristics, evidence suggests that entrepreneurs have a *vision* and *mindset* to see problems in the market/society/environment as opportunities for creation of value. Thus, they sense economic potential in problems (see Box 2.1).

Table 2.1. Internal and external factors influencing entrepreneurship.

Internal	External
• Individual personality: Certain personality traits are associated with high-impact entrepreneurship • Practical entrepreneurial skills: Entrepreneurship competences, resilience, and the drive to pursue opportunities can be acquired through education and experience	• Local cultural attitudes towards entrepreneurship: Countries that celebrate entrepreneurs and their successful enterprises tend to have higher rates of entrepreneurship • Role models: Successful entrepreneurs act as role models and can influence career choices by providing individuals with tangible evidence that they too can succeed as entrepreneurs • Exposure at school, university and in the family: Familiarity with the concept of start-ups and entrepreneurship helps avoid misconceptions about being an entrepreneur • Supportiveness of local start-up ecosystem: Before deciding whether to launch a start-up, individuals would assess if the ecosystem around them or in their targeted area is supportive of entrepreneurship

---

Box 2.1. How entrepreneurs view problems.

- What is the problem?
- Whom does it affect?
- How does it affect them?
- What costs are involved?
- Can it be solved?
- Would the marketplace pay for a solution? (Kuratko, 2016, p.109).

In addition to the unique mindset in regard to perception of problems, entrepreneurs share a distinct range of attributes which can be classified into three categories (Figure 2.1):

- Innate attributes – these are psychological and behavioural characteristics that may be genetic.
- Acquired/learned attributes – these can be developed through experience, education, training, and exposure to entrepreneurial environments.
- Undesirable attributes – these attributes have negative effects on successful entrepreneurship and are less present in successful entrepreneurs.

Innate attributes

Entrepreneurs may be born with certain innate characteristics including good health, energy, emotional stability, tolerance of stress, charisma, intelligence and creativity. It is important to note that while these can support entrepreneurship, innate characteristics are not enough for successful venture creation. The benefit of such innate attributes stems from their positive effect on the acquired attributes, for example, (i) natural creativity can support entrepreneurs in learning to become innovative; (ii) intelligence can support problem solving skills; and (iii) energy can support drive and determination.

Acquired attributes

Spinelli and Adams (2016) argued that 'the making of an entrepreneur occurs by accumulating the relevant skills, know-how, experiences, and contacts over a period of years and includes large doses of self-development' (p. 37). Thus, the successful characteristics of entrepreneurs are those that can be learned through education, training and experience, building on human capital assets (see Chapter 6). Such acquired attributes include:

Vision and passion: While vision and passion are distinct characteristics, they go hand-in-hand in that an entrepreneur needs to establish a vision of where the organization is heading, establish goals and objectives, and have the passion and motivation to realize this vision. Entrepreneurs have a vision in regard to the realization of the opportunity, not necessarily a fixed outcome of what

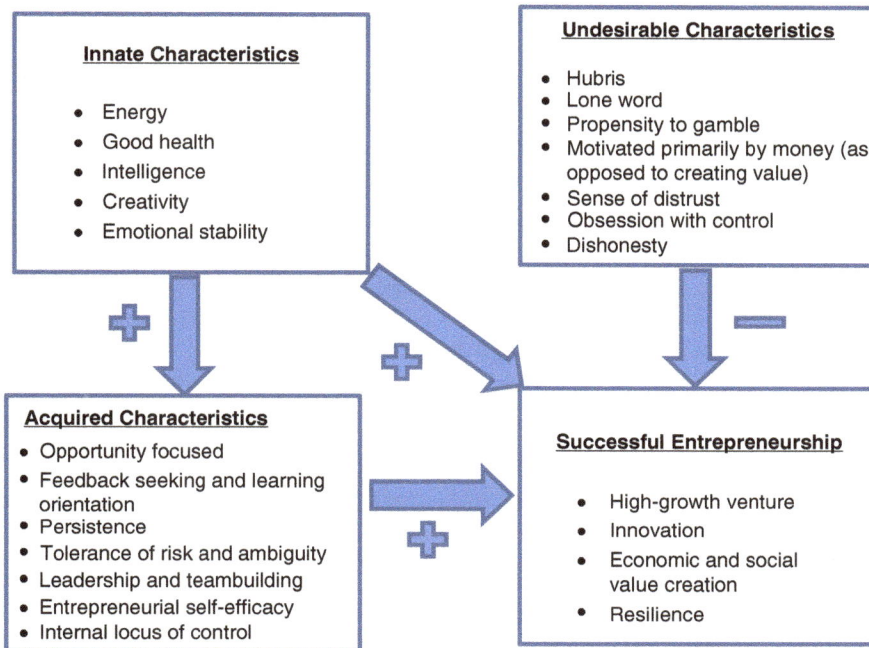

Figure 2.1. Entrepreneurial attributes – innate, acquired, undesirable. (Source: author developed, drawing from Goulding 2015; Spinelli and Adams, 2016; Frederick *et al.*, 2019.)

the business will look like. This vision can change and adapt throughout the life cycle of the business and the changing dynamics of the environment.

Entrepreneurial passion is described as 'a discrete emotion that is quite intense, having been described as an underlying force that fuels our strongest emotions; the intensity felt when engaging in activities that are of deep interest; or the energy that enables entrepreneurs to achieve peak performance' (Frederick *et al.*, 2019, p. 50). Having passion is fundamental to the entrepreneurial psyche.

Opportunity focused: Another clear defining characteristic of entrepreneurs is their orientation toward identifying opportunities; they perceive problems in a different context and see an opportunity for creating change. Entrepreneurs start with the opportunity, not with a business or product. The opportunity is what drives the business model formation. The opportunity becomes the direction of what business is established, how it is established, for whom it is set up, what products are to be developed, etc.

Persistence: A key characteristic of entrepreneurs is the 'never give up' attitude. They fight through adversity and persist in pursuit of the opportunity. They also recognize that success is not a linear process and there will be bumps, set-backs and failures. Persistence does not imply that they are stubborn and single-minded, but rather that they are persistent in finding solutions to problems, adapting, adjusting, and therefore shifting direction when needed.

Feedback seeking and learning orientation: Entrepreneurs understand that learning is a constant and iterative process. They learn from mistakes, from experimentation and through trial and error. They evaluate what works and does not work and seek feedback and different perspectives to inform their decision making.

Need for achievement: Entrepreneurs are intrinsically motivated and self-starters. They have a desire to compete and to set goals, and drive to achieve them. Need for achievement is the driving force for entrepreneurial motivation and success, and also influences perceptions toward risk and reward.

Internal locus of control: Entrepreneurs have a strong belief in their capabilities and that their fate is in their own hands. They believe success is within their control and that they can influence and shape business outcomes.

Entrepreneurial self-efficacy: Like internal locus of control, entrepreneurs have high levels of entrepreneurial self-efficacy (ESE) – belief in their capabilities to successfully accomplish the tasks of entrepreneurship (Hallak *et al.*, 2012). Self-efficacy plays an important role in entrepreneurial motivations and decision making. ESE is multi-dimensional and includes an individual's capabilities toward: (i) developing new product and market opportunities; (ii) building an innovative environment; (iii) initiating investor relationships; (iv) defining core purpose; (v) coping with the unexpected; and (vi) developing critical human resources (DeNoble *et al.*, 1999).

Tolerance of risk and ambiguity: – Entrepreneurs are capable of assessing and calculating risks, and look at ways to minimize and share risk (e.g., by attracting investors). They are also capable of managing stress and conflict and are not fearful of uncertainty.

Resilience and adaptability: Entrepreneurs display high levels of resilience. Resilience is defined as a 'dynamic adaptation process that allows entrepreneurs to continue to look towards the future despite harsh market conditions and despite the destabilizing events they must continually face' (Ayala and Manzano, 2014, p.127). Resilience is an important characteristic for entrepreneurs, especially in the tourism and hospitality industry where there is constant disruption, and businesses are susceptible to external events (Hallak *et al.*, 2018). Entrepreneurs with high resilience develop higher degrees of tolerance for ambiguity and can better adapt to change (McInnis-Bowers *et al.*, 2017).

Leadership and teambuilding: Entrepreneurs may be shrewd business operators but they recognize the need to motivate and inspire others to share the vision in pursuit of the opportunity. They need to build teams, hire staff, attract investors, gain the support of government, banks, lenders, etc. Therefore, a key criterion of entrepreneurship is the ability to engage with people and demonstrate leadership capabilities (see Chapter 7).

Undesirable attributes

These are attributes that have a negative effect on successful entrepreneurship and are seldom observed among high-impact entrepreneurs. They include hubris, lone wolf, propensity to gamble, distrustful, dishonest and obsessed with control. Other undesirable characteristics include having unrealistic optimism, and being pompous and grandiose. Evidence also suggests that entrepreneurs who are motivated purely by financial gain, as opposed to creating value, are less likely to build organizations of substantial value.

What do Investors Look for in Entrepreneurs?

Venture capitalists and investors in entrepreneurial start-ups also assess the potential of an investment based on the EPIC (Execution, Perspective, Intellect, Communication) characteristics of the lead entrepreneurs (Visontay, 2013) (Box 2.2).

Motivations for Entrepreneurship

There are diverse motivations as to why people engage in entrepreneurship. The drive can be a need for independence, push and pull motivations, opportunity-driven entrepreneurs vs. necessity, etc. Opportunity-driven entrepreneurs start a business mainly to meet and satisfy a market opportunity whereas necessity-driven entrepreneurs start a business mainly for financial income (Nasiri and Hamelin, 2018). Opportunity-driven entrepreneurs are motivated by pull factors while necessity-driven entrepreneurs are motivated by push factors (Tony, 2014). Van der Zwan *et al.* (2016) refer to pull motivations as positive factors towards entrepreneurship while push factors may be the negative factors that drive one into entrepreneurship. According to the push and pull framework of entrepreneurship, opportunity-driven entrepreneurship occurs when people are pulled into starting businesses by attractive opportunities whereas necessity-driven entrepreneurship occurs when people are pushed into starting a venture by negative forces (Gras *et al.*, 2021).

Box 2.2. EPIC characteristics of the lead entrepreneurs. (Source: Vistonay, 2013.)

Execution: From an investor's perspective, the entrepreneur needs to be a person that follows through on ideas and pursues an opportunity rather than working on unfinished projects or moving on to new ideas. This differentiates between those with floating ideas, and those that act and implement.

Perspective: This aligns with the entrepreneurial attributes of learning orientation and adaptability. Investors will favour entrepreneurs with good intuition, learn from trial-and-error, and are willing to adapt and shift gears. An individual that is wedded to an idea and is not willing to learn and adapt is not favoured by investors.

Intellect: Investors support individuals with a capacity to learn quickly, make informed decisions and demonstrate proficiency in a wide range of business-related tasks.

Communication: Entrepreneurs, as leaders, must be able to effectively communicate and inspire others to follow with the vision of the organization. The business objectives and strategy need to be clearly explained and understood by all stakeholders, including customers, employees and investors.

Table 2.2. Pull and push factors for entrepreneurship motivation. (Source: author's compilation.)

Pull factors (internal/dispositional attribution)	Push factors (external/situational attribution)
• Need for independence and autonomy – freedom to make and control decision making • Need for achievement or recognition – entrepreneurs feel a sense of personal satisfaction and self-esteem • Personal development – learning opportunities to understand various business operations • Availability of business and market opportunities • Financial rewards – some people engage in entrepreneurship to achieve their financial goals. • Availability of business information, and accumulated experience, skills and knowledge • Passion – turning a hobby into an income-generating venture.	• Unemployment • Forced redundancy and retirement • Job dissatisfaction (unfavourable employment working conditions) • Family-related • Need for financial security • Limited set of skills or qualifications

The various pull and push factors for entrepreneurship motivation suggested by Kirkwood (2009) and Duan *et al.* (2020) are given in Table 2.2.

Shane *et al.* (2003) found pull factors including locus of control, self-efficacy, need for independence, passion, vision and need for achievement to be among the significant drivers for entrepreneurship. With an increase in unemployment, redundancy rates and early retirement, the possibility of getting into paid employment diminishes, pushing people into necessity entrepreneurship (Dawson and Henley, 2012). Family-related motives have been found to strongly influence one's ability to start a business (Dawson and Henley, 2012; Orhan and Scott, 2001).

Characteristics of Entrepreneurial Organizations

As previously explained, not all business owners are entrepreneurs and not all organizations are entrepreneurial. For organizations, there are certain characteristics that differentiate between 'entrepreneurial' vs. 'solid-state' enterprises. The distinguishing characteristics include:

- Innovation
- Opportunity seeking
- Tolerance of risk
- Proactivity
- Networks and stakeholder engagement
- Entrepreneurial culture
- Vision and strategy.

Innovation: Entrepreneurial firms are able to create and develop innovative business ideas. Dai *et al.* (2014) found evidence that the innovation level of a firm has a significant impact on its international scope – high-innovation firms have a higher international scope.

Opportunity seeking: Opportunity seeking involves: (i) scanning the environment; (ii) screening and selecting the best possible opportunity; and (iii) seizing and generating ideas. Entrepreneurial firms actively search for ideas that can be turned into new business opportunities.

Tolerance of risks: Entrepreneurial firms have high tolerance of risk, and management is willing to commit resources to manage risk and uncertainty (Hurtado-Palomino *et al.*, 2021).

Proactivity: Entrepreneurial firms are constantly forward-looking, anticipating future market demand and trends in pursuit of opportunities (Dai *et al.*, 2014).

Networks and stakeholder engagement: Through building business networks that facilitate information and knowledge sharing, entrepreneurial firms can access resources and information about opportunities, markets, customers and suppliers through networks (Moensted, 2010).

Entrepreneurial culture: Entrepreneurial firms establish an 'entrepreneurial culture' – shared values, beliefs, attitudes (Brownson, 2013). An entrepreneurial culture supports entrepreneurial behaviours in terms of innovation, proactiveness, risk taking and opportunity seeking (Beugelsdijk, 2010).

Mobilization of resources: Entrepreneurial firms are able to identify and access resources needed for venture creation. For example, mobilization of financial and human resources through networks and partnership enables small tourism firms to overcome limited resource constraints (Casanueva *et al.*, 2014).

Vision and strategy: Leaders of entrepreneurial firms are visionary and strategically orientated (ability to initiate and manage organizational change). Vision and strategy are hallmarks of entrepreneurial firms and important for successful performance (Al-Dhaafri and Alosani, 2021).

Entrepreneurial Orientation

Entrepreneurial organizations think and act 'entrepreneurially' through a focus on innovation, aggressively entering new markets, and accepting a measure of strategic and financial risk in the pursuit of new opportunities (Miller, 1983). Lumpkin and Dess (1996) define entrepreneurial orientation (EO) as 'processes, practices, and decision-making activities that lead to new entry in terms of launching a new venture either in an existing firm or a start-up' (p. 136). According to Covin and Lumpkin (2011), EO is conceptualized as a multidimensional construct of five dimensions: innovativeness, proactiveness, risk taking, competitive aggressiveness and autonomy (Box 2.3).

A popular measure of entrepreneurial orientation used to assess a continuum of entrepreneurship and to discriminate between entrepreneurial and

---

Box 2.3. EO as a multi-dimensional construct of five dimensions.

---

1. Innovativeness – introducing new products and services, creativity and process improvement
2. Proactiveness – forward-looking, seeking opportunities, anticipating future market demand and changing status quo.
3. Risk taking – willingness to commit resources to risky uncertain projects. Risk taking is seen as a positive that supports exploration and experimentation.
4. Competitive aggressiveness – focus on outperforming competitors, out-manoeuvring competitor organizations
5. Autonomy – providing autonomy and empowerment to employees in the organization. It involves allowing employees freedom to take actions towards organizational goals.

'conservative' or 'solid-state' firms is presented by Hughes and Morgan (2007). This scale measures:

Risk taking

- The term risk taker is considered a positive attribute for people in our enterprise.
- People in our enterprise are encouraged to take calculated risks with new ideas.
- Our enterprise emphasizes both exploration and experimentation for opportunities.

Innovativeness

- We actively introduce improvements and innovation in our enterprise.
- Our enterprise is creative in its methods of operation.
- Our business seeks out new ways of doing things.

Proactiveness

- We always try to take the initiative in every situation (e.g., against competitors, in projects when working with others).
- We excel at identifying opportunities.
- We initiate actions to which other organizations respond.

Competitive aggressiveness

- Our enterprise is intensely competitive.
- In general, our enterprise takes a bold or aggressive approach when competing.
- We try to out do and out-manoeuvre the competition as best as we can.

Autonomy

- Employees are permitted to think without interference.
- Employees perform jobs that allow them to make and instigate changes in the way they perform their work tasks.
- Employees are given freedom and independence to decide on their own how to go about doing their work.
- Employees are given freedom to communicate without interference.
- Employees are given authority and responsibility to act alone if they think it to be in the best interests of the enterprise.
- Employees have access to all vital information.

Pathways to Entrepreneurship

Often when we think about entrepreneurship we are referring to new business start-ups, also referred to as new venture creation. Although the business is 'new' in that it did not exist prior to creation, most 'new' businesses are me-too businesses that replicate existing business models, processes and products and aim to generate sales by capturing market share from other similar businesses. An example would be the opening of a new restaurant with similar menu items to other competitor restaurants. The business can capture market share by competing against other restaurants on products or price, etc. A lack of innovation and unique selling proposition means that me-too businesses will struggle to grow their customer base. According to the US Small Business Administration Office of Advocacy, approximately one in five new businesses failed within their first 12 months, and almost 50% closed within five years (US Small Business Administration Office of Advocacy, 2018).

The following section describes the various options available for business ownership, with an analysis of the advantages and disadvantages of each path to entry. While most people see business start-up as the main approach, there are in fact several options for entering into entrepreneurship (Box 2.4).

New venture creation/business start-up: As the name suggests this is where an individual creates a new business in pursuit of a market opportunity. Depending on the type of business, it may be online or have a physical premises. Start-up costs for the new venture also vary depending on the capital investment required (see Chapters 8 and 9). New venture creation has both challenges and advantages. These are outlined in Table 2.3.

Box 2.4. Entrepreneurship pathways.

- New venture creation (business start-up)
- Purchasing an existing business
- Investing (buying-in) an existing business
- Inheriting (or taking over) an existing business
- Buying a franchise

Table 2.3. New venture creation.

Disadvantages	Advantages
A new business starts without a customer base	A start-up begins with a clean slate and does not carry any of the baggage of an existing business
Business may have new or inexperienced staff	Provides opportunities for the entrepreneurs to structure the business model, hire new staff, appoint managers, etc.
It takes time (and money) to build up brand recognition	Opportunity to build a new brand
It is difficult to establish trade credit with suppliers	Adopt the latest technologies
Accessing debt financing is less accessible, and expensive	Opportunity to start with 'innovation', rather than carryovers from the past
The business needs time to build up its cashflow, while covering its ongoing purchases and expenses	Allows crafting of a business that can best exploit the identified opportunity in the market

Purchasing (or buying-in) an existing business: Another path to entry into entrepreneurship is to purchase an existing business. Entrepreneurs can decide to purchase an existing business with a current customer base, sales/revenues/contracts, suppliers, employees. The entrepreneurs can determine if the business is a 'good buy', and purchase with an intention to implement ideas on making improvements. In some cases, the cost of purchasing an existing business may be less than the cost of establishing a new business, when considering start-up capital investment requirements. In the tourism industry, where location is important, purchasing an existing business, e.g., restaurant, hotel, bed and breakfast, in a desirable location may be the only option, as trying to find an unoccupied site to create a new business may not be possible.

There are several channels for finding businesses for sale including business brokers or commercial listings such as https://www.commercialrealestate.com.au/business/ (accessed 10 November 2022).

The major advantages of purchasing an existing business are that there is an established customer base, its systems are in operation, there are existing relationships with suppliers, it may come with experienced staff, and the business is currently trading and generating cashflow. The business listed for sale may also be successful, but the owners are keen to sell in order to move on to other priorities, e.g., retirement, travel, family commitments, etc.

Purchasing an existing business does not necessarily mean buying 100% of the business. There may be an opportunity to *buy-in*, investing as co-owner/shareholder, then gradually increasing share of equity. When it comes to financing a business purchase (or start-up), borrowing money to acquire an existing business may be easier to obtain than for a start-up, especially if the existing business is trading and generating profit.

Below is an indicative list of factors to consider when buying an established business:

- Understand the reasons why the business is for sale
- Conducting due diligence
- Consider the market outlook and trends
- Understand the current customers and suppliers
- Analyse the business's reputation and brand image
- Check all business licences and permits.

Purchasing an existing business has both advantages and disadvantages. Some are highlighted in Table 2.4.

Franchising

A third option for starting a business is to purchase a business franchise. Franchising is a business model that allows a business to operate under the name/brand of another company. A franchisee is the business/organization that enters into a legal agreement with a franchisor (parent organization) to own and operate a business under the franchisor's name. The franchisee pays for the rights to use the franchisor's name. Depending on the agreement, the franchisor provides assistance with marketing, strategy, technology, access to customers, etc. The term of the franchise agreement is determined in the contract. The franchisor sells the rights to use the company brand. They control the intellectual property, brand, products, IP, business processes, etc. Examples of franchise companies in tourism include Cruise Planners, Europcar, Tim Hortons, Subway, Four Seasons Hotels and Resorts, etc.

Table 2.4. Buying an existing business. (Source: adapted from https://www.business.qld.gov.au/starting-business/buying-business/buying-business-guide/due-diligence (accessed 13/7/2022).)

Advantages	Disadvantages
• Established, ready-to-use plans and procedures • Instant/immediate cashflow • Ability to assess the financial viability of the business • Established customer base, brand image, suppliers, staff, assets • Existing mature market for the product • Availability of experienced employees • Requires less cash outlay as the owner will not need to purchase new equipment or machinery	• Might require business model adjustment and assets improvement • Mostly requires a large financial budget to cover the acquisition costs • The business could be attractive but poorly managed with unskilled employees • External factors, rising competition or a declining industry can impede future growth • Poor performing businesses require a lot of initial investment to make them profitable • Business may also come with baggage, poor reputation or disgruntled customers

Table 2.5. Franchising. (Source: author's compilation.)

Advantages	
Franchisor	Franchisee
Market expansion (uses the franchisee expertise for marketing and growing the brand)	Perceived to be low risk (established reputation and brand name)
Source of extra income from franchising fees, royalties	Easy set-up – little experience is required since the franchisor usually provides training
Increased brand awareness through franchisee distribution and marketing strategies	Shared marketing costs
Reduced risk as part of the marketing risk is assumed by the franchisee	Established target market
	Potentially lower start-up costs

Disadvantages	
Reduction of market share to franchisee	High start-up costs in terms of franchise fees, licence fees, human resources training costs
Loss of brand control	Restrictions on daily business operations dictated by franchisor
	No guaranteed agreement renewal
	Profit sharing with franchisor
	Reputation damage to the head company can spread to entire franchising network

Franchising has advantages and disadvantages to both the franchisor and franchisee. Some are highlighted in Table 2.5.

Bootstrapping

As discussed throughout this chapter, there are several pathways to entrepreneurship. An increasingly popular approach is to start small, or with a part-time venture (i.e. side hustle), in order to test a concept, experiment, adaptation, before moving into large-scale operations. This has been conceptualized as 'minipreneurship', or 'bootstrapping'.

Bootstrapping, or starting a business on a shoestring budget, is defined as 'a means of starting a new venture through highly creative acquisition and use of [sometimes other people's] resources' (Frederick *et al.*, 2019, p. 114). Following a bootstrapping approach, the entrepreneur pursues a business opportunity with minimum start-up capital, relying on resourcefulness, networks and thinking outside the box. This minimizes the entrepreneur's risk exposure in the start-up stage, allowing the business to start small, or part-time, and then scale up gradually. Some examples of bootstrapping are given in Box 2.5.

Box 2.5. Bootstrapping examples.

- Running a business from home instead of leasing expensive premises
- Paying employees with company shares or non-cash benefits
- Doing what you can yourself
- Using your own funds, or borrowing from family and friends as opposed to from banks
- Buying on consignment
- Minimizing accounts receivables
- Delay accounts payable payments
- Using government grants
- Working with universities in collaborative market/product research
- Leasing, as opposed to buying, equipment

Advantages of bootstrapping

1. Business ownership – there is no ownership dilution.
2. Management control – the business owner has and maintains full control of management decision making.
3. Financial risk – low financial risk in case of business failure since the business owner has low initial investments.
4. Testing the opportunity – allows for flexible experimentation with new products and new markets.

Disadvantages of bootstrapping

1. Risk of failure is solely borne by the business owner.
2. Limited capital may hinder growth opportunities.
3. Business may lack technical skills and expert advice to develop products.
4. The business can remain a part-time or mini-venture and eventually dwindle away.
5. Susceptible to larger, more intense, competitors.

Summary

This chapter presented an overview of entrepreneurship, including definitions, characteristics and attributes. It presented the differences between entrepreneurs and small-business owners, as well as the contrast between entrepreneurial and solid-state organizations. Paths to business entry were discussed, including new venture creation, purchasing an existing business, franchising and bootstrapping. The chapter concluded with an example of bootstrapping in the tourism and hospitality industry, and how a business can start up with minimal resources to test a concept in the market.

Box 2.6. An example of bootstrapping.

Let us now provide an example of bootstrapping a tourism or hospitality business. Joe Gaucci is a high school teacher living in Brisbane, Australia. His grandmother, Ginevra, came from Naples, Italy, and he grew up enjoying her home cooking, especially her pizzas and pastas, made the traditional way. Joe has identified an opportunity in the market to open a restaurant that is based around his grandmother's recipes. Not wanting to quit his job or to take major financial risks, knowing that the restaurant industry is highly competitive and that many have opened (and closed) in his area, Joe wants to experiment with the concept with minimum start-up capital.

Joe proceeds with registration of a restaurant business and calls it 'Nonna Ginevra', paying tribute to his grandmother and her recipes. He gets help from an IT-savvy colleague from work to set up the business website. The menu list for the restaurant is deliberately kept small – five pizzas and three pasta dishes. Joe is not prepared or willing to invest $200, 000 for a full restaurant fit-out; thus, he adopts an online only business model where he leases kitchen premises from a dark kitchen facility. Rather than purchasing products direct from suppliers, one of Joe's past students has a family that runs a supermarket. Joe makes an agreement to source his products direct from the supermarket at wholesale prices. Now, Joe has a registered business name, company website, leased kitchen premises, and suppliers for ingredients. Nonna Ginevra provides delivery only. Rather than investing in delivery vans or hiring delivery staff, Joe contracts online delivery platforms Uber Eats, Deliveroo and Menulog. He advertises mostly through social media platforms such as Facebook and Instagram.

His cousin's husband is an amateur photographer and helps to photograph images of the menu items. Nonna Ginevra opens for trade only on Fridays and Saturdays. Total start-up costs for Nonna Ginevra were $6000. Joe funded this from his savings, $4000, and by selling some of his shares, $2000. The business begins trading and over time builds an online fanbase of loyal customers. It grows in its review rankings and establishes a presence on TripAdvisor and Zomato. After 6 weeks Joe expands his trading days to Thursday–Sunday, and he hires two university students (who study hospitality management) to assist him part-time.

The example of Nonna Ginevra highlights how bootstrapping, and creative use of resources, can provide pathways into entrepreneurship by starting at a small and manageable scale. Joe maintains his full-time employment as a school teacher, but has now secured a second income through Nonna Ginevra.

Discussion Questions

1. Are individuals born to be entrepreneurs or can they be trained?

2. What are some of the undesirable attributes of entrepreneurs and what impact do they have on business success?

3. Describe characteristics of entrepreneurial organizations in contrast to solid-state businesses.

4. What are the advantages of a business start-up (new ventures) in contrast to buying an existing business or a franchise?

5. Find three examples of businesses in tourism that began through bootstrapping.

References

Al-Dhaafri, H. and Alosani, M.S. (2021) Role of leadership, strategic planning and entrepreneurial organizational culture towards achieving organizational excellence: evidence from public sector using SEM. *Measuring Business Excellence* 26(3).

Alrawadieh, Z., Altinay, L., Cetin, G. and Simsek, D. (2021) The interface between hospitality and tourism entrepreneurship, integration and well-being: a study of refugee entrepreneurs. *International Journal of Hospitality Management* 97, 103013.

Altinay, L. (2010) Market orientation of small ethnic minority-owned hospitality firms. *International Journal of Hospitality Management* 29(1), 148–156.

Audretsch, D., Belitski, M. and Desai, S. (2015) Entrepreneurship and economic development in cities. *The Annals of Regional Science* 55(1), 33–60.

Australian Government Office of Chief Scientist (2015) Available at https://www.chiefscientist.gov.au/sites/default/files/Boosting-High-Impact-Entrepreneurship.pdf (accessed 10 November 2022).

Ayala, J.C. and Manzano, G. (2014) The resilience of the entrepreneur. Influence on the success of the business: a longitudinal analysis. *Journal of Economic Psychology* 42, 126–135.

Beugelsdijk, S. (2010) Entrepreneurial culture, regional innovativeness and economic growth. In: A. Freytag and R. Thurik (eds) *Entrepreneurship and Culture*. Springer, Berlin, Heidelberg, pp. 129–154.

Brownson, C.D. (2013) Fostering entrepreneurial culture: a conceptualization. *European Journal of Business and Management* 5(31), 146–155.

Casanueva, C., Gallego, Á., Castro, I. and Sancho, M. (2014) Airline alliances: mobilizing network resources. *Tourism Management* 44, 88–98.

Covin, J.G. and Lumpkin, G.T. (2011) Entrepreneurial orientation theory and research: reflections on a needed construct. *Entrepreneurship Theory and Practice* 35(5), 855–872.

Dai, L., Maksimov, V., Gilbert, B.A. and Fernhaber, S.A. (2014) Entrepreneurial orientation and international scope: the differential roles of innovativeness, proactiveness, and risk-taking. *Journal of Business Venturing* 29(4), 511–524.

Dawson, C. and Henley, A. (2012) "Push" versus "pull" entrepreneurship: an ambiguous distinction? *International Journal of Entrepreneurial Behavior & Research* 18(6), 697–719.

DeNoble, A., Jung, D. and Ehrlich, S. (1999) Entrepreneurial self-efficacy: the development of a measure and its relationship to entrepreneurial action. In: R.D. Reynolds, W.D. Bygrave, S. Manigart, C.M. Mason, G.D. Meyer, H.J. Sapienze and K.G. Shaver (eds) *Frontiers of Entrepreneurship Research*. P&R Publications, Waltham, Massachusetts.

Duan, J., Yin, J., Xu, Y. and Wu, D. (2020) Should I stay or should I go? Job demands' push and entrepreneurial resources' pull in Chinese migrant workers' return-home entrepreneurial intention. *Entrepreneurship & Regional Development* 32(5–6), 429–448.

Frederick, H., O'Connor, A. and Kuratko, D. (2019) *Entrepreneurship: Theory/Process/Practice*. 5th Asia-Pacific edn. Cengage Learning Australia Pty Limited.

Goulding, P. (2015) 'Entrepreneurial' traits. In: M. Brookes and L. Altinay (eds) *Entrepreneurship in Hospitality & Tourism: A Global Perspective*. Goodfellow Publishers, Oxford, UK, pp. 5–17.

Gras, D., Nason, R., O'Donnell, P.J., Slade Shantz, A. and Sunny, S.A. (2021) Reconceptualizing necessity entrepreneurship. *Academy of Management* 2021 (1), 15368.

Hallak, R., Brown, G. and Lindsay, N.J. (2012) The place identity – performance relationship among tourism entrepreneurs: a structural equation modelling analysis. *Tourism Management* 33(1), 143–154.

Hallak, R., Assaker, G., O'Connor, P. and Lee, C. (2018) Firm performance in the upscale restaurant sector: the effects of resilience, creative self-efficacy, innovation and industry experience. *Journal of Retailing and Consumer Services* 40, 229–240.

Hisrich, R.D., Peters, M.P. and Shepherd, D.A. (2013) *Entrepreneurship*, 9th edn. McGraw-Hill Education, New York, NY.

Hougaard, S. (2005) *The Business Idea: The Early Stages of Entrepreneurship*. Springer, Heidelberg.

Hughes, M. and Morgan, R.E. (2007) Deconstructing the relationship between entrepreneurial orientation and business performance at the embryonic stage of firm growth. *Industrial Marketing Management* 36(5), 651–661.

Hurtado-Palomino, A., De la Gala-Velásquez, B. and Merma-Valverde, W.F. (2021) The synergistic effects of innovativeness, risk-taking and proactiveness on performance of tourism firms. *Tourism Planning & Development*, 1–22.

Kibedi, G.B. (1979) Development of tourism entrepreneurs in Canada. *The Tourist Review* 34(2), 9–11.

Kirkwood, J. (2009) Motivational factors in a push-pull theory of entrepreneurship. *Gender in Management* 24(5), 346–364.

Koh, K.Y. and Hatten, T.S. (2002) The tourism entrepreneur: the overlooked player in tourism development studies. *International Journal of Hospitality & Tourism Administration* 3(1), 21–47.

Lerner, M. and Haber, S. (2001) Performance factors of small tourism ventures: the interface of tourism, entrepreneurship and the environment. *Journal of Business Venturing* 16(1), 77–100.

Lumpkin, G.T. and Dess, G.G. (1996) Clarifying the entrepreneurial orientation construct and linking it to performance. *Academy of Management Review* 21(1), 135–172.

McInnis-Bowers, C., Parris, D.L. and Galperin, B.L. (2017) Which came first, the chicken or the egg? Exploring the relationship between entrepreneurship and resilience among the Boruca Indians of Costa Rica. *Journal of Enterprising Communities: People and Places in the Global Economy* 11(1), 39–60.

Miller, D. (1983) The correlates of entrepreneurship in three types of firms. *Management Science* 29(7), 770–791.

Moensted, M. (2010) Networking and entrepreneurship in small high-tech European firms: an empirical study. *International Journal of Management* 27(1), 16.

Nasiri, N. and Hamelin, N. (2018) Entrepreneurship driven by opportunity and necessity: effects of educations, gender and occupation in MENA. *Asian Journal of Business Research* 8(2), 57–71.

Orhan, M. and Scott, D. (2001) Why women enter into entrepreneurship: an explanatory model. *Women in Management Review* 16(5), 232–247. Available at: https://doi.org/10.1108/09649420110395719 (accessed 10 November 2022).

Schaper, M. and Volery, T. (2007) *Entrepreneurship and Small Business,* 2nd Asia Pacific Rim edn. John Wiley & Sons, Milton, Queensland, Australia.

Shane, S., Locke, E.A. and Collins, C.J. (2003) Entrepreneurial motivation. *Human Resource Management Review* 13(2), 257–279.

Shaw, G. and Williams, A. (1998) Entrepreneurship, small business, culture and tourism development. In: D. Ioannides and K. Debbage (eds) *The Economic Geography of the Tourism Industry: A Supply-side Analysis*. Routledge, London, pp. 235–255.

Simms, D.M. (1981) Tourism, entrepreneurs, and change in Southwest Ireland. Unpublished doctoral dissertation, State University of New York, Albany, New York.

Solvoll, S., Alsosn G.A. and Bulanova, O. (2015) Tourism entrepreneurship – review and future directions. *Scandinavian Journal of Hospitality and Tourism* 15(1), 120–137. DOI: 10.1080/15022250.2015.1065592.

Spinelli, S. and Adams, R.J. (2016) *New Venture Creation: Entrepreneurship for the 21st Century,* 10th edn. McGraw-Hill/Irwin, New York.

Tony, O.A. (2014) The secrets and values of successful entrepreneurs in Nigeria. *International Journal in Management and Social Science*, 2.

US Small Business Administration Office of Advocacy (2018). Available at: https://advocacy.sba.gov/ (accessed 10 November 2022).

Van der Zwan, P., Thurik, R., Verheul, I. and Hessels, J. (2016) Factors influencing the entrepreneurial engagement of opportunity and necessity entrepreneurs. *Eurasian Business Review* 6(3), 273–295.

Visontay, G. (2013) How to recognise an EPIC start-up founder. Available at: https://www.smartcompany.com.au/startupsmart/advice/startupsmart-legal/how-to-recognise-an-epic-start-up-founder/ (accessed 11 July 2022).

World Economic Forum (2014) The bold-ones: high-impact entrepreneurs who transform industries. World Economic Forum Report, World Economic Forum, Geneva, Switzerland.

3 Creativity and Innovation

> …everyone is an entrepreneur only when he actually 'carries out new combinations,' and loses that character as soon as he has built up his business, when he settles down to running it as other people run their businesses. (Schumpeter, 1934, p. 78)

Introduction

Modern tourism firms today are increasingly knowledge-based, meaning their competitive advantage over other firms is increasingly dependent upon the unique skills and knowledge they possess. To effectively deploy these unique skills and knowledge requires creativity, which in turn is wielded to develop and implement innovation, pushing firms ahead of the pack thus achieving a competitive advantage (Martins and Terblanche, 2003).

The phenomena of creativity, innovation and tourism entrepreneurship are inextricably linked but also conceptually different (Dino, 2015). 'Creativity' and 'innovation' have been used interchangeably (Martins and Terblanche, 2003). However, the two constructs are not the same and consideration should be given as to their use, seeing as there are nuanced differences between them.

'Creativity' refers to the generation of new and novel ideas, whereas 'innovation' is the implementation of creativity (i.e. new and novel ideas) in a specific context to create value (Dino, 2015). Within an enterprise, innovation is defined as:

the intentional introduction and application within a role, group, or organization of ideas, processes, products, or procedures, new to the relevant unit of adoption, designed to significantly benefit the individual, the group, the organization, or wider society. (West and Farr, 1990 cited in Martins and Terblanche, 2003, p. 67).

© Rob Hallak and Craig Lee 2023. *Managing Tourism Enterprises: Start-up, Growth and Resilience* (R. Hallak and C. Lee)
DOI: 10.1079/9781789249446.0003

Entrepreneurship is defined as 'the identification and capture of opportunities for useful and actionable outcomes' (Dino, 2015, p. 139). While perspectives on entrepreneurship tend to focus on business start-ups and profit maximization, a wider definition of entrepreneurship identifies it as 'a process that addresses important social needs in a way that is not dominated by direct financial benefits for the entrepreneurs and, simultaneously, catalyses social change' (Edwards-Schachter *et al.*, 2015, p. 29).

The entrepreneurship process and associated entrepreneurial competencies and capabilities can be understood through different theoretical lenses:

1. Psychological traits theory – this focuses on profiling enterprises based on individual level characteristics.
2. Cognitive-behavioural and functionalist theories – this focuses on understanding entrepreneurial behaviours.
3. Social cognitive theories – this focuses on an individual's personal development of their knowledge and capabilities and how they interact with their environment (Edwards-Schachter *et al.*, 2015).

Building a culture of entrepreneurship thus requires the coalescence of creativity, innovation and entrepreneurship (Edwards-Schachter *et al.*, 2015). 'Creativity' and 'innovation' are important to entrepreneurship in order to facilitate recognition and solving of consumer problems and to identify and fill market gaps with appropriate products and services. Thus, creativity, innovation and entrepreneurship strengthen each other in a value-adding ecosystem (Dino, 2015). Creativity (i.e. new and novel ideas) without commercialization (i.e. innovation) results in just another idea, while 'innovation' that is not based on novel or original ideas will struggle to make any impact or create value (i.e. usefulness) in the market. As such, the process of entrepreneurship helps identify where value can be created and commercialized (Dino, 2015).

Learning Outcomes

After completing this chapter, you should be able to:

* Distinguish between the concepts of creativity and innovation
* Identify the sources of information for new business ideas
* Understand the different types of innovations that can be developed by tourism enterprises
* Identify the barriers to creativity and the innovation process.

Creativity

Creativity is defined as the act of generating or recognizing ideas, alternatives or possibilities that may be useful in solving problems, communicating with others and entertaining ourselves and others (Franken, 1982, p. 396). At the individual level, creativity can be operationalized as 'personal creativity', referring to the individual experience of coming up with an idea. Creativity can also be operationalized as 'consensual creativity', referring to the validation of ideas as new by external parties such as colleagues, workers and society (Simonton, 2016).

The concept of creativity involves creative thinking, creative processes and creative outcomes (Edwards-Schachter *et al.*, 2015). To generate creative ideas, several phases are involved and can be thought of as an 'idea journey'. This journey can include 'idea generation', 'idea elaboration', 'idea championing' and 'idea implementation', with the 'idea creator' required to utilize different social networks throughout the phases (Perry-Smith and Mannucci, 2017). In order to determine what ideas qualify as being creative, one needs to understand what ideas are considered not creative (Simonton, 2016). Creative ideas are a 'multiplicative product of originality, utility and surprise', whereas uncreative ideas are routine or habitual, serendipitous responses (Simonton, 2016, p. 87).

In a business context, creativity can occur at multiple levels including the person, enterprise, industry, profession, or broader (Martins and Terblanche, 2003). At the enterprise level, creativity is defined as 'the generation of new and useful/valuable ideas for products, services, processes, and procedures by individuals or groups in specific organizational context' (Martins and Treblanche, 2003, p. 67). Additionally, factors external to the enterprise also play a role in creativity. Plucker *et al.* (2004, p. 90) define creativity as 'the interaction among aptitude, process, and environment by which an individual or group produces a perceptible product that is both novel and useful as defined within a social context'. In this sense, creativity is 'constructed in a complex socio-cultural process' (Edwards-Schachter *et al.*, 2015).

Actors from outside the enterprise that have input into the creative process include customers, clients, professional bodies and cross-boundary networks (Anderson *et al.*, 2014). Creative ideas can be generated from monitoring and imitating competitors, gathering customer feedback, consulting with suppliers, or accessing university and government research (Von Hippel, 1988; Chesbrough *et al.*, 2006). Recent evidence suggests that group-level creativity produces better outcomes in terms of innovation and performance for service-based organizations (Hon and Lui, 2016). In addition, research has also shown that creativity has a stronger association with performance in smaller firms compared to larger firms as there are fewer layers of communication, supporting rapid implementation of creative ideas (Gong *et al.*, 2013).

Innovation

Innovation is closely linked with the concept of entrepreneurship (Hébert and Link, 2006). Schumpeter defined innovation as the introduction of new products or production methods, the opening of a new market or source of new materials, and the creation of new organizational structures in industry. According to the entrepreneurship theory of innovation, in a capitalist system a key driver of economic development is through the act of the entrepreneur in introducing innovation within the marketplace (Schumpeter, 1952).

Entrepreneurs primarily strive to develop new innovations to break the status quo and achieve an economic or competitive advantage (Hébert and Link, 2006). This act disturbs or destroys existing economic structures, resulting in the creation of new economic structures by successfully putting untried methods into practice. This process is labelled by Schumpeter (1952) as 'creative destruction'. On a related note, this also acts as a defining feature that separates entrepreneurs from business owners and/or managers. Entrepreneurs introduce new innovations into the economy and have the ability to continuously innovate, whereas business owners and/or managers do not (Sundbo *et al.*, 2007).

The key element to define an innovation is that it must be a 'new' idea. Being 'new' encompasses an idea that is perceived as new to an individual regardless of when it was first used or discovered (Rogers, 2003). In addition, for an idea to be considered an innovation it must be successfully implemented and utilized for an economic benefit (Kanter, 1983; Damanpour, 1987). This separates the concept of innovation from invention. Inventions refer to the manifestations of creativity and new ideas (Damanpour, 1987). Inventions can be based on new ideas and produce unseen products and services but have no value or usefulness over existing offerings currently on the market. However, when an invention is developed for practical and commercial use, is introduced to the market, is accepted, and results in economic benefits, only then can it be considered an innovation (Sundbo, 1998).

Sources of Information for Innovation

A key step in the process of developing innovations is generating new ideas (Hyland *et al.*, 2006). New ideas can come from 'internal sources', generally referring to actors within an enterprise, and from 'external sources', referring to actors outside the enterprise (Bommer and Jalajas, 2004). Theories of innovation suggest that the likelihood for innovation to occur is driven by internal sources (Amara and Landry, 2005). Ideas can emerge from investments into a dedicated internal research and development (R&D) department (Galende and de la Fuente, 2003). Ideas can also be sourced from the enterprises' employees (Zhou *et al.*, 2013).

Obtaining new ideas from external sources is also recognized as important to the innovation process. Innovations can occur through the constant inward and outward flow of knowledge and information from beyond an enterprises' boundaries (Santamaría *et al.*, 2009). External idea sources can include an enterprise's suppliers, customers and competitors, as well as universities, governments, private laboratories and other countries (Von Hippel, 1988). In terms of the act of obtaining information from external sources, enterprises can look to copy a competitor's idea, consult with customers to develop and refine innovations, or they can access publicly available research (Chesbrough *et al.*, 2006, p. 7).

Studies have shown that a mix of both internal and external sources of information is associated with a productive innovation process. For example, Lee *et al.* (2010) found internal research departments, customers, affiliates and the manufacturing department to be the top sources of innovative ideas for Korean SMEs in the science and technology sectors. A study by Bommer and Jalajas (2004) indicated that small and large firms both placed similar importance on their top sources of information, which were customers, employees, internal R&D, competitors and marketing departments. Overall, these studies demonstrate that employees (internal sources) and customers (external sources) are frequently cited as being among the top sources for collecting information.

Types of Innovation

There are several ways that innovations can be categorized. Innovations can be classified in terms of how 'new' or 'novel' they are to the environment, whether they are 'incremental' or 'radical', as well as being content- and industry-specific – such as service innovations (see Witell et al., 2016). Innovations can also be categorized as 'exploratory' or 'exploitative'; exploratory innovations are innovations developed to meet the needs of emerging customers or markets, while exploitative innovations are developed to meet the needs of existing customers or markets (Jansen et al., 2006). Frameworks for innovation can also be industry-specific – for example, culinary innovations encompass dimensions of artistic aspiration, continuous and discontinuous conditions, learning and networking, adoption and diffusion, as well as newness and change (Stierand and Lynch, 2008).

The Organization for Economic Cooperation and Development (OECD) (OECD and Eurostat, 2005) classifies innovations according to five types: *product, service, process, management* and *marketing* innovations (Schumpeter, 1934; Hjalager, 2010).

Product/service innovations relate to the introduction of new or significantly improved products and services (Hall, 2009). These can be the development or introduction of new materials, intermediate products, or new components or product features (Camisón & Monfort-Mir, 2012). Product/service innovations are generally directly observable by customers and are considered as new (Hjalager, 2010).

Process innovations relate to the development and introduction of new processes that take place 'behind the scenes' with the goal of increasing efficiency and productivity (Hjalager, 2010). This can include the introduction of new equipment or increased automation, new and more efficient methods of production, or the use of new energy sources (Camisón and Monfort-Mir, 2012).

Organizational/managerial innovations relate to the introduction of new or improved methods in an enterprises' organizational structure or systems, configuration of work, or developing new external relations (Hall, 2009). For many tourism enterprises, a main challenge in doing business is developing ways to lower staff turnover, increase flexibility and control costs (Hjalager, 2010). Thus, organizational/managerial innovations also focus on developing new ways of coordinating internal collaborations, training and empowering staff, career progression, and rewarding workers with appropriate pay and benefits (Ottenbacher and Gnoth, 2005; Hjalager, 2010).

Marketing innovations relate to the introduction of new marketing methods, which include changes in product design, promotional strategies and price (Camisón and Monfort-Mir, 2012). Marketing innovations can also involve developing novel types of marketing or behaviour in the market, which include relationships between other parties such as state and other regulatory systems, societal organizations or specific customer segments (Sundbo, 1998).

Benefits of Innovation

Research has shown introducing new products/services, processes, and marketing innovations to be strongly associated with firm growth in entrepreneurial SMEs (Varis and Littunen, 2010). Developing new product innovations works to attract new customers in current and/or new customer segments, increasing an enterprise's market share and sales growth, which in turn increases profits (Wolff and Pett, 2006). Introducing new products will also require the ability to penetrate new markets, which can be provided by marketing innovations (Varis and Littunen, 2010). Introducing marketing innovations functions to increase the purchase and consumption of an enterprise's products and services, which in turn generates increased profits (Gunday et al., 2011).

Other than increasing sales, innovations can also function to reduce costs or improve an enterprise's innovation development capabilities. Developing and implementing process innovations can increase profits for an enterprise through improved efficiencies and reduced costs (Johne and Davies, 2000). Introducing management innovations can create new organizational structures that can make building an entrepreneurial culture more effective, facilitating the development of innovation in other areas, thus playing a key role in enhancing an enterprise's innovative capabilities (Gunday et al., 2011).

Barriers to Creativity and Innovation

The association between creativity and innovation is not always straightforward. Rather, it is characterized by tensions, contradictions and trade-offs (Gong et al., 2013; Revilla and Rodriguez-Prado, 2018). For example, when an enterprise is at the idea-generation phase, exploration, creativity and divergent thinking are required. However, when the innovation process gets to the development and implementation stage, exploitative, convergent and process-oriented thinking is required to ensure an innovation is successfully commercialized (Revilla and Rodriguez-Prado, 2018). An enterprise's strategy, structures, support mechanisms and behaviour that encourages innovation will either support or hinder creativity and the innovation process (Martins and Treblanche, 2003).

Research suggests that for SMEs the ability to innovate is context-dependent, and factors such as a firm's age, types of innovation being developed, and the cultural context play significant roles in influencing the success of developing innovations (Rosenbusch *et al.*, 2011). Creating an innovation orientation in an enterprise encompasses embracing ambitious goals, allocating resources in areas to create more value, challenging firm culture, and effective risk taking (Rosenbusch *et al.*, 2011). Thus, innovation requires significant investment in time and resources, as well as creating risk for the enterprise.

Tourism enterprises may operate with a limited resource base both in funding and knowledge and may not have the competencies to establish formal research and development departments (Whittaker *et al.*, 2016). These constraints create barriers to both creativity and the development and implementation of new innovations (Lee *et al.*, 2016). The innovation development process can also be restricted due to high development costs, lack of government support, and difficulties in protecting intellectual property (Oke, 2004; Madrid-Guijarro *et al.*, 2009).

Summary

This chapter has reviewed the role of innovation and creativity in tourism enterprises. Creativity focuses on the generation of new and novel ideas, whereas 'innovation' is the implementation of creativity (i.e. new and novel ideas) in a specific context with the outcome of creating value. We summarize the innovation development process in Figure 3.1.

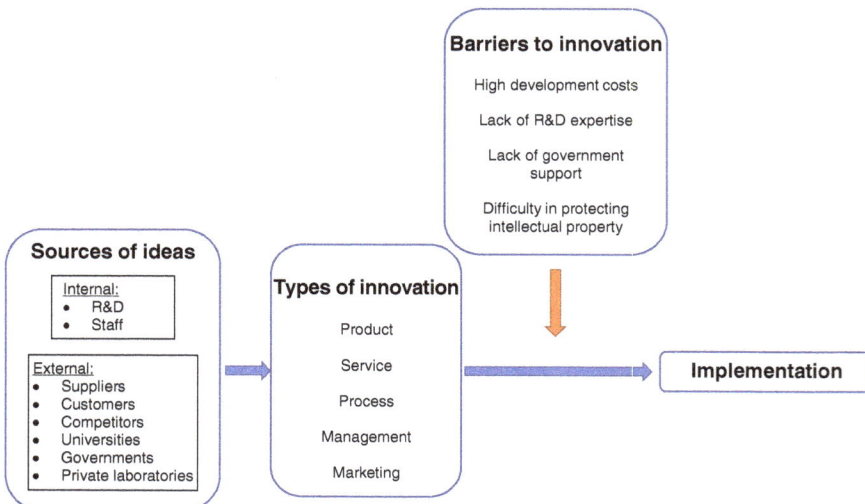

Figure 3.1. Innovation in tourism firms.

The innovation development process begins with the generation of new and creative ideas. These can come from internal or external sources, such as internal research and development, employees, suppliers, customers, competitors, governments and universities. Innovation can come in various forms, such as innovations in products, services, processes, marketing techniques and management structures. These innovations can also be categorized according to their level of novelty, whether incremental or radical, exploratory or exploitative.

Innovation confers various benefits to tourism enterprises. New products can attract new customers or new market bases, increasing market share and sales growth. Process innovations increase profits by reducing costs associated with the production process. Marketing innovations increase the consumption of the tourism enterprise's products and services, while management innovation can create new organizational structures that foster creativity and innovation. While innovation is desirable, there are also barriers that tourism enterprises need to overcome to innovate. The innovation process can be hampered by high development costs (e.g., in time and money), lack of government support, difficulty in protecting intellectual property, and low staff or customer acceptance.

Review Questions

1. How can tourism enterprises build a culture of creativity within the organization?

2. What external sources of information may be useful for tourism enterprises to develop ideas for innovation?

3. Do some research and find out what are the current innovations in products, services, processes, management and marketing in the tourism industry.

4. How might tourism entrepreneurs overcome some of the barriers associated with the innovation development process?

CABI case study: A small German business hotel on the cutting edge of sustainability.

The German Creativhotel Luise shows how an independent hotel can reach sustainability in all aspects of its business. It also explains how this can be a profitable model to share with other hotels.

Authors: Julien Andre, Justine Duval, Marine Jeannon, Mo Yang, Marta Valls I Pi

Affiliation: Skema Business School

Origin: This case study is based on interviews with Ben Förtsch, owner & Managing Director of Creativhotel Luise. If a source is not provided for any data below, it will be from the information provided by Ben.

© CAB International 2021

Continued

CABI case study: continued.

Background

Creativhotel Luise is an independent business hotel in a quiet location with natural surroundings, five minutes from the centre of the small town of Erlangen, Germany.

 The hotel has been family-run for generations and strongly committed to sustainability since the late 1980s. Since 2010, the Creativhotel Luise has calculated and compensated its CO_2 footprint and claims to have become the first climate-positive hotel in Germany. CO_2 emissions per overnight stay are only 11.88 kg, which corresponds to climate-efficiency Class A. Viabono certifies the hotel's CO_2 footprint scope 3, considering all direct and indirect emissions, which is calculated on a yearly basis.

 The green-consciousness of the family is emphasized by Ben Förtsch, the owner of the hotel: 'Since the Luise is a family-run hotel, the focus is on its responsibility towards future generations.' The hotel is managed by Ben, of the third generation, a man of enthusiasm, always keen to participate in new projects, whether it is DIY, gardening or photography. He likes to take things that no-one has a use for and make artwork, which is displayed throughout the hotel.

The Sustainability Context in Germany

Germany's sustainability goals are expressed in its National Sustainable Development Strategy, the short- and long-term objectives of which include inter-generational equity, quality of life, global cohesion and social responsibility. By 2030, the federal government wants renewable energy to represent 60% of total production of energy. In 2019, Germany passed the Climate Change Act, the main intention of which is to reduce greenhouse gases by 55% by 2030, as compared to their 1990 level. Incentives will be introduced for businesses and agencies that operate in an environmentally friendly way.

Sustainability in Business Hotels

Studies by the environmental technology company Greenprint suggest that around 75% of Millennials and 63% of Generation Zs are willing to pay more for sustainable goods. As the interest of customers in sustainability is growing, lots of businesses are investing in sustainable programmes and measures in the hospitality industry.

 Hotels often make efforts to improve their environmental, economic and social impact. However, depending on the hotel type and target, customers might have different expectations and criteria when looking for a place to stay. Business travellers may not necessarily be interested in sustainability. Their stay is often short (one or two nights) and price, location, amenities and services (such as Wi-Fi or room availability) may be more important criteria when choosing the place. According to Ben, only 5–10% of Creativ's guests are really committed to sustainability; 60–70% say they are concerned about these issues but do not consider sustainability as a major factor in their choice. Finally, his impression is that 20–30% of his guests – those that come during the big exhibitions and fairs – do not care about such matters at all. So to what extent is it relevant for a business-oriented hotel, such as Creativhotel, to invest in sustainability?

Continued

CABI case study: continued.

Hotel Chains vs. Independents

Businesses involved in tourism are under increasing pressure to do more to contribute to solving social and environmental problems, and a lot of leading hotel chains are now taking concrete action. They have developed diverse initiatives and programmes to reduce their environmental footprint and improve their social and economic impact. For instance, Hyatt has set ambitious environmental sustainability goals to achieve by 2020 (https://about.hyatt.com/en/hyatt-thrive/our-planet.html). The chain aims to lower energy and water consumption as well as gas emissions. Marriott International also developed the Serve 360 programme (https://serve360.marriott.com/, accessed 10 November 2022) focusing on four core actions: nurture the world (by delivering aid and support to local communities); empower through opportunity (by fighting against unemployment, underemployment and inequality); sustain responsible operations; and welcome all (by promoting understanding of other cultures and human rights). Moreover, they have been certified by LEED (Leadership in Energy and Environmental Design) Volume Program, a green-building certification.

It is easier for hotel chains to develop strong sustainability programmes. Their size, skills and financial assets allow them to foster partnerships with a wide range of organizations to drive sustainable actions quickly and efficiently. Ben agrees that hotel chains have the means to implement strong efficiency-oriented processes. Small independent hotels cannot compete on some levels but, on the other hand, have the freedom to be more flexible and creative. Independent hotels may use a different approach towards sustainability, taking advantage of the fact that the owners and managers are close to the customers and have more interaction with them. They can personally encourage guests to be more committed to sustainability. For instance, Ben often takes his clients for a ride in his autonomous electric car, a Tesla. The idea is to encourage them to think about these issues, to try them out and to make up their own minds.

Creativhotel Luise is a member of Klima Hotels and of Green Pearls – an online platform for sustainable hotels that provides some marketing help. As a member of Green Pearls, the hotel is committed to four main goals: environmental protection; offering local/authentic experiences; 'giving back'; and cultural commitment. The hotel is also certified by three labels: Klimaschutz-Unternehmen e.v, Green Brands and Viabono.

Environmental Practice

For the Förtsch family, all policies and actions can be improved and made more sustainable:

- They own an e-car and provide charging stations at the hotel. They have also established a partnership with the Car Sharing Community in Erlangen.
- Thanks to Klima Hotels, they are able to compensate for CO_2 emissions through a reforesting project in Panama, with others of the same label ('The Climate Forest').
- A solar-power system to provide hot water and heating was installed in the 1990s by Ben's parents. The hotel has recently replaced it and installed new solar electricity panels, which provide 20–30% of their energy needs.
- Another energy source is the hot steam from the local energy plant, with which they have a contract, whose electricity comes from wind or water.
- A rainwater collection system provides water for guest toilets and for the garden.
- They have centralized their air conditioning and heating, which is reduced automatically during the night to save energy.

Continued

CABI case study: continued.

When applying these measures, they want their customers to be involved. A good example of that is their different approach to the towel stickers on the bathrooms. Many hotels have stickers on bathrooms asking guests to leave the towel on the floor if they need a new one or to keep it on the rack if they can keep using the same one to 'save the planet'. The Hotel Luise created their own, saying:

You can save the planet and save us a lot of energy and money by not leaving your towels on the floor. You already know that. But what you should also know is that it makes us happy that you are an everyday hero, making the world a better place by not putting the towel on the ground.

Ben insists that employees working at the hotel share the same values and vision, applying sustainable practices in their own everyday life. For instance, many of them cycle to work. In general, all these policies are implemented with pleasure and humour and they show – in Ben's words – 'how beautiful sustainability can be'.

Being Creative: The 'Renewable Room'

Although it is just a small, independent hotel in a small town, Ben wants the Hotel Luise to be a leader and innovator and to justify the 'creative' in Creativhotel. The best example is most certainly their commitment to recycling, leading to the creation of the 'renewable hotel room'.

The initiative is based on the theories of McDonough and Braungart. In 2002, the architect William McDonough and the chemist Michael Braungart published *Cradle to Cradle: Remaking the Way We Make Things*. The principle rests on two requirements: first, that 'everything should be a resource for something else', and secondly, the use of clean and renewable energy. In practical terms, for a hotel, it means that everything built or integrated should be repairable and recyclable.

The Creativhotel Luise sees itself as being at the beginning of the cradle-to-cradle process. The first elements that correspond to the cradle-to-cradle principle are of the interior design. They do not contain dangerous substances; they are built to last and are also stable, safe and easy to repair. If they are made of wood, they come from sustainable forestry or recycling.

This renewable room takes the cradle-to-cradle principle to a new level. Everything it contains is made of raw materials that are 100% biodegradable or recyclable. Ben explains that 'only the electronics and the electricity do not follow this principle' because of the impossibility of doing so nowadays.

At present, only six renewable rooms are available at the hotel. To develop more, they will need to 'make some modifications, to make it cheaper and to start replacing materials used in the transformation of old rooms with recycled materials'. The renewable room is currently more expensive than other rooms, but the goal is to bring such rooms down to the standard price.

Ben sees the cradle-to-cradle concept as the way forward in sustainable hospitality. He would like to refurbish all old rooms on the basis of this principle, to progress towards a 100% renewable hotel. If the Hotel Luise can figure out how to apply it to the entire hotel without it being too expensive, it could be applied in other hotels and even (why not?) in international hotel chains. This practice could seriously reduce the impact of travelling on the environment.

'Imagine the day,' says Ben, 'when you would like to change your bed and you are able to bury the old one in your garden, knowing it will disintegrate with no negative impact on the soil and on the environment.'

Continued

CABI case study: continued.

Social Measures

The social side of sustainability is just as important. They have two commitments to improve their social environment. One is the Charta der Vielfalt, the German Diversity Charter (https://www.charta-der-vielfalt.de/en/, accessed 10 November 2022), committing the company to good practices regarding staff diversity. The other is the FamilienPakt Bayern, the Family Pact of Bavaria (https://www.familienpakt-bayern.de/), which attests that the company is a family-friendly workplace.

Instead of using the term work–life balance, Ben tries to 'implement work within life, to make it as enjoyable as possible'. This makes it easier for staff to identify with the philosophy of the company and, in turn, transmit it to the guests.

This has a positive impact on the 35 staff and local residents. Employees have unlimited contracts and are treated equally, with above-average pay and qualified training provided by the hotel. Most of their employees are women (80–90%) and work part-time (approximately 85% of all staff). The hotel does not employ seasonal workers. It also employs people who might have more difficulties than others (i.e. older employees, disabled people or single mothers). Nightshifts are mostly done by students, so they can do their homework during the shift once their work for the night at the hotel is done.

Another practice that the Hotel Luise has always kept to and is proud of is having the housekeeping done by in-house staff, instead of externalizing the service as is usually the case in the industry. This has a positive impact on the hotel, as the cleaning staff feel part of the company and the hotel, and it reflects in the quality of their service.

In terms of social practices outside the company, they support different local, social and cultural projects. Some examples are:

- they donate their old furniture and electronic devices to students or people in need;
- they support the small local shops and the local swimming team;
- they tend to buy locally and sell some of these local products on their website; and
- they belong to a network where participant hotels benefit from advantageous prices when they stay with them (around 70% off).

Economic Sustainability

In Ben's words, the Creativhotel Luise is 'not that profit-oriented'. One of their goals is indeed to generate profit, but mainly so that they can reinvest it in the hotel and renovate it to be sustainable over the long term.

When it comes to costs, their biggest one is the employees, who represent 40% of total expenditure. This is due to the high proportion of part-time employees in their total staff and the good wages they provide. However, a way for them to reduce this cost is to have only a three-level hierarchy: the team, the team leaders and the manager – meaning that they do not have to pay for any other managerial positions.

Other ways for them to reduce costs include 'restructuring our processes to be more efficient'. For instance, at breakfast, they do not use a tablecloth. Not only does that allow them to save energy but it also saves on soap, detergent, ironing, time, etc. They use a bio-degradable paper in the centre of the table instead. That allows them to have nice aesthetics for an economical price.

Continued

CABI case study: continued.

Even though calculating the return on investment of their sustainable practices can be complex, they still take them into consideration when running their business. For instance, regarding the room design, usually seen as 5–10 years of usage in hotels, they try to make it usable for more than 10 years.

In terms of KPIs (Key Performance Indicators), they use the same as most hotels, so they can compare themselves to others. However, that does not mean that if one of their own indicators is lower than their competition they must change their own performance.

In Ben's words, even though there might be specific situations where investing in sustainability might not be that profitable, sometimes 'you invest with your heart to make it a true and honest concept. It also creates a good atmosphere for employees, and you can feel it.' For instance, that is why they spend around €3000–4000 of their profits every year on the CO_2 compensation scheme (planting trees in Panama). Apart from the marketing message, they do not get a return from this investment, but it is a small price for them to make the hotel have a positive impact.

References

Charta der Vielfalt. Available at: https://www.charta-der-vielfalt.de/en/ (accessed 10 June 2021).
Business Wire. 'GreenPrint survey finds consumers want to buy eco-friendly products, but don't know how to identify them'. Available at: https://www.businesswire.com/news/home/20210322005061/en/GreenPrint-Survey-Finds-Consumers-Want-to-Buy-Eco-Friendly-Products-but-Don%E2%80%99t-Know-How-to-Identify-Them#:~:text=75%25%20of%20Millennials%20are%20willing,impact%20of%20products%20they%20buy (accessed 10 June 2021).
Hyatt Hotels. 'Our Planet'. Available at: https://about.hyatt.com/en/hyatt-thrive/our-planet.html (accessed 10 June 2021).
Marriott Hotels. 'Serve 360'. Available at: https://serve360.marriott.com/ (accessed 10 June 2021).

Discussion questions

1. Identify and categorize the types of innovations that Creativhotel Luise has implemented in their business.
2. What are the benefits that Creativhotel Luise has derived from the innovations that they have implemented?
3. What are the barriers to innovation that the owner Ben Förtsch discussed in the case study?

References

Amara, N. and Landry, R. (2005) Sources of information as determinants of novelty of innovation in manufacturing firms: evidence from the 1999 Statistics Canada Innovation Survey. *Technovation* 25(3), 245–259. DOI: 10.1016/S0166-4972(03)00113-5.

Anderson, N., Potocnik, K. and Zhou, J. (2014) Innovation and creativity in organizations: a state of the science review, prospective commentary, and guiding framework. *Journal of Management* 40(5), 1297–1333. DOI: 10.1177/0149206314527128.

Bommer, M. and Jalajas, D.S. (2004) Innovation sources of large and small technology-based firms. *IEEE Transactions on Engineering Management* 51(1), 3–18. DOI: 10.1109/TEM.2003.822462.

Camisón, C. and Monfort-Mir, V.M. (2012) Measuring innovation in tourism from the Schumpeterian and the dynamic-capabilities perspectives. *Tourism Management* 33, 776–789. DOI: 0.1016/j.tourman.2011.08.012.

Chesbrough, H., Vanhaverbeke, W. and West, J. (2006) *Open Innovation: Researching a New Paradigm*. Oxford University Press, Oxford, UK.

Damanpour, F. (1987) The adoption of technological, administrative, and ancillary innovations: impact of organizational factors. *Journal of Management* 13(4), 675–688. DOI: 0.1177/014920638701300408.

Dino, R.N. (2015) Crossing boundaries: toward integrating creativity, innovation and entrepreneurship research through practice. *Psychology of Aesthetics, Creativity and the Arts* 9(2), 139–146. DOI: 10.1037/aca0000015.

Edwards-Schachter, M., Garcia-Granero, A., Sanchez-Barrioluengo, M., Quesada-Pineda, H. and Amara, N. (2015) Disentangling competencies: interrelationships on creativity, innovation and entrepreneurship. *Thinking Skills and Creativity* 16, 27–39. DOI: 10.1016/j.tsc.2014.11.006.

Franken, R.E. (1982) *Human Motivation*. Cengage Learning, Massachusetts.

Galende, J. and de la Fuente, J.M. (2003) Internal factors determining a firm's innovative behaviour. *Research Policy* 32(5), 715–736. DOI: 10.1016/S0048-7333(02)00082-3.

Gong, Y., Zhou, J. and Chang, S. (2013) Core knowledge, employee creativity and firm performance: the moderating role of riskiness orientation, firm size and realised absorptive capacity. *Personnel Psychology* 66, 443–482. DOI: 10.1111/peps.12024.

Gunday, G., Ulusoy, G., Kilic, K. and Alpkan, L. (2011) Effects of innovation types on firm performance. *International Journal of Production Economics* 133, 662–676. DOI: 10.1016/j.ijpe.2011.05.014.

Hall, C.M. (2009) Innovation and tourism policy in Australia and New Zealand: never the twain shall meet? *Journal of Policy Research in Tourism, Leisure and Events* 1(1), 2–18. DOI: 10.1080/19407960802703466.

Hébert, R. and Link, A. (2006) The entrepreneur as innovator. *The Journal of Technology Transfer* 31(5), 589–597. DOI: 10.1007/s10961-006-9060-5.

Hjalager, A. (2010) A review of innovation research in tourism. *Tourism Management* 31, 1–12. DOI: 10.1016/j.tourman.2009.08.012.

Hon, A.H.Y. and Lui, S.L. (2016) Employee creativity and innovation in organisations: review, integration and future directions for hospitality research. *International Journal of Contemporary Hospitality Management* 28(5), 862–885. DOI: 0.1108/IJCHM-09-2014-0454.

Hyland, P.W., Marceau, J. and Sloan, T.R. (2006) Sources of innovation and ideas in ICT firms in Australia. *Creativity and Innovation Management* 15(2), 182–194. DOI: 10.1111/j.1467-8691.2006.00378.x.

Jansen, J., Van Den Bosch, F. and Volberda, H.W. (2006) Exploratory innovation, exploitative innovation, and performance: effects of organizational antecedents and environmental moderators. *Management Science* 52, 1661–1674. DOI: 10.1287/mnsc.1060.0576.

Johne, A. and Davies, R. (2000) Innovation in medium-sized insurance companies: how marketing adds value. *International Journal of Bank Marketing* 18, 6–14. DOI: 10.1108/02652320010315316.

Kanter, R.M. (1983) *The Change Masters: Corporate Entrepreneurs at Work*. George Allen and Unwin, London, UK.

Lee, C., Hallak, R. and Sardeshmukh, S.R. (2016) Innovation, entrepreneurship, and restaurant performance: a higher-order structural model. *Tourism Management* 53, 215–228. DOI: 0.1016/j.tourman.2015.09.017.

Lee, S., Park, G., Yoon, B. and Park, J. (2010) Open innovation in SMEs: an intermediated network model. *Research Policy* 39(2), 290–300. DOI: 10.1016/j.respol.2009.12.009.

Madrid-Guijarro, A., Garcia, D. and Van Auken, H. (2009) Barriers to innovation among Spanish manufacturing SMEs. *Journal of Small Business Management* 47, 465–488. DOI: 10.1111/j.1540-627X.2009.00279.x.

Martins, E.C. and Terblanche, F. (2003) Building organisational culture that stimulates creativity and innovation. *European Journal of Innovation Management* 6(1), 64–74. DOI: 10.1108/14601060310456337.

Oke, A. (2004) Barriers to innovation management in service companies. *Journal of Change Management* 4, 31–44. DOI: 10.1080/1469701032000154953.

OECD and Eurostat (Organization for Economic Cooperation and Development and Statistical Office of the European Communities (2005) *Oslo Manual: Guidelines for Collecting and Interpreting Innovation Data* (3rd edn). OECD Publishing, Paris.

Ottenbacher, M.C. and Gnoth, J. (2005) How to develop successful hospitality innovation. *Cornell Hotel and Restaurant Administration Quarterly* 46(2), 205–222. DOI: 10.1177/0010880404271097.

Perry-Smith, J.E. and Mannucci, P.V. (2017) From creativity to innovation: the social network drivers of the four phases of the idea journey. *Academy of Management Review* 42(1), 53–79. DOI: 10.5465/amr.2014.0462.

Plucker, J.A., Beghetto, R.A. and Dow, G.T. (2004) Why isn't creativity more important to educational psychologists? Potentials, pitfalls, and future direction in creativity research. *Educational Psychologist* 39, 83–96. DOI: 10.1207/s15326985ep3902_1.

Revilla, E. and Rodriguez-Prado, B. (2018) Building ambidexterity through creative mechanisms: contextual drivers of innovation success. *Research Policy* 47, 1611–1625. DOI: 0.1016/j.respol.2018.05.009.

Rogers, E.M. (2003) *Diffusion of Innovations*, 5th edn. Free Press, New York US.

Rosenbusch, N., Brinkmann, J. and Bausch, A. (2011) Is innovation always beneficial? A meta-analysis of the relationship between innovation and performance in SMEs. *Journal of Business Venturing* 26, 441–457. DOI: 10.1016/j.jbusvent.2009.12.002.

Santamaría, L., Nieto, M.J. and Barge-Gil, A. (2009) Beyond formal R&D: taking advantage of other sources of innovation in low- and medium-technology industries. *Research Policy* 38(3), 507–517. DOI: 10.1016/j.respol.2008.10.004.

Schumpeter, J.A. (1934) *The Theory of Economic Development: An Inquiry into Profits, Capital, Credit, Interest, and the Business Cycle*. Harvard University Press, Cambridge, UK.

Schumpeter, J.A. (1952) *Capitalism, Socialism and Democracy*, 4th edn. Allen & Unwin, London, UK.

Simonton, D.K. (2016) Defining creativity: Don't we also need to define what is not creative? *Journal of Creative Behaviour* 52(1), 80–90. DOI: 10.1002/jocb.137.

Stierand, M.B. and Lynch, P. (2008) The art of creating culinary innovations. *Tourism & Hospitality Research* 8, 337–350. DOI: 10.1057/thr.2008.28.

Sundbo, J. (1998) *The Theory of Innovation: Entrepreneurs, Technology and Strategy*. Edward Elgar, Cheltenham, UK and Northampton, Massachusetts.

Sundbo, J., Orfila-Sintes, F. and Sørensen, F. (2007) The innovative behaviour of tourism firms: comparative studies of Denmark and Spain. *Research Policy* 36(1), 88–106. DOI: 10.1016/j.respol.2006.08.004.

Varis, M. and Littunen, H. (2010) Types of innovation, sources of information and performance in entrepreneurial SMEs. *European Journal of Innovation Management* 13, 128–154. DOI: 10.1108/14601061011040221.

Von Hippel, E. (1988) *The Sources of Innovation*. Oxford University Press, New York.

Whittaker, D.H., Fath, B.P. and Fiedler, A. (2016) Assembling capabilities for innovation: evidence from New Zealand SMEs. *International Small Business Journal* 34, 123–143. DOI: 10.1177/0266242614548931.

Witell, L., Snyder, H., Gustafsson, A., Fombelle, P. and Kristensson, P. (2016) Defining service innovation: a review and synthesis. *Journal of Business Research* 69, 2863–2872. DOI: 0.1016/j.jbusres.2015.12.055.

Wolff, J.A. and Pett, T.L. (2006) Small-firm performance: modeling the role of product and process improvements. *Journal of Small Business Management* 44(2), 268–284. DOI: 10.1111/j.1540-627X.2006.00167.x.

Zhou, Y., Hong, Y. and Liu, J. (2013) Internal commitment or external collaboration? The impact of human resource management systems on firm innovation and performance. *Human Resource Management* 52(2), 263–288. DOI: 10.1002/hrm.21527.

4 Marketing, Service Quality and Distribution

Introduction

This chapter focuses on the marketing functions of tourism enterprises. It describes elements of the marketing mix (7Ps), as well as a discussion of marketing challenges facing tourism enterprises. The chapter also introduces the concept of 'entrepreneurial marketing' and how this contrasts with traditional marketing approaches. In addition to marketing, the chapter expands on service quality, as well as distribution channels, in the context of tourism and hospitality organizations.

Learning Outcomes

After completing this chapter, you should be able to:

- Describe the 7P elements of the marketing mix
- Explain the marketing challenges experienced by small-business operators
- Distinguish between entrepreneurial marketing and traditional marketing
- Understand the entrepreneurial marketing dimensions
- Define the concept of service quality
- Understand distribution systems in tourism.

Marketing for a Small Business (vs. a Large Organization)

Marketing is a fundamental business process regardless of firm size. Small and large organizations must undertake marketing activities to help identify potential customers, and then create need-satisfying market offerings. However, it is important to note that the way small businesses market their products/services can be different from larger established businesses. Marketing focuses on

© Rob Hallak and Craig Lee 2023. *Managing Tourism Enterprises: Start-up, Growth and Resilience* (R. Hallak and C. Lee)
DOI: 10.1079/9781789249446.0004

creating need-satisfying exchanges by understanding and then meeting their customers' demands. Marketing informs the business about its customers and competitors to enable it to develop superior value propositions for the customer. Marketing involves market research, product development, selling products, product distribution, public relations and customer support. Marketing is essential in all stages of a business's life cycle.

Marketing Mix

The marketing mix is a combination of elements that a business can use to implement its marketing strategies to achieve its marketing objectives. The 7Ps marketing mix has been commonly applied in services marketing (see Table 4.1). The 7Ps marketing mix is an extension to Kotler's (2011) traditional 4Ps (price, product, promotion and place) commonly used for products to include services-focused elements (people, process and physical evidence) (Pholphirul *et al.*, 2021).

Marketing Challenges for Small Businesses

Marketing strategies between small and large businesses vary greatly in several ways due to their inherent characteristics (strategic and tactical).

Lack of marketing budget: Lack of financial resources to carry out marketing research and a feasibility analysis before product introduction to the

Table 4.1. The 7Ps of marketing mix.

Elements	Description
Product	What is being sold. This may be tangible, intangible or an experience.
Price	Charges paid for products or services. When setting prices, it is vital to understand how much customers are prepared to pay for your product, the profit margins target, and costs associated with selling the product. This may include credit payment and instalment payments.
People	This includes everyone directly or indirectly involved in selling the product or service and providing customer service.
Place (or distribution)	Channels or means used to make the products available to customers. This could refer to a shopfront, an online store, a warehouse, or a cloud-based platform.
Promotion	Actions taken to inform the market about what is being sold, including advertising and public relations
Physical evidence	Everything that customers see when interacting with your business. This includes the physical or online facilities where products or services are provided, the design of the facilities, company logo and branding, product packaging, social media presence and more.
Process	Functions involved in delivering your product or service to customers. This includes aspects like your sales funnel, your payment systems, your distribution approach and the way you manage customer relationships.

Source: author's compilations.

market. The budget constraints also hinder the owner's ability to hire the right marketing skills talent. Small businesses are normally characterized by a small number of staff or a single owner-manager. This implies that in most cases there is no specified staff to perform the marketing role.

Limited access to communication techniques: Choosing the right market strategies for the product. Most small-business owners are not sure of how to gather and evaluate available marketing information. As a non-marketer, small-business operators will experience challenges in identifying the effective platform of communication.

Limited resources to implement marketing activities: Marketing is a dynamic process in an evolving environment. Things that worked yesterday may cease to work today. Small businesses may struggle with acquiring the resources (including skills and finance) to develop and implement continuous marketing activities.

Entrepreneurial Marketing

Entrepreneurial marketing (EM) is at the intersection of entrepreneurship and marketing disciplines (see Table 4.2). With EM, an entrepreneur initially conceives a unique idea and develops it into a product that is introduced to the market (new product is tested in main market). Morris *et al.* (2002, p. 5) define entrepreneurial marketing as 'proactive identification and exploitation of opportunities for acquiring and retaining profitable customers through innovative approaches to risk management, resource leveraging and value creation'. This definition incorporates four dimensions from the entrepreneurship literature and three from marketing literature (in blue in Figure 4.1).

Table 4.2. Entrepreneurial marketing versus traditional marketing.

Entrepreneurial marketing	Traditional marketing
Requires creativity, energy, and determination to develop ideas and brands	Manages an established brand and advertising
Captures first customers; develop a client base and long-term relationships	Manages existing customers
Develops new products, pricing strategies, distribution channels, communication, training and design	Manages existing promotions, products, pricing, places, people, processes and physical environment (the 7Ps)
Continuous market experimentation; market pilots	Focuses on targeting the same market
Limited resources; entrepreneur/founder-driven	Resources dedicated toward marketing
Communication with customers is more fluid and spontaneous; two-way communication process	Communication with customers are standardized, one-directional; more difficult to create one-on-one relationships
Satisfaction and awareness goals	Financial and market share goals

Source: adapted from Morris *et al.*, 2002; Becherer *et al.*, 2012

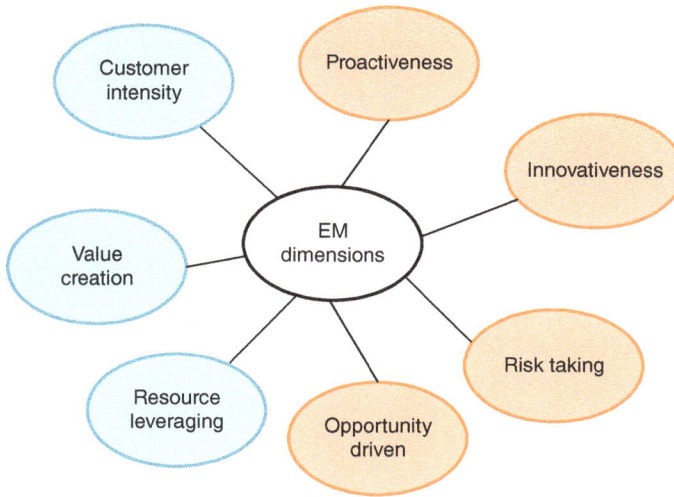

Figure 4.1. Dimensions of entrepreneurial marketing. (Source: developed by authors.)

Dimensions of Entrepreneurial Marketing

Proactiveness: Refers to taking actions in anticipation of future opportunities. Proactiveness is forward-looking. An entrepreneurial marketer anticipates and redefines future market opportunities and then develops marketing strategies to exploit them.

Opportunity driven: This dimension focuses on recognizing and pursuing opportunities of presently untapped markets. Opportunity recognition and pursuit is fundamental to entrepreneurship.

Innovativeness: Core to entrepreneurship, this dimension focuses on creativity in idea generation and development. Innovativeness can be in the form of new products, new processes, new technology and new markets. An entrepreneurial marketer always concentrates on marketing actions that lead to new markets, new technology, new products or new processes.

Risk taking: Willingness to take calculated risks attached to possible gains in pursuit of new opportunities. The level of risk an entrepreneurial marketer is willing to take influences the marketing actions employed to exploit opportunities.

Resource leveraging: Using limited resources to maximum advantage. According to Morris *et al.* (2002), entrepreneurial marketers can leverage limited resources in several ways such as recognizing resources not seen by others, using certain resources to find other resources and extending resources much more than others (Becherer *et al.*, 2012). Resource-constrained tourism businesses are more likely to devise innovative and proactive marketing strategies and thus be able to do more using limited resources, complementing resources with one another to increase their value.

Customer intensity: Customer intensity, or customer-centric, is a key dimension of EM and a central element of marketing (Morrish *et al.*, 2010). An entrepreneurial marketer takes customers as top priority of marketing actions, which are adaptive, flexible and creative to suit customers' preferences.

Value creation: Value creation is a core marketing activity. Entrepreneurial marketers need to find untapped customer value propositions and find new ways to create or discover value.

Entrepreneurial Marketing Practices in Small Businesses

Entrepreneurial marketing is a low-cost approach whereby businesses create and/or use low-cost campaigns to promote their product or service. Entrepreneurial marketing follows a customer-based approach whereby the product or service is developed first before identifying a target market (business builds interest in their product or service through trial and error). It does not require a large budget allocation to increase sales from this approach. Because of a lack of marketing resources, small businesses adopt entrepreneurial marketing practices to sell products to their customers. Small-business marketing practices tend to be low-cost, directly targeted to customers (sometimes by networking), and apply viral marketing (Gilmore *et al.*, 2001; Rollins *et al.*, 2014).

In a tourism context, entrepreneurial marketing enables the leveraging of customer preference knowledge, market intelligence and product knowledge to deliver superior value to the customer through brand differentiation (Thomas *et al.* 2013). Boutique hotels in particular can benefit from entrepreneurial marketing, in terms of service delivery and effective segmentation (Kurgun *et al.* 2011). Entrepreneurial marketing is effectively used when there are limited marketing resources (Jaafar, 2012).

How can businesses implement entrepreneurial marketing?

With entrepreneurial marketing, a business can use viral marketing to leverage the power of social media and other similar channels to market its product or service. This marketing tactic is fast and reaches many people, and the product becomes popular very quickly. There are numerous ways to implement entrepreneurial marketing. Ionita (2012) suggests ways shown in Box 4.1.

Box 4.1. Ways to implement entrepreneurial marketing.

- *Networking/relationship marketing*: This is a one-on-one, person-to-person technique of promoting and creating a new product.
- *Guerrilla marketing*: This involves novel and unconventional tactics that businesses (mostly small) use to introduce and attract buyers for a new product. The tactics are designed to evoke surprise, wonder or shock.
- *Expeditionary marketing*: This tactic enables businesses to identify and expand into new markets. It helps to discover information and opportunities about new markets.

What are the outcomes of entrepreneurial marketing for business performance?

Entrepreneurial marketing provides several benefits for small businesses including:

1. *Performance efficiency* – in terms of return on investment and return on assets.
2. *Growth* – in terms of increase in sales growth, increase in market share, employee growth.
3. *Profit* – in terms of increased return on sales, increase in net profit margins and gross profit margins.
4. *Reputation* – in terms of high reputation, social media reviews, employees are proud to be part of the business. (Sadiku-Dushi *et al.*, 2019)

Service Quality

Products or services in tourism have unique characteristics that differentiate it from manufacturing and other service-oriented organizations. Intangible products and services make them harder for testing and evaluation. Heterogeneous services dependent on human performance make it difficult to apply standard specifications of quality and eliminate deviations from the norm. Mistakes in the service process cannot be identified and corrected before they reach the consumer because of simultaneity. Many mistakes are accidental or unexpected and are a part of business. These must be mitigated through service recovery strategies. In contrast, manufacturing mistakes can be discovered and corrected before the products are purchased. Because of these characteristics, managing service quality is essential for any tourism enterprise.

Berry (1988) stated the following about service quality:

- Customers define quality
- Quality is a journey
- Quality is everyone's job
- Quality, leadership and communication are inseparable
- Quality and integrity are inseparable
- Quality is a design issue
- Quality is keeping the service promise.

Customer service has a direct impact on customer satisfaction (Box 4.2). In turn, this increases repeat purchase and positive word-of-mouth, ultimately increasing the company's bottom line.

Service quality is subjective and judged by the guests. Guests' expectations are conceptualized at three levels:

Essential services: Services that are the core of the service business. These meet the fundamental requirements to continue operations. For example, hotels should maintain reasonable opening hours to check in guests with reservations.

Expected services: Services that guests assume the service provider should offer to provide adequate service. While not mandatory, these services need to be offered

---

Box 4.2. The functions of customer service.

Delivering good customer service works to:

- Improve guest convenience
- Enhance a tourism provider's image
- Ensure customer security
- Generate repeat visitation or purchase
- Establish a competitive edge
- Generate customer demand.

---

to stay competitive because of guest expectations. For example, multiple payment options, full information on the services, facilities and surrounding location.

Optional/desired services: Services that are an added bonus that enhance the value of a guest's visit. This expresses the uniqueness of the service provider and creates a competitive advantage.

Service quality model

Service is an intangible construct; hence it is difficult to measure service quality objectively. However, measuring the service quality expectations and perceptions of the service recipient is important as it helps organizations to identify problems in current systems and manage them effectively, for both customer retention and attracting new customers. One of the most frequently cited models for measuring customer service, SERVQUAL, developed by Parasuraman *et al.* (1985, p. 46), suggests that 'the quality that a consumer perceives in a service is a function of the magnitude and direction of the gap between expected service and perceived service'. The wider the gap between what the customer expects and what the customer actually experiences, the larger the dissatisfaction will be and vice versa (Table 4.3).

The SERVQUAL model consists of five factors that contribute to service quality:

1. *Tangibles*: Appearance of physical facilities, equipment, personnel and communication materials.
2. *Reliability*: Ability to perform the promised service dependably and accurately.
3. *Responsiveness*: Willingness to help customers and provide prompt service.
4. *Assurance*: Knowledge and courtesy of employees and their ability to convey trust and confidence.
5. *Empathy*: Caring, individualized attention the firm provides to its customers.

Service Performance

Service quality reflects the difference between guests' expectations and the actual services received. The extent to which expectations and service performance are similar or different influence the satisfaction levels of guests, based on a 'better-than/worse-than' comparison. Service is perceived as exceptional

Table 4.3. Example of a SERVQUAL measure for a hotel.

Tangibles
The hotel has up-to-date equipment
The hotel's physical facilities are visually appealing
The hotel's employees are well-dressed and appear neat
The hotel's physical environment is clean
Reliability
When the hotel staff promise to do something by a certain time, they do it
The hotel shows sincere interest in solving guests' problems
The hotel performs the service right first time
The hotel provides its services at the time it promises to do so
The hotel keeps its records accurately
Responsiveness
The hotel's employees make information easily obtainable by guests
The hotel's employees give prompt service to guests
The hotel's employees are always willing to help guests
The hotel's employees are never too busy to respond to guests' requests
Assurance
The behaviour of the hotel's employees instils confidence in guests
Guests feel safe in their stay at the hotel
The hotel's employees are polite to guests
The hotel's employees have knowledge to answer guests' questions
Empathy
The hotel gives guests individual attention
The location of the hotel is convenient for guests
The hotel's employees give guests personal service
The hotel has its guests' best interests at heart
The hotel's employees understand the specific needs of their guests

Source: Adapted from: Kumarasinghe *et al.*, (2019). Comparing local and foreign perceptions of service quality of five-star hotels in Sri Lanka.

when expected services have been surpassed in quality and quantity. Service is perceived as adequate when expectations are sufficiently met with the services provided. However, one must keep in mind that what is adequate today may not be tomorrow. Thus, adequate service is not a standard that lets companies excel. Services are unsatisfactory when the service performed does not match expectations. Despite this, service failures can be an opportunity for service recovery that can enhance customer satisfaction if the failures are remedied.

Distribution channels

Distribution channels in tourism refer to a system of intermediaries that facilitate the sale and delivery of tourism services from suppliers to consumers (Buhalis and Laws, 2001). Distribution channels are important to consider because they serve as part of the marketing mix that makes tourism products and services available to customers, are the link between the suppliers of tourism products and services to their end-users, and are the bridge between supply and demand (Gartner and Bachri, 1994). Information technology has significantly impacted the structure of distribution channels, increasing choice and shifting more power to tourists, making it crucial for tourism enterprises to understand the tourist to develop a successful distribution strategy.

For example, under the traditional tourism distribution model, tourists relied on intermediaries such as travel agents to access the products and services offered by tourism enterprises (e.g., tours, accommodation) through global distribution systems (GDSs) (Law *et al.*, 2015). In today's tourism distribution model, the internet allows tourists to directly access the products and services of tourism enterprises, effectively cutting out the middlemen, or to use online intermediaries such as online travel agencies (OTAs) (e.g. Expedia, Tripadvisor, etc.).

Intermediaries

Intermediaries refer to actors that bundle together two or more elements of supply (e.g., a tour, airline seat, accommodation) and sell it to the customer (i.e. middlemen) (Cooper, 2016). Intermediaries are important in tourism distribution channels because in many cases it is not feasible for tourism enterprises to sell their products and services directly to tourists across every market. Therefore, according to Song (2012), intermediaries function to:

Match supply with demand: Tourists demand a wide range of products and services when engaging in tourism. However, suppliers can only provide a specific range of products and services to meet tourist needs. As such, tourism intermediaries can package several tourism products and services to meet tourism demand, increasing sales for all enterprises involved.

Improve efficiency: Intermediaries reduce the number of transactions and associated costs that tourists need to make. For example, instead of making individual purchases for airline tickets, accommodation and tours, intermediaries can bundle these services together and sell them in one transaction at one price to tourists. This reduces expense and search time for the customer.

Facilitate information exchange: Tourism enterprises may sell their products and services to markets far beyond their location. Thus, intermediaries assist in transferring information to customers that can be costly or too complex for smaller tourism enterprises to manage. For example, a small tourism operator may not have the capacity to advertise their products and services to a large and diverse market such as China. In this case, the tour operator can engage the services of an intermediary who specializes in distribution in China to disseminate information about their products and services at a much lower cost. Additionally, intermediaries can also collect information from tourists and pass it back to suppliers, enabling tourism enterprises to improve their product/service quality.

Provide extra services: Intermediaries can provide service beyond just facilitating buying and selling. For example, tourism enterprises can extend credit to allow delayed payments to intermediaries. Intermediaries can also offer members in the channel finance, credit, insurance and consultancy services to tourism enterprises and consumers.

Distribution channel structure

The structure of a distribution channel refers to the way in which tourism supplies reach the consumer. This can be categorized into direct and indirect channels. Direct channels have the simplest and shortest structure, where a tourism enterprise sells its products and services directly to the customer without involving intermediaries (see Figure 4.2). For example, low-cost airlines allow customers to book and pay for air tickets from their own website.

Indirect channels involve tourism enterprises working with their intermediaries to sell their products and services to customers. The number of intermediaries between the tourism supplier and customer denotes the number of 'levels' within the indirect channel. Referring to Figure 4.2, for the distribution channel presented in the middle, the sole travel agent sitting between the path from the tourism supplier to the customer denotes a one-level channel. In the same vein, for the distribution channel presented at the bottom, the tourism wholesaler and travel agent sitting between the path from the tourism supplier to the customer denote a two-level channel. Note that, in practice, a tourism supplier is likely to sell its products through both direct and indirect channels, making for a complex and interconnected distribution system.

Developing distribution channels

As distribution channels can range from simple direct channels to more complex, interconnected distribution systems, it is imperative for tourism enterprises to take a strategic approach to planning its methods of distribution.

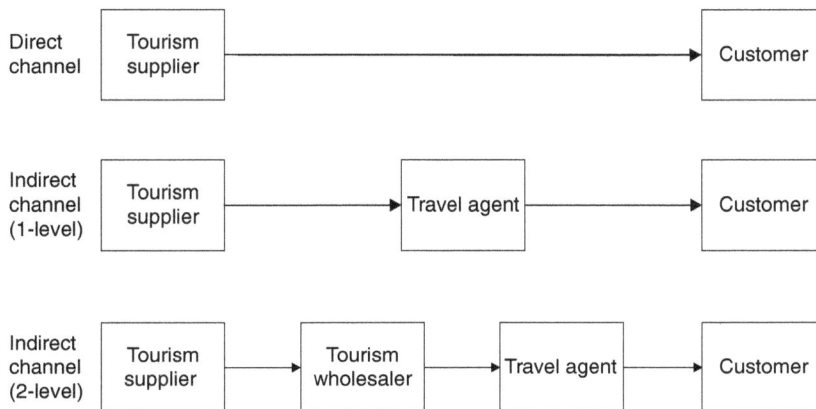

Figure 4.2. Tourism industry distribution channels.

This is to ensure that the types of channels selected will achieve a balance between reach, profitability and cost. There are several strategies tourism enterprises can use to set distribution channels as illustrated by Cooper (2016):

Intensive distribution strategy: This strategy is where the tourism enterprise's products and services are sold through every available channel.

Exclusive distribution strategy: This strategy is where the tourism enterprise's products and services are sold through a limited number of highly appropriate/specialized channels that meet the tourism enterprise's desired image or type of clientele.

Selective distribution strategy: This strategy is a hybrid of the previous two approaches, where the tourism enterprise's products and services are sold through multiple channels, but each channel closely meets the tourism enterprise's desired marketing image and objectives.

Evaluating distribution channels

For any strategy pursued, the effectiveness of the tourism enterprise's distribution channels should be evaluated on a regular basis to ensure value for money is being achieved. Evaluating channel members within a distribution system will allow the tourism enterprise to decide which intermediaries' contracts to renew, which to discontinue, and whether new channels need to be established. Evaluation of distribution channels can include the sales revenue or volume, number of new customers gained, profit margins achieved, service quality, number of customer complaints, commissions paid, and expenditure on promotions and marketing (Song, 2012).

Summary

This chapter presented the essentials of marketing, entrepreneurial marketing, service quality and distribution. Different perspectives on these concepts in small businesses have been provided, as well as explaining the differences between entrepreneurial marketing and traditional marketing. The chapter concluded with a brief discussion of the service quality model, as well as a discussion of the distribution channels, distribution channel structure and how to develop a distribution channel for a small business in tourism.

Discussion Questions

- What is entrepreneurial marketing? How is it different from traditional marketing? Discuss using examples.
- Using examples, discuss the entrepreneurial marketing dimensions.
- With your classmates, discuss the 7Ps of the marketing mix.
- In your class groups, come up with a hypothetical example of a tourism business and develop its distribution channel.

Case study: Supporting informed destination development using visitor intelligence.

A study to articulate the importance of visitor intelligence data in tourism business and destination development

Author: Nicole L. Vaugeois and Pete Parker

Affiliation: Vancouver Island University, Nanaimo, British Columbia, Canada

Origin: Vancouver Island University World Leisure Centre of Excellence

© N.L. Vaugeois and P. Parker, 2015

The Issue, Opportunity or Trend

Communities that are serious about tourism need to obtain and use market research to understand who their current visitors are and how satisfied they are with their experience. Having access to local visitor data provides numerous benefits to the range of tourism stakeholders in a destination. Armed with research data, destination marketing organizations (DMOs) are able to maximize the return on investment of their often limited and unstable marketing funds by participating in programmes that align with their desired target markets. Tourism businesses can use the evidence of consumer demand to make strategic decisions enabling the growth of their business, or to assist in obtaining financial support from funding institutions. Municipal bodies are able to identify the types of activities that visitors engage in and their relative satisfaction with community infrastructure and amenities. And collectively, all stakeholders can utilize marketing intelligence to design tourism development plans including strategic initiatives to satisfy current visitors or tap into new markets. While these benefits may seem obvious to some, the reality is that very few communities have developed a system to obtain information from their visitors on an ongoing basis. This is particularly true of many rural areas at early stages of tourism development. Unfortunately, these destinations often have limited budgets for marketing and a lack of intellectual capital to undertake much needed market research. In the absence of local market data, they often rely on macro-level data sources on visitors in urban areas, or from provincial and national sources. These data are unlikely to represent the profile of their own visitors and if used to guide decisions, could result in risky and ineffective investments for the communities. There is a need for tourism researchers to design models to gather visitor data at the community level on an ongoing basis that results in enhanced marketing intelligence for stakeholders. The purpose of this case study is to describe the design and implementation of an innovative and successful model developed by multiple tourism stakeholders on Vancouver Island, Canada. After highlighting some insights from the literature, the context of the case study will be described and then details on the design and implementation of the model will be detailed, including the outcomes that have emerged.

Literature

The literature on visitor experience has expanded rapidly in recent years (Sharpley and Stone, 2010), largely in response to the growing interest in understanding the multi-dimensional nature of experience. Tourism researchers have made tremendous contributions to understand the nature of the visitor experience including tourist satisfaction (Alegre and Garau, 2010; Rucks and Geissler, 2011; Zabkar *et al.*, 2010), segmentation, psychographics

Continued

Case study: continued.

and niche markets (Andriotis and Agiomirgianakis, 2008; Arimond *et al.*, 2003; Canadian Tourism Commission, 2015) and spatial analysis (Edwards and Griffin, 2013). Additionally, the focus on methodological advancements in this research has also expanded the ability of researchers to analyse and interpret visitor data (Stradling *et al.*, 2007; Priporas and Vassiliadis, 2013). Many of the studies used to produce this knowledge are conducted as single investigations on visitors with the intent of enhancing academic knowledge about visitor experience. While useful and necessary, there remains a need to ensure that those involved in destination marketing can access visitor research to improve their investment decisions (Liburd, 2011). In particular, destinations require enhanced knowledge about the origin of their visitors, their satisfaction levels, travel activities, spending and trip-planning behaviours to enable them to make more informed investments in tourism marketing. Despite the numerous opportunities that exist for academics and destination marketing organizations to work together to combine their resources and skill sets to gather, share and utilize visitor research, there are limited examples of collaboration in the literature. This case study contributes to this gap and may inspire further knowledge exchange in destination marketing as called for by Hudson (2013).

The Innovation

Case context

Vancouver Island, British Columbia, relies heavily on tourism as a core contributor to the economy. The region provides visitors with adventure, culinary and agritourism experiences in both terrestrial and marine settings. Despite the fact that the last provincial visitor research was undertaken in British Columbia in 1995, the Vancouver Island region has been proactive in researching and profiling its visitors. In 2003, a region-wide visitor research model provided tourism stakeholders with comprehensive data on visitors in all four seasons. Then, in 2008, a region-wide study provided updated information on visitors led by the regional DMO, Tourism Vancouver Island. While useful, these efforts relied on significant funding from external sources and, as such, have been difficult to maintain on an ongoing basis. Additionally, these regional studies were not focused on providing individual communities with results on their visitors *per se*. Many of the communities in the region are small and at early stages of tourism development and support for continuous investment in tourism by local government varies widely. As such, the budgets to invest in tourism marketing or market research are often limited and highly unstable, and the capacity to undertake market research among staff members (if they exist) is usually quite weak. While the regional economy highlights opportunities for growth of small business, tourism businesses often have difficulty obtaining financing due to their inability to provide evidence of visitor demand in their business plans. While significant investments in tourism have been made, they have largely been based on outdated visitor data, one-off studies by consultants and guesswork. In an effort to address these systemic issues and enhance the availability of marketing intelligence, researchers piloted a visitor experience study (VES) with the City of Nanaimo and the community of Tofino in 2013. After a successful pilot, the model was refined and expanded in 2014 to include the community of Ucluelet and the Cowichan Valley, and in 2015 to include nine communities in the Vancouver Island region. The innovative model was developed using a collaborative approach with multiple stakeholders who shared an interest in understanding community and regional visitor experience.

Continued

Case study: continued.

Stakeholders Involved

The success of this innovation is due in large part to the collaboration of multiple stake-holders who share an interest in community and regional tourism development. The original model was designed as part of a Cooperative Work placement by a fourth-year student, Nichola Evernden, at Vancouver Island University, who worked with her supervisor, Dr Nicole Vaugeois, and the DMOs, Tourism Nanaimo and Tourism Tofino. After the success of this pilot in 2013, the partnership sought the skills of a private consultancy called the Sociable Scientists to help expand the model with additional communities. In 2014, the model was expanded to include the community of Ucluelet and the Cowichan Valley, and following that, in 2015, additional communities included Port Alberni, Parksville, Qualicum Beach, Courtenay, Campbell River and the communities within the sub-region of North Vancouver Island. Each of the partners in this initiative have a clear role in the VES. The Community DMO initiates the study within their community when they are seeking market research. They are also responsible for encouraging buy-in from local businesses, select-ing ballot locations, providing input on the survey and determining and obtaining incentive prizes. The Sociable Scientists signs a contract with each community and coordinates the data-collection process. The university is responsible for the data analysis and preparation of the visitor profiles and assists in presentations back to the communities.

Approach Used and the Impact

The model was developed in a collaborative manner utilizing the resources and capacities of researchers at a local university, a private research consultancy, DMOs and tourism businesses. The model's innovative design incorporates the participation of businesses, the use of pre-consent ballots, incentive prizes and a post-experience online visitor survey. The model has evolved over time due to continuous evaluation by the stakeholders. Its evolution is described in three stages.

Stage 1: Initial Pilot

The initial pilot of the model was done in 2013 with Vancouver Island University (VIU), Tourism Tofino and Tourism Nanaimo. In this first stage, the partners met via teleconference calls to discuss the need for the data, to clarify roles for the pilot and to determine timelines for the data collection and reporting. Both communities needed better data but had limited funds or staff time to contribute to the project. They decided to pool a modest investment towards a salary for a Cooperative Education student to pilot the project in both communities. Nichola Evernden, a fourth-year student in the Bachelor of Tourism Management at VIU did her Cooperative Education work term on contract with Tourism Tofino. The original survey was designed based on the instrument used in the 2003 Vancouver Island study so that comparable data would emerge. As the 2003 study was done using in-field intercepts, the instrument was redesigned to take place as a web-based survey using Survey Monkey as the platform. The survey instrument was modified with input from the DMOs to ensure that it represented, for example, attractions and community-specific amenities. The resulting survey gathered data on visitor motivations, travel planning behaviour and informational sources, overall experience, satisfaction, group composition, spending and suggested enhancements.

Continued

Case study: continued.

The sample of visitors was obtained via convenience sampling methods and the use of ballot boxes at 10–12 locations within each community. The DMO partners selected a range of businesses and attractions within their community that visitors were likely to frequent while on vacation. These included, for example, coffee shops, retail outlets, tour operators, visitor information centres, accommodations, special events, marinas and parks. Each business was approached to request their participation in the study by hosting a ballot box for a 12-week data-collection period. These were often placed in the guest reception area or an area where visitors might be waiting. These ballot boxes were customized with visuals and branding by the DMO and via email. In exchange, visitors were able to enter their name to win a series of prizes determined by the destination, which included both experiences and tangible products. These ballots were gathered bi-weekly by the destination and sent to the researchers who then sent a request to participate in the study to the emails provided. Data were later analysed in Statistical Package for the Social Sciences (SPSS) by the university partner and results were shared in an 8–10-page user-friendly visitor profile for the community. Results were also shared publicly in a stakeholder event.

Stage 2: Expanding the Model to Include Sub-regions

Early in 2014, the partnership expanded to include a private research consultancy called the Sociable Scientists. This was done to allow the model to expand across the region as the private firm could take over the contract process with communities and hire Nichola Evernden (now graduated with her degree). This expansion of the model to a business focus proved to be critical for the success of the model as it allowed for a strong client-centred focus to emerge whereby future contracts for the firm were dependent upon the provision of successful research in each community. Now, communities signed a business contract with the Sociable Scientists where for a modest investment of approximately CAN$5000–$6000, the community then received the VES for one data-collection period.

Based on the success of the first year and with the inclusion of a new partner, the decision was made to invite the first communities to share their experience with the VES team at a meeting to which other DMOs within the region were invited. This meeting allowed for these communities to learn more about the model, why visitor data is critical and to hear from their colleagues on how it worked for them and how they have been using the new data. After this gathering, two new DMOs signed on for 2014 data collection including Ucluelet and a sub-region called the Cowichan Valley. This shift allowed the partners to see if the model would work in a small region as opposed to a single community. In this case, additional ballot locations were added to ensure that locations throughout the sub-region were incorporated.

Stage 3: Expansion across the Island

The second expansion of the model occurred in 2015 where, after another evaluation gathering, additional communities decided to participate in the 2015 process. This resulted in the VES model to incorporate the majority of communities and sub-regions of Vancouver Island. In this stage, a sub-region in the north was able to gain buy-in from a number of the communities and obtain external funding support through the Island Coast Economic Trust. Similarly, the Parksville Qualicum Beach sub-region was able to gather support from community

Continued

Case study: continued.

partners to contribute to the VES. This buy-in would not have been possible without the success of the first two stages and the validation of the value of the model by the previous DMOs.

Key Findings

The VES model has produced numerous insights about visitors coming to the communities and sub-regions of Vancouver Island, as well as numerous insights about how to engage community-based research. The model has gathered data from visitors in each of the locations with sample sizes ranging from 225 to 1544 completed surveys and response rates of 37–58% (average response rate is 48%) as shown in Table 4.4. Since the original pilot, participating communities have continued their involvement in subsequent years, indicating their satisfaction with the model. With experience and continuous evaluation, the sample sizes have increased over time.

The visitor profiles that have emerged through the VES indicate that communities are wise to understand their own, versus regional, visitors. Variables that often differ among the destinations include length of stay, visitor spending, inspiration to visit, trip-planning behaviour and suggested enhancements. Variables that are fairly consistent among the profiles include visitor origin, group size and composition, and modes of travel used. For example, visitors in the 2015 visitor profile to the Parksville Qualicum Beach area were more inspired by beaches, sandcastles and family experiences; 27% had planned their trip 1–6 months in advance and spent, on average, $649 per day per group. Visitors to the North Island were more inspired by nature, wilderness, whales and beauty; 43% had planned their trip 1–6 months in advance and spent an average of $611 per day per group. The City of Nanaimo

Table 4.4. Data collection over the period of the BES evolution 2013–2015 including completed surveys and response rates.

Community and data-collection period	Completed surveys	Response rate from ballots received
2013		
Nanaimo	225	41%
Tofino	475	52%
2014		
Nanaimo	307	37%
Tofino	401	53%
Ucleuelet	661	50%
Cowichan	582	58%
2015		
Nanaimo	241	47%
Tofino	733	48%
Cowichan	609	48%
Parksville Qualicum Beach	1544	47%
Vancouver Island North	522	54%
Campbell River	462	50%
Comox Valley	324	50%
Port Alberni	230	43%

Continued

Case study: continued.

visitors were more inspired by friends, family and shopping; 39% had planned 1–6 months ahead and had an average spend of $489 per day. These few comparisons illustrate some of the insights that have been gained at the community level and justify the value of engaging community-based research to understand visitors.

For many of the communities, the VES has provided the DMOs with the first community specific data sets on visitors to enable them to understand their current visitors. The insights produced on visitors have aided tourism stakeholders to make more strategic marketing and development decisions at the business, community and regional level. Feedback from the DMOs has expressed strong support for the model based on comparing the value of the information with the financial investment required and the ease of application for their staff. The initial communities continued the use of the model to gather data on visitors in a different season, and they actively recruited additional communities to adopt the model in the second and subsequent seasons.

The survey instrument used in the VES is similar in each community, but with some customization options. The response categories for the attractions and activities that visitors participate in for example, are customized for each community. The instrument has been adapted in, a number of communities to gather data on subsets of visitors; for example, those attending a special event. In these cases, survey logic is used to identify visitors attending a specific event and then those visitors are asked a few additional questions enabling the community to understand specific event visitors. Similarly, some of the communities are interested in the Canadian Tourism Commission Explorer Quotient, a market segmentation tool that uses psychographic profiles to understand visitor motivations and trip behaviour (see https://www.destinationcanada.com/sites/default/files/archive/2013-01-01/Tools_ExplorerQuotient_Profiles_2015_EN.pdf?msclkid=efea4e4faba211ecaba0b0e6e2f403aa, accessed 11 November 2022). For these communities, similar to the special event process, the end of the survey asked respondents if they were willing to answer a few more questions, and if they did, they were routed out of the Survey Monkey site temporarily to take the EQ survey to find out what type of explorer they were. They were then routed back into the VES survey to provide their EQ type before completing the survey. This allowed the communities investing in the EQ model to verify their visitor types and respond to their needs accordingly. In 2015, the model also incorporated a question to provide a Net Promoter score as this indicator has become more valued by Destination BC as a metric of positive visitor experience. The model continues to grow in application to additional communities with the intention of moving to other regions of the province. Interest from the Northwest Territories and Ontario, Canada and the Republic of Ireland has also emerged, providing opportunities to test the model in different contexts. Additionally, the model is being considered for sector-specific implementation (e.g., marine tourism, golf).

In summary, the evolution and success of the VES model has been possible due to a number of success factors including:

1. The engagement of multiple partners with clear roles;
2. Community buy-in, engagement and ownership of the results;
3. The affordability and value of the investment for DMOs;
4. The format and speed of the reporting of the results;
5. The ongoing nature of the model with opportunities to buy-in whenever a community wants;
6. Insights gained and opportunities to learn from other communities;
7. Professionalism and client-centered approach by the Sociable Scientists;
8. Continual evaluation and enhancements of the model; and
9. Credibility of data due to involvement by the university.

Continued

Case study: continued.

Implications and Lessons Learned

This case study will close by sharing some of the implications and lessons learned in the initiative in the hope that others can incorporate them in future research design.

Perhaps the most important implication to share is that communities can obtain data on their visitors through the use of such models. The immediate impacts of this innovation have been in the communities where the VES has been applied. These communities, and the tourism stakeholders within, have benefitted from learning more about who their visitors are, why and how they travelled to the destination, their satisfaction, spending levels and suggested improvements. These insights have aided them in aligning marketing and product development decisions with the needs of visiting markets. For example, the data has been cited in the Tourism Master Plan in Tofino and in marketing plans of the DMOs. The data provides a valid proxy for use in future funding applications for communities. For example, communities could use the suggested enhancements provided by visitors as priority infrastructure projects and the evidence from the VES may assist them in supporting their case. The application of this model in the Vancouver Island context highlights a number of opportunities to enhance visitor research methods in contexts outside of BC. The model is potentially scalable to understand sector groups, events, regions and tourism routes. The design of the model also highlights the need to modernize research methodology in visitor research to provide communities and regions with accessible, affordable and localized data sets. Similarly, it illustrates the need to enhance research capacity and knowledge sharing between tourism researchers and destination marketing organizations. Where communities can obtain the participation of a local university or college that can aid in the design, data collection and analysis, there are likely many more opportunities to arrive at a similar win-win scenario. The need for this type of collaboration aligns with calls to get more academic researchers and destination marketing bodies collaborating on studying visitor research (Fyall et al., 2012). The emphasis on co-creating the study with community-based partners and the format used in knowledge mobilization also addresses criticisms in the literature (Hudson, 2013).

The future application of the VES in the Vancouver Island region looks promising. The partners will continue to evaluate its evolution and plan to scale the model to be applied in sectors and regions off the island. The community data sets are accessible for students at VIU to use in classroom and thesis projects, which may provide value-added insights as the data is mined around their study questions. In 2016, the university planned to combine the community data from 2015 into a macro data set to mine for additional questions on visitors to the entire island. For example, this data set could provide insights on the visiting friends and relatives market, nature-based visitors or any number of other niche markets. Monitoring the evolution of the VES has enabled the partners to learn a number of important lessons that are valuable to share with others that may consider adapting it in their own context. In closing this case, the lessons learned in the VES from 2013–2015 include:

1. Engage multiple tourism stakeholders and utilize their respective strengths and resources;
2. Identify clear roles for each stakeholder in the model;
3. Gain business and venue buy-in and train them in their role;
4. Consider engaging a university for added credibility;
5. Place ballot boxes where visitors are likely to see them during their stay and move them if they are not working;
6. Gather data from visitors' post-experience to achieve more valid results on the entire experience (as opposed to intercepts at early stages or mid-way through a visit);
7. Use attractive incentive prizes to garner attention and participation from visitors;

Continued

Case study: continued.

8. Track and create stories from the participants who win the incentive prizes;
9. Create user-friendly reports and share widely; and
10. Engage in regular check-in and evaluation of the model by the various stakeholders.

References

Alegre, J. and Garau, J. (2010) Tourist satisfaction and dissatisfaction. *Annals of Tourism Research* 37(1), 52–73.

Andriotis, K. and Agiomirgianakis, G. (2008) Measuring tourist satisfaction: a factor-cluster segmentation approach. *Journal of Vacation Marketing* 14(3), 221–235.

Arimond, G., Achenreiner, G. and Elfessi, A. (2003) An innovative approach to tourism market segmentation research: an applied study. *Journal of Hospitality and Leisure Marketing* 10(3-4), 25–56.

Canadian Tourism Commission (2015) *Explorer Quotient*. Available at: https://www.destinationcanada.com/sites/default/files/archive/2013-01-01/Tools_ExplorerQuotient_Profiles_2015_EN.pdf?msclkid=efea4e4faba211ecaba0b0e6e2f403aa (accessed 10 November 2015).

Edwards, D. and Griffin, T. (2013) Understanding tourists' spatial behaviour: GPS tracking as an aid to sustainable destination management. *Journal of Sustainable Tourism* 21(4), 580.

Fyall, A., Garrod, B. and Wang, Y. (2012) Destination collaboration: a critical review of theoretical approaches to a multi-dimensional phenomenon. *Journal of Destination Marketing and Management* 1(1–2), 10–26.

Hudson, S. (2013) Knowledge exchange: a destination perspective. *Journal of Destination Marketing and Management* 2(3), 129–131. DOI: http://dx.doi.org.ezproxy.viu.ca/10.1016/j.jdmm.2013.08.002

Liburd, J.J. (2011) Tourism research 2.0. *Annals of Tourism Research* 39(2), 883.

Lugosi, P. and Walls, A.R. (2013) Researching destination experiences: themes, perspectives and challenges. *Journal of Destination Marketing and Management* 2(2), 51–58.

Parasuraman, A., Zaithaml, V.A. and Berry, L. (1985) A conceptual model of service quality and its implications for future research. *Journal of Marketing* 49(4), 41–50.

Priporas, C. and Vassiliadis, C.A. (2013) An analysis of visitor behaviour using time blocks: a study of ski destinations in Greece. *Tourism Management* 34, 61–70.

Rucks, C.T. and Geissler, G.L. (2011) The overall theme park experience: a visitor satisfaction tracking study. *Journal of Vacation Marketing* 17(2), 127–138.

Sharpley, R. and Stone, P.R. (2010) *Tourist Experience: Contemporary Perspectives*. Routledge, Abingdon, UK.

Stradling, S.G., Anable, J. and Carreno, M. (2007) Performance, importance and user disgruntlement: a six-step method for measuring satisfaction with travel modes. *Transportation Research Part A* 41(1), 98–106.

References

Becherer, R.C., Helms, M.M. and McDonald, J.P. (2012) The effect of entrepreneurial marketing on outcome goals in SMEs. *New England Journal of Entrepreneurship* 15, 7–18.

Berry, L.L. (1988) Delivering excellent service in retailing. *Retailing Issues Letter* 1(4).

Buhalis, D. and Laws, E. (2001) *Tourism Distribution Channels: Practices, Issues and Transformations*. Continuum, London.

Cooper, C. (2016) *Essentials of Tourism*. Pearson Education Limited, London.

Gartner, W.C. and Bachri, T. (1994) Tour operators' role in the tourism distribution system: an Indonesian case study. *Journal of International Consumer Marketing* 6(3/4), 161–179.

Gilmore, A., Carson, D. and Grant, K. (2001) SME marketing in practice. *Marketing Intelligence & Planning* 19, 6–11.

Ionita, D. (2012) Entrepreneurial marketing: a new approach for challenging times. *Management & Marketing* 7(1), 131.

Jaafar, M. (2012) Entrepreneurial marketing and accommodation businesses in East Peninsular Malaysia. *Tourism and Hospitality Research* 12(2), 89–100.

Kotler, P. (2011) Philip Kotler's contributions to marketing theory and practice. In: Malhotra, N.K. (ed.) *Review of Marketing Research: Special Issue – Marketing Legends*. Emerald Group Publishing Limited Bingley, UK.

Kumarasinghe, S., Lee, C. and Karunasekara, C. (2019) Comparing local and foreign perceptions of service quality of five-star hotels in Sri Lanka. *Journal of Quality Assurance in Hospitality & Tourism* 20(1), 44–65.

Kurgun, H., Bagiran, D., Ozeren, E. and Maral, B. (2011) Entrepreneurial marketing: the interface between marketing and entrepreneurship: a qualitative research on boutique hotels. *European Journal of Social Sciences* 26(3), 340–357.

Law, R., Leung, R., Lo, A., Leung, D. and Fong, L.H.N. (2015) Distribution channel in hospitality and tourism: revisiting disintermediation from the perspective of hotels and travel agencies. *International Journal of Contemporary Hospitality Management* 27(3), 431–452.

Morris, M.H., Schindehutte, M. and LaForge, R.W. (2002) Entrepreneurial marketing: a construct for integrating emerging entrepreneurship and marketing perspectives. *Journal of Marketing Theory & Practice* 10, 1–19.

Morrish, S.C., Miles, M.P. and Deacon, J.H. (2010) Entrepreneurial marketing: acknowledging the entrepreneur and customer-centric interrelationship. *Journal of Strategic Marketing* 18(4), 303–316.

Parasuraman, A., Zeithaml, V. and Berry, L. (1988) SERVQUAL: a multiple item scale for measuring consumer perceptions of service quality. *Journal of Retailing* 64 (1), 12–40.

Pholphirul, P., Rukumnuaykit, P., Charoenrat, T., Kwanyou, A. and Srijamdee, K. (2021) Service marketing strategies and performances of tourism and hospitality enterprises: implications from a small border province in Thailand. *Asia Pacific Journal of Marketing and Logistics*.

Rollins, B., Anitsal, I., Anitsal, M.M. and Meral, M. (2014) Viral marketing: techniques and implementation. *Entrepreneurial Executive* 19(1), 1–17.

Sadiku-Dushi, N., Dana, L.P. and Ramadani, V. (2019) Entrepreneurial marketing dimensions and SMEs performance. *Journal of Business Research* 100, 86–99.

Song, H. (2012) *Tourism Supply Chain Management*. Routledge, Abingdon, UK.

Thomas, L.C., Painbéni, S. and Barton, H. (2013) Entrepreneurial marketing within the French wine industry. *International Journal of Entrepreneurial Behavior & Research* 19(2).

5 Business Strategy and Growth

Firms inherit positions that constrain and shape their choices, but do not determine them. They have considerable latitude in reconfiguring the value chain with which they compete, expanding or contracting their competitive scope, and influencing important dimensions of their industry environment. Strategy is not a race to occupy one desirable position, but a more textured problem in which many positions can be chosen or created. Success requires the choice of a relatively attractive position given industry structure, the firm's circumstances, and the positions of competitors. It also requires bringing all the firm's activities into consistency with the chosen position. (Porter, 1991, pp. 104–105)

Introduction

The business environment presents both opportunities and threats for tourism enterprises. Opportunities arise in identifying gaps in the market and providing products and services to fill these gaps, establishing a competitive advantage. Threats result from movements of competitors into market gaps before you, or changes in the business environment that threaten the operations of a business. For example:

- Traditional accommodation providers (e.g., hotels and motels) are challenged by digital accommodation platforms such as Airbnb.
- Local brick-and-mortar travel agencies are competing against online travel agencies (OTAs) such as Expedia and Booking.com that have worldwide reach.

While it is impossible to perfectly predict how business environments will change, tourism enterprises must analyse their external environment

© Rob Hallak and Craig Lee 2023. *Managing Tourism Enterprises: Start-up, Growth and Resilience* (R. Hallak and C. Lee)
DOI: 10.1079/9781789249446.0005

systematically and regularly to anticipate and respond to environmental changes. The elements of the business environment include:

- The macro-environment
- The industry (or sector) environment
- The firm's market and immediate competitors
- The firm itself.

Examining the competitive market structure has been called the position-based view (González-Rodríguez *et al.*, 2018). In this view, the external environment is believed to play a significant role in influencing an enterprise's business performance, and the structure of the market determines the business strategy a company should adopt (Porter, 1991). Thus, firms are continuously adapting their business to respond to changes in the external environment, seeking a set of strategic activities that will enable a firm to obtain optimal performance (González-Rodríguez *et al.*, 2018).

Learning Outcomes

After completing this chapter, you should be able to:

- Utilize a PESTEL analysis to analyse the macro-environment
- Utilize a Porter's five forces framework to analyse the industry environment
- Utilize a SWOT analysis to analyse the firm's capabilities.
- Understand the different types of business strategies available to tourism enterprises
- Identify the types of strategies a tourism enterprise can use for business growth.

Understanding the Macro-environment

PESTEL analysis

The macro-environment can be analysed using a PESTEL analysis (Aguilar, 1967). PESTEL stands for:

- **P**olitical
- **E**conomic
- **S**ocial
- **T**echnological
- **E**cological
- **L**egal.

This framework helps managers identify the market and non-market factors within the six factors listed above that may impact the organization. Market factors refers to actors that directly influence a tourism enterprise, such as customers, competitors and suppliers. The firm's interactions with these groups are primarily for economic reasons, through competition for resources, revenues and profits. Non-market factors represent actors that sit outside of those within market factors, but whose actions can still influence the firm. These are represented, for example, by governments, regulatory bodies, NGOs, the media and the local community.

Information to conduct a PESTEL analysis can be gathered from primary or secondary sources.

Primary sources are obtained directly from individuals or organizations, such as: discussions or interviews with managers, employees, customers, supplies, consultants, analysts, academics, government officials, etc.

Secondary sources are obtained from information that has been published/made available, such as: industry reports, consultancy reports, annual reports, news articles, industry magazines, academic articles, etc.

Political

The political aspect of the macro-environment represents the role of governments and other political factors that can influence the tourism enterprise (Box 5.1). Managers can analyse political risks associated with whole countries (e.g., politics in Australia) or specific industries or sectors within a country (e.g., hotel industry in the Middle East). One can also look at potential effects of political factors outside of a country's national borders, which could influence conditions within a firm's country (e.g., war or political unrest in a neighbouring country blocking trade and access to suppliers).

Economic

The economic aspect of the macro-environment represents the forces that can influence a tourism enterprise based on the state of the economy and business prospects within a particular region/country/industry (Box 5.2). Within this factor, an awareness of economic cycles is important as economic growth rates tend to increase and decrease at regular intervals. Economies riding high growth rates eventually plateau and decline, while economies slipping into recession will eventually move into the recovery phase and experience an uptick. The key trend for managers to identify will be recognizing the current state of the economy and predicting (as much as possible)

Box 5.1. Political issues to consider.

- National or regional policies of governing parties
- Changes in government
- International trade policies
- Immigration and border policies
- Wars
- Political stability/instability
- Terrorism

the economic turning points so that preparations can be made to maximize business potential during upturns or prevent/prepare for negative impacts during downturns.

The tourism industry is highly susceptible to economic cycles because:

It is a discretionary spend industry. Because spending on tourism products and services are considered non-essential expenditure for consumers, during economic downturns consumers tend to decrease or defer spending. For a tourism enterprise, this means a loss of revenue due to shrinking markets. However, after a period of reduced spending coinciding with a growing economy, there is likely to be a strong recovery as pent-up demand and an increase in discretionary income is released into the market.

It is a high fixed-cost industry. During economic downturns, tourism enterprises tend to suffer as the high fixed costs of running a business (e.g., in rent, equipment and labour) are difficult to reduce as quickly in relation to the fall in revenue.

Social

The social aspect of the macro-environment represents the demographic, psychographic and geographic characteristics of a population that can influence the tourism enterprise's market (Box 5.3). These factors will determine the nature of supply and demand within the tourism industry. It is also important to consider that these social aspects also impact the potential pool of labour a tourism enterprise relies upon when sourcing employees.

Box 5.2. Economic issues to consider.

- Gross domestic product (GDP) growth rates
- Inflation rates
- Interest rates
- Mortgage rates
- Currency exchange rates
- Consumer price index (CPI)
- Stock market movements
- Taxation
- Unemployment rates
- Prices of commodities

Box 5.3. Social issues to consider.

- Demographic characteristics related to: age, gender, education, ethnicity, religion, population growth, income
- Psychographic characteristics related to: lifestyles of generational cohorts (e.g., Gen X and Y, Baby Boomers), well being, political leaning
- Geographic characteristics related to: weather and climate, elevation, bodies of water.

Technology

The technology aspect of the macro-environment represents the extent to which technology plays a role in the way products and services in tourism are produced, marketed, distributed and consumed (Box 5.4). Technology is utilized on both the demand and supply sides. On the demand side, customers increasingly search, book or purchase tourism products over the internet (e.g., through OTAs such as Expedia, TripAdvisor, etc.). On the supply side, tourism enterprises have benefitted from technology through enhanced efficiency and productivity. For example, the relatively low cost and wide distribution of internet marketing has enabled tourism enterprises to reach customers across the globe to promote their products and services.

Ecological

The ecological aspect of the macro-environment represents the extent to which 'green' issues, such as pollution, waste, energy saving and climate change, are a major factor in the markets in which the tourism enterprise operates (Box 5.5). Ecological pressures force tourism enterprises to redevelop or redesign their business's policies, procedures and systems to be more environmentally conscious. These pressures can be seen as an opportunity to establish a competitive advantage (e.g., creating a positive brand image resulting in customer loyalty and satisfaction), especially as customers are becoming more eco-friendly in their lifestyles and purchase decisions. Or, these pressures can be seen as an

---

Box 5.4. Technology issues to consider.

- Extent of spending on research and development by firms, industries or countries
- Extent of patenting activity on national patent registers
- New hardware technology developed and introduced to market
- New software technology developed and introduced to market
- Development and/or introduction of new products and services within a particular industry

---

Box 5.5. Ecological issues to consider.

- Climate change
- Greenhouse gas emissions
- Global warming
- Sea level rises
- Rate of deforestation
- Waste disposal
- Recycling policies
- Availability of 'green' technologies
- Customer demand for 'green' products and services
- Availability of suppliers of 'green' products and services

additional cost to doing business (e.g., having to invest in greener technology, sourcing more environmentally friendly products).

Legal

The legal aspect of the macro-environment represents the extent laws, regulations and informal norms within a society influence the ability of tourism enterprises to conduct business (Box 5.6). Legal aspects related to laws and regulations can cover labour and taxation laws and corporate governance. Informal norms, representing patterns of expected behaviour within a society, are also covered under this aspect.

Industry Analysis

An industry is defined as any concentration of firms that operate in the same segment of the economy and produce similar products and services. In contrast, a sector refers to a large segment of the economy that can contain multiple industries that operate together, either directly or indirectly, to allow a sector to function. For example, the tourism sector consists of the airline, tour, hotel, food and beverage, and retail industries among others.

To assess the attractiveness of entering an industry and to determine a competitive strategy, managers can utilize the Porter five forces framework.

Porter's five forces

Porter's five forces framework (Porter, 1980) helps to analyse an industry and identify attractiveness in terms of five competitive forces (see Figure 5.1):

- Extent of rivalry between competitors
- Threat of entry
- Threat of substitutes
- Power of buyers
- Power of suppliers.

Through this analysis, the five forces are then determined by managers to be high/strong, medium or low/weak. When the five forces are deemed as high

---

Box 5.6. Legal issues to consider

- Labour and employment law (e.g., minimum-wage policies, leave policies)
- Taxation law
- Rules on business ownership
- Competition law
- Consumer protections
- Corporate governance laws.

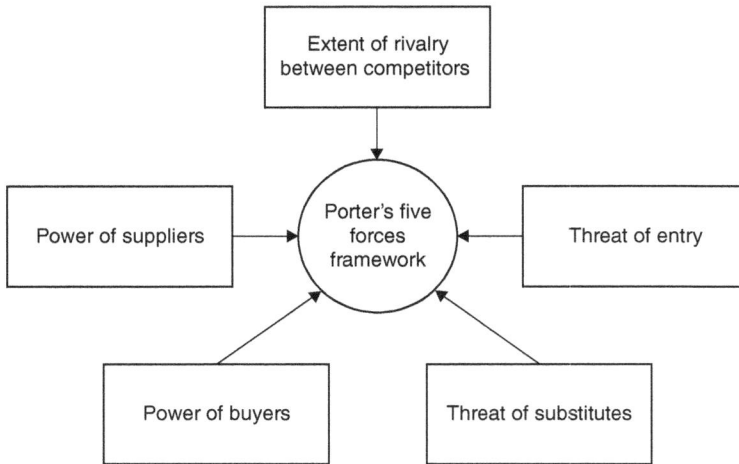

Figure 5.1. The Porter five forces framework.

and strong, an industry is said to be unattractive for entry. This is because excessive rivalry between competitors, powerful buyers and suppliers, the ease by which consumers can switch to substitutes, and the threat of new entrants into the industry will combine to significantly reduce profitability.

In contrast, when the five forces are deemed as low and weak, an industry is said to be attractive for entry. This is because little or no rivalry, with customers and suppliers with relatively low bargaining power, the lack of substitutes for a firm's products and services, and high barriers to entry result in first-mover advantages and the potential to establish a monopoly.

Extent of rivalry between competitors

The extent of rivalry between competitors looks at the level of competition for markets and resources between existing players in the industry. There are several factors to assess to determine the level of competition.

First, managers should examine the concentration and size of existing competition. When there are many competitors of equal size, the industry may face intense rivalry as competitors aim to beat each other. When there are few competitors, the industry may have one or two dominant organizations and smaller competitors survive by focusing on niche markets to avoid competing with the larger firms.

Second, managers should chart the growth phase of the industry. When an industry is still growing, firms can coexist as there is enough growth in the market to satisfy all firms' needs. When an industry's growth is declining, all firms in the industry are competing for a shrinking market, and firms will have to grow by capturing market share from competitors leading to competition and rivalry.

Third, the barriers to exit should be assessed. When the cost of exiting an industry is high (i.e. high barriers to exit), incumbent firms will try to survive as much as possible. This leads to excess supply lingering in the market, resulting in reduced prices and more substitutes available to consumers, causing firms to compete fiercely for market share. When the barriers to exit are low, losses when exiting an industry will be less severe, making it easier for firms to make the decision to leave, thus taking their excess capacity out of the industry.

Fourth, the level of fixed costs to operate should be examined. In industries with high fixed-cost structures, in times of declining revenues firms will seek to reduce costs by increasing sales volumes. This typically results in lowering prices for products and services, forcing competitors to do the same.

Threat of entry

The threat of entry refers to how easy it is for a new firm to enter the industry. Entry barriers are the factors that a firm entering the industry need to overcome to be competitive and profitable. An industry with high barriers to entry is attractive for incumbents or for new entrants who can overcome these barriers because there is a reduced threat of new competition within the industry. There are several factors to assess when determining the level of the threat of entry.

First, managers should determine the scale and experience required to enter the industry and that of incumbent firms. When firms already in the industry have achieved large-scale production, it becomes expensive for new firms to compete with them until they can achieve a similar scale. If achieving such scale requires high capital investments, then the effect of scale is further compounded. Similarly, for incumbent firms, their experience of being in the industry gives them a cost advantage as they have had the time to establish how to operate in the industry more efficiently. This gives them a competitive advantage over new entrants who are inexperienced and will be operating less efficiently on start-up.

Second, managers should assess how easy it is to access suppliers or distribution channels. In some industries, the incumbent firms may have control over the supply and distribution channels, either through the establishment of strong supplier/exclusive relationships or through vertical integration. This can become a barrier to new entrants as new firms would not be able to source suppliers or distribute their products and services in the industry.

Third, the extent to which legislation or government actions influence the barriers to entry must be considered. Legislation or government regulation that discourages new entry, such as patent protection, protectionist policies, or direct government action, can create high barriers to entry. In contrast, deregulation can reduce barriers to entry, making industries more vulnerable to entry by new firms.

Fourth, existing firms may enjoy incumbent advantages such as a loyal consumer base, a stronger and more established brand identity, more locations/outlets, unique sources for materials, and proprietary technology. These may be too far along or too strongly established for new entrants to overcome.

Fifth, managers should also determine the extent and strength to which incumbents will likely retaliate against new entrants. If potential entrants assess that incumbent firms will retaliate (e.g., through price wars, marketing campaigns, etc.) or that it would be too costly to counter such retaliation, they may be discouraged from entering the industry.

Threat of substitutes

The threat of substitutes refers to products or services that offer similar benefits to an industry's products and services and may come from within or outside the industry. This threat manifests when it is easy for customers to switch to the substitutes. This threat can also indirectly affect incumbent firms when the mere presence of a substitute limits how much can be charged for a product or service within an industry. When switching costs for customers are seen as low, then this becomes a threat. There are several factors to assess when determining the threat of substitutes.

First, the extent to which products and services between competitors are differentiated should be examined. When products and services across competitors in an industry are poorly differentiated, rivalry among firms increases as there is little cost for consumers to switch to competitors, or there is little reason to be loyal to any particular brand. This causes firms within the industry to compete primarily on price.

Second, the price-to-performance ratio of products and services is important. If substitutes that command higher prices also offer higher performance advantages, then customers will still switch regardless of the price differential. Thus, new entrants will have to compete on quality rather than simply offering lower prices.

Third, managers should also assess the effects of substitutes outside the industry of interest. It is critical for managers to look beyond their industry to consider substitutes that may not seem related at first glance. For example, in the restaurant industry, substitutes for food and beverage services can come from meal delivery services and ready-to-eat meals from supermarkets.

Power of buyers

The power of buyers refers to the extent to which parties that buy a firm's products and services can influence the firm's prices. Buyers in this sense refers to the firm's immediate customers, not the final/ultimate customer. Several factors influence the power of buyers.

First, managers should determine if the firms deal with a concentrated set of buyers. If a few customers constitute most of a firms' sales, then the power of the buyer increases as the firm selling the products and services are reliant on them for most of their profits. In a similar manner, if a particular firm's products and services account for a large percentage of the buyers' overall purchases, their buyer power also increases. This is because the buyers will be more inclined to make purchases from firms that can provide bulk-purchasing discounts, which squeezes a firm's profits.

Second, the cost of switching should also be determined. When products and services among competitors are undifferentiated or standardized, this lowers the costs of switching. Additionally, when buyers have full information or are very knowledgeable about prices and product/service performance, then switching costs also fall because buyers are aware of all possible substitutes they have access to within an industry. Thus, if buyers in an industry can easily switch between suppliers, they will possess more leverage during negotiations.

Third, managers should determine the reliance of buyers to their suppliers. Buyers who are unsatisfied with the products and services of suppliers may threaten to become their own supplier. Thus, if buyers could meet their supply needs themselves or develop such capabilities, they have high buyer power.

Fourth, the performance of the buyers' own operations and the importance of the supplied materials also influences buyer power. Buyers who are facing unprofitable situations will be pressured to reduce costs as much as possible, increasing their buying power, as they will attempt to buy at the lowest prices possible. Additionally, if the quality of the supplier's products and services that becomes the buyer's input has minimal impact on the quality of the buyer's output, then this increases their power. This is because there would be no incentive for buyers to pay top dollar for higher-quality supplies, leading them to seek the cheapest source possible.

Power of suppliers

The power of suppliers relates to the extent to which parties that supply a firm's products and services can control the price of supplies. Suppliers refer to parties who provide the inputs a firm needs to produce its products and services. This includes raw materials, equipment, labour and financing. The power of suppliers is the inverse of the power of buyers.

First, managers should determine whether there is a concentrated set of suppliers. When an industry has only a few suppliers that dominate the sources of supply, then they will have more power over their buyers.

Second, the cost of switching between suppliers also determines supplier power. When it becomes expensive or highly disruptive to supply-chain efficiency to switch from one supplier to another, then the buyer becomes dependent and has a weaker position. This means they will be willing to pay the supplier's rate to maintain efficiency and productivity over and above the increased cost of supplies.

Third, in industries where products and services are highly differentiated, supplier power increases. This is because if there are no or very few sources of input to develop the buyer's unique products and services, buyers become dependent on their supplier's resources, increasing the supplier's leverage at the negotiating table.

Fourth, managers should determine the reliance of suppliers to their buyers. Suppliers who are unsatisfied with their buyers may threaten to cut out the buyer and develop their own products and services to market. Thus, their supplier power increases if it is conceivable that they could cut out the buyer and enter the industry themselves.

Understanding a Firm's Environment

SWOT analysis

A SWOT analysis is a method for analysing an organization's resources and environment according to its strengths, weaknesses, opportunities and threats (Phadermrod *et al.*, 2019). Strengths and weaknesses are the internal factors that enhance or obstruct an enterprise to achieving their goals and can be controlled. Opportunities and threats are the external factors that enable or disable an enterprise achieving their goals and are uncontrollable. Listing favourable and unfavourable internal and external factors can allow tourism enterprises to better understand how strengths can be leveraged to capture new opportunities and understand how weaknesses can hinder efforts to achieve organizational goals (Helms and Nixon, 2010).

A SWOT analysis is typically conducted using a 2 × 2 grid (Figure 5.2). In the top row, managers first brainstorm the internal strengths and weaknesses of the enterprise. This can include the company's products and services, brand image, organizational structure, financial resources and expertise. Next, in the bottom row, managers consider the opportunities and threats in the marketplace such as trends in the market, emergence of new technologies, changes in consumer behaviours, capabilities of competitors, and environmental, political or social issues. Through listing the four factors in the grid, an enterprise can identify its core competencies that assist in decision making, planning and setting organizational strategies.

Business strategies

Once an enterprise understands its external and internal environment, it can proceed to select the appropriate strategy that is consistent with its desired market position. There are four general strategies that tourism enterprises can pursue. These are cost leadership, differentiation, focus, and hybrid strategies (Okumu *et al.*, 2010; Johnson *et al.*, 2017).

Strengths	Weaknesses
(What's good about your business?)	(What's not so good about your business?)
Opportunities	**Threats**
(What external factors can you take advantage of?)	(What external factors can cause problems for you?)

Figure 5.2. A SWOT analysis is a method for analysing an organization's resources and environment.

Cost leadership

A cost leadership strategy refers to firms deriving a competitive advantage primarily by maintaining a low-cost position. Low cost in this sense means having lower costs of production compared to competing firms in the same market. As a result, this allows the firm to charge lower prices. The focus of this business strategy is to achieve high efficiency and productivity. In terms of selling products and services, the objective is to target high sales volumes due to the lower profit per sale, and also so the marginal costs of production can be reduced through increased economies of scale.

For example, easyJet, a British low-cost airline group, expressly states that its strategy is to use its structural cost advantage relative to other airlines to offer customers more affordable fares (https://corporate.easyjet.com/about/strategy, accessed 12 Novemner 2022).

Differentiation

A differentiation strategy focuses on firms providing unique products and services to their customers compared to their competitors. A competitive advantage is achieved when the firm can charge premium prices for its products and services, or if the firm can sell more of a product at a higher price compared to the competition. Another advantage associated with a differentiation strategy is the building of customer loyalty. This creates price-inelastic consumers, and this customer base can help sustain a firm through a downturn in demand. In this strategy, firms focus on investing more in research and development than the industry average and are market-driven to offer unique products and services. Thus, reducing per-unit cost of production is not a primary concern for firms pursuing a differentiation strategy.

For example, the Ritz-Carlton Hotel Company, a luxury hotel brand, states that its business credo is:

> The Ritz-Carlton is a place where the genuine care and comfort of our guests is our highest mission.

We pledge to provide the finest personal service and facilities for our guests who will always enjoy a warm, relaxed, yet refined ambience.

The Ritz-Carlton experience enlivens the senses, instils well-being, and fulfils even the unexpressed wishes and needs of our guests.

(https://www.ritzcarlton.com/en/about/gold-standards, accessed 12 November 2022)

Focus strategy

A focus strategy refers to firms focusing their efforts on a particular market segment, with the sole objective of only catering to this specific market. In such a strategy, an enterprise will develop its products and services to the specific needs of its target market to the exclusion of all others. Within this strategy, the focus can be cost-driven or differentiation-driven. A cost-driven focus strategy aims to position a firm to deliver cost savings to a particular segment of the market. A differentiation-driven focus strategy aims to position a firm to deliver unique products and services to serve the specific needs of a tightly defined market segment that the broader differentiators do not serve well enough.

For example, the tour company Contiki provides tour packages sold exclusively for 18–35-year-olds (contiki.com).

Hybrid strategy

It may be possible for firms to pursue a hybrid strategy, combining cost, differentiation, and focus strategies. However, firms are generally discouraged from doing so as attempting to pursue multiple strategies tends to lead to a loss of focus, efficiency, and product and service quality by being 'stretched too thin'. However, in some cases a hybrid strategy combining different strategies can be achieved (e.g., horizontal integration through mergers and acquisitions).

Business growth

Not only do enterprises need to survive in the marketplace, but they should also seek to grow and thrive. Growth can relate to increasing sales, profitability, opening new outlets/locations, etc. To grow a business, there are four general strategies that can be implemented according to whether a business seeks to grow their current customer base or seek new markets, and whether they will do so by using existing or new products and services. The combination of these two initiatives results in market penetration, market development, product development and conglomerate diversification strategies.

Market penetration

A market penetration strategy for business growth refers to increasing the penetration of a firm's existing products and services within an existing market. This usually entails increasing a firm's market share with its current range of products and services. The benefits accrued from penetrating further into existing markets can come in the form of greater economies of scale, higher experience-curve benefits, and an increase in power in relation to the firm's buyers and suppliers.

The execution of a market penetration strategy usually involves taking market share from competing firms. Thus, managers can expect retaliatory actions. Additionally, legal constraints such as anti-monopoly laws can constrain the amount by which a firm can increase their market share.

Product development

A product development strategy for business growth refers to when firms deliver modified/improved/updated or new products and services to their existing markets. This establishes new streams of revenue for a firm within its existing customer base.

The risks associated with this growth strategy is the costs involved to develop and bring new products and services to market. New product development usually requires mastery of new information, processes and techniques. It may also require new sources of input, equipment/machinery and/or

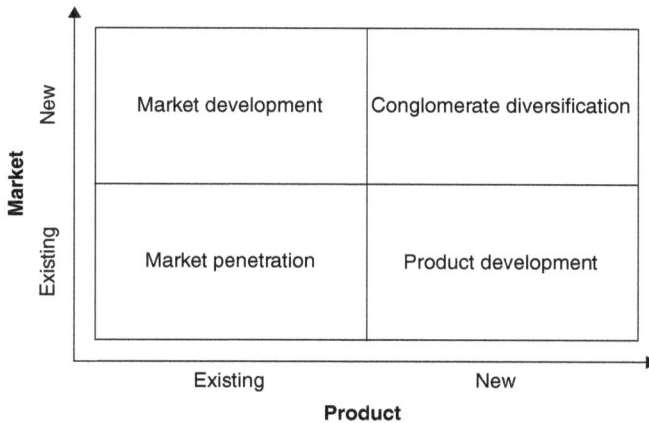

Figure 5.3. Business growth strategies matrix. (Source: author developed.)

organizational restructuring. This involves heavy investment and the risk of project failures if the new product or service fails to gain traction within their current customer base.

Market development

A market development strategy for business growth involves offering a firm's existing products and services to new markets. This will also, typically, involve some modifications to existing products and services to cater to the new market.

New markets can take the form of new users or new geographical markets. New users means a firm finds new users outside of its current markets to consume the products and services it has on offer. New geographical markets means a firm sells its products and services in different locations (e.g., through internationalization), but will generally sell to the same 'profile' of consumers within the new geographical market.

The potential risks associated with a market development strategy is the lack of understanding of the targeted 'new users'. This makes it difficult for firms to find the right marketing skills and branding to attract new users. Additionally, if spreading to new geographical markets, it can be difficult for firms to coordinate between their different markets and the different needs of users in different geographical locations, even if the firm tries as much as possible to find 'similar' user profiles.

Conglomerate diversification

Conglomerate diversification can also be called unrelated diversification, where a firm decides to grow by going beyond its existing markets and products and services. This strategy is generally enacted in practice through mergers and acquisitions.

For the acquiring firm, conglomerate diversification can create value by scattering the firm's risk across a variety of industries, making a company less dependent on any one business. This means that profits from higher-performing businesses/industries can be diverted to offset losses from lower-performing businesses/industries, or help lower-performing businesses invest in improvement.

For the acquired firm, being merged or acquired can create value through benefits associated with being part of a larger group. For example, consumers can have greater confidence in a firm's products and services when they perceive the company as being backed by a larger, more stable and wealthier firm. Additionally, a larger size may enable easier access and lower costs for financing, as the acquiring firm can act as a guarantor for the acquired firm.

The drawbacks associated with a conglomerate diversification strategy is that the parent company can suffer from an absence of a clear strategy to turn diversification into a competitive advantage, especially if they do not have the capacity and expertise to manage a diverse set of businesses across different industries.

Summary

This chapter reviewed the business environment that presents both opportunities and threats for tourism enterprises. Opportunities arise from gaps in the market that tourism enterprises can identify and fill with their products and services to achieve a competitive advantage. Threats result from changes in the business environment, or actions taken by competitors in the market. To be prepared for changes in the business environment, tourism enterprises must analyse their external environment systematically and regularly in order to anticipate and respond to environmental changes. This can be done at the macro-environmental level through a PESTEL analysis, at the industry level using Porter's five forces framework, and at the firm level using a SWOT analysis. Once opportunities and threats are identified, tourism enterprises can then develop their business strategies to respond. This can include a cost leadership, differentiation, focus, or hybrid strategy. Enterprises must not only use business strategies to survive, but they must also improve their performance and viability through business growth. This can be executed through market penetration, product development, market development and conglomerate diversification.

Review Questions

1. Conduct a PESTEL analysis for an industry within tourism at the national level (e.g., hotel industry in China, cruise industry in the Bahamas, etc.).
2. Conduct a Porter's five forces analysis for an industry within tourism at the local level (e.g., boutique hotel market in Cape Town, South Africa, fine-dining restaurant market in Tokyo, Japan, etc.).
3. Conduct a SWOT analysis for a tourism business in your area.
4. Conduct an internet search to find examples of tourism enterprises that have adopted a cost leadership, differentiation, and focus strategy.
5. Do some research and find out which tourism enterprises have engaged in, or are part of, a conglomerate diversification business growth strategy.

Case study: A Korean travel agency helps make leisure activities accessible to all.

Amuse Travel addresses the growing South Korean market for leisure services for customers with special needs: not just for travellers with disabilities, but also seniors with restricted mobility, and families with children.

Authors: Linlin Zhao[1], Fathimath Shiraani[2], Mo Yang[1], Katie Seabolt[1] and Yu Sun[1]

Affiliations: [1]Skema Business School, Sophia Antipolis, France
[2]University of Otago, New Zealand

Origin: For Skema: written on the basis of material provided by Amuse Travel Company.

© CAB International 2021

Important note on disability language

The Amuse Travel website and staff use different terms (such as 'person with special needs' and/or 'disabled members') inconsistently to describe people with disability experience(s). Preference for these terms is debatable as disability language is often contested and under continuous scrutiny (Shiraani, 2021).

It is important to note that there is no universally accepted terminology to define people with disabilities. There is a concern that people use language 'loosely, inconsistently and interchangeably, euphemistically with erroneous understandings and nuances' (Gillovic *et al.*, 2018, p. 616). In the absence of agreed definitions, various disability nomenclatures are used, and of these, some are considered more acceptable than others.

Much of the contemporary literature, both academic and non-academic, tends to use 'politically correct' *disability-first* (i.e. disabled person) or *person-first* language (i.e. persons with disabilities or people with disabilities) (Iriarte *et al.*, 2016, p. 8). The authors of this case study consistently deploy person-first phrasing (e.g., people with disabilities, tourists with disabilities) with the exception of direct quotes. The decision to employ person-first terminology was made after considering the language used in South Korea's disability statutory acts, such as the Act on Welfare of Persons with Disabilities (Statutes of the Republic of Korea, 2014) and the Anti-Discrimination Against and Remedies for Persons with Disabilities Act (Ministry of Health and Welfare, 2011).

The terminology used to refer to older people is similarly contentious. Some use the term 'older' or 'elderly', as we have done in the sentence above (Bouhalis and Darcy, 2011). Some gerontologists, however, prefer the term 'old', claiming that it is a powerful way to reclaim and normalize ageing.

Unless otherwise mentioned, all data for this case study are extracted from three sources: personal interview with Mr Kim; Mr Oh's radio interview on Korean Broadcasting System (KBS); and information available on Amuse Travel's official website and in its brochures.

Background

The company

Amuse Travel is a for-profit travel agency founded in October 2016 by Mr Oh. The company aims to create a favourable environment for three traveller groups: people with disabilities, families travelling with children, and senior citizens. In Mr Oh's words, 'By using our services,

Continued

Case study: continued.

parents with children, the elderly, people with disabilities and their families can travel safely and comfortably'. Focusing on the three customer groups, the company offers various travel packages, and this case study describes four of them: 'accessible tours', 'care trips', 'senior programmes' and 'data business'.

Government initiatives and support

Since the late 1980s, South Korea has strengthened its social welfare system for people with disabilities. There is a greater level of financial and support mechanisms in place, such as welfare centres, vocational training, and incentives to hire people with disabilities. Additionally, people with disabilities enjoy other benefits such as exemption from automobile tax, income tax and inheritance taxes, reductions on the gift tax and import duty, medical insurance, and free public transport. There are discounts on telephone and mobile phone subscriptions based on disability level and age. Further, volunteers and nurses are available to help people with disabilities go out and to assist with everyday care needs (e.g. take a bath, see a doctor).

Despite the numerous government-led changes and support systems, travel for people with disabilities in South Korea can be difficult. However, this, potentially, will change, particularly for people with physical disabilities, with the South Korean government's initiatives launched in 2015 to renovate tourist sites to enhance mobility. Such government action has helped companies like Amuse Travel to provide better travel options and has encouraged customers who were previously reluctant to travel.

Accessible tourism

Improving access for people with disabilities has become an important issue in all countries, not just those dependent on the tourism industry. Destinations and attractions around the world are increasingly aware of the need to make their offering accessible to all, with a particular focus on people with disabilities, older visitors, and families with young children. This is a work in progress, and it is generally accepted that much more needs to be done (NTG, 2021). Regarding those with disabilities, the work of the tourism industry on accessibility is, at least in part, driven by legislation regarding the rights of disabled people to access places and experiences.

Creation and development of the company

Mr Oh, in particular, believes that all people should have the opportunity to travel equally and enjoy themselves without discrimination or struggle. While working as an office worker, he engaged in voluntary activities, but that did not fully satisfy his desire to contribute to society. Hence, Mr Oh decided to create a travel agency that would serve disadvantaged groups in the community based on an idea expressed by one of his acquaintances who did volunteer work with him: 'I started as a volunteer, helping some friends that were physically challenged', says Mr Oh. 'Afterward, parents of their friends asked me to take their children as well, and I received more and more requests. That is how I started this business.'

The mission

According to Mr Kim, 'People with disabilities often have limited choices and experience difficulties when travelling. More than 40% of tourists with disabilities in Korea say that they have

Continued

Case study: continued.

experienced discrimination when travelling. Amuse Travel's slogan is Travel for all, Travel for good, which means helping these people travel easily and comfortably. At the same time, providing professional services with good quality at a reasonable price.'

By providing the most suitable tour packages and additional services with credible and accurate tourism information for travellers, Amuse Travel aims to become Asia's leading full-concierge travel agency focused on inclusion and enjoyment of travel. In his radio interview, Mr Oh tells the story of travelling with a person with physical disabilities who grabbed his hands and said, 'Captain, it is so fun and great to travel with you. I hope there will be many more programmes like this'.

The staff

Amuse Travel has 17 employees: 15 work in the office in Seoul, and two work remotely from Jeju and Andong. The office staff work in two different teams. One team, consisting of four employees, is dedicated to the 'care trip' programmes and focuses primarily on families. The other team (with eight to nine staff) looks after accessible tours for customers with disabilities, the senior programmes, and the data business. These programmes and services are described below in detail.

Amuse Travel supports and values staff training and development. 'If an employee needs a certificate in order to carry out their work effectively, our company will support them in getting the necessary qualification', says Mr Kim. 'They are encouraged to get certification and stay up-to-date through online study, including YouTube lectures. Our company also has partnerships with professors who specialize in education for the disabled.'

Amuse Travel's Programmes and Services

Accessible tours

Most standard travel packages designed for mass tourists are less user-friendly for people with disabilities. Thus, Amuse Travel customizes its service package according to the needs and expectations of tourists with disabilities. The following points exemplify considerations made by Amuse Travel when serving people with disabilities:
- For wheelchair users – visits to attractions that are classified as 'barrier-free'
- For tourists with visual disabilities – voice commentator and things to smell, hear or touch, rather than see
- For tourists with hearing disabilities – travelling with a sign-language interpreter, delivering travel information correctly, focusing on visuals
- For tourists experiencing pervasive developmental disorders (PDD) – activity-oriented tours to stimulate the five senses.

The staff of Amuse Travel try to work collaboratively with their customers to make the travel experiences easy and enjoyable. Mr Oh gives the example of rail biking at the Gimhae Nakdong River Rail Park. 'We help [customers with physical disabilities to] wear seat belts and provide them with more comfortable seats, working in cooperation with the local staff'.

According to Amuse Travel, one of the most popular tourist attractions for blind people is Mulle-gil ('The Water Road') in Chuncheon (the capital city of Gangwon province, South Korea). In Chuncheon, tourists can enjoy canoes on the lakes. The lakeside city of Chuncheon is filled with sounds of nature such as running water and peaceful sounds of people paddling

Continued

Case study: continued.

in the lakes. 'Visually impaired tourists love these elements', says Mr Oh. 'And for rafting in Dong river, we've arranged a rafting route that disabled people can easily access.'

Amuse Travel, equally, looks after carers accompanying tourists with disabilities. As per Mr Oh, 'taking a trip with someone with mobility problems can also be difficult for the person accompanying' and 'caregivers can get tired after a while. In such circumstances, we may take over, so that [carers] can also have some time for themselves.'

Care trips (Dolbom)

Dolbom travel, translated as 'care trip', is a service for parents with children. A personal helper takes care and entertains the children while parents enjoy free time with an optional wellness programme on offer.

Family travel groups usually consist of four to six people travelling together. In contrast, the senior programmes described below comprise larger groups of up to 40 or even 60 people.

The senior programme

The senior programme offers trips for aged customers with a more relaxed schedule than the other tour packages. It includes both domestic and international tourists assisted by helpers.

Mr Oh tells this story in his interview with KBS Radio: 'A family that travelled with older parents through our service told me that their older mother was delighted and pleased. The mother found her previous trip quite difficult, even saying that she wanted to die. But after using our tour package she said she wanted to live longer, looking forward to the next trip.'

The data business

In addition to providing leisure and travel services to different groups, Amuse Travel contributes to the broader mission of making travel more accessible in South Korea, particularly for people with disabilities. The company collects video data with GoPro and a 360 camera. The staff members film paths, circuits and facilities at tourist attractions (including slopes, stairs, blockages, road surface materials) when they go out on tours and then rate them to establish an accessibility index to assist travellers with disabilities.

'We've visited many locations so far and collected extensive data on some 100 tourist sites', says Mr Oh. 'The data includes information on slopes, ground conditions, the facilities' size and whether the stairs, restrooms are accessible by wheelchairs (including electric ones) at those sites. I'd guess that we've collected such information from more than 40% of South Korean tourist sites. Our tour packages provide safer and more enjoyable travel courses tailored to those with special needs, based on the data.'

Similarly, Mr Kim stated, 'We are collecting P.O.I. [points, lines, polygons] map data with Ministry of Land, infrastructure, and transport for accessible tourists. It is walking-based data that is quick and easy to update, from which practical data sets can be constructed. We have collected about 100,000 pieces of mobility information for vulnerable groups. In this way, we contribute to improving the infrastructure needed for barrier-free travel.'

Beyond data collection, Amuse Travel undertakes other initiatives of public interest. For example, it has made a voice-recorded braille brochure and a tactile map for Ulleung Island – one of the least developed areas in terms of infrastructure for visitors with disabilities.

Continued

Case study: continued.

Challenges and Opportunities

Multiple factors challenge Amuse Travel's care- and trust-based services. Some of them include childcare issues and the more recent event of COVID-19.

Childcare issues

As highlighted earlier, part of Amuse Travel's business involves taking care of children. The childcare service faces trust issues. 'It is important to gain the trust of the children's parents, but it is not easy to do so', says Mr Kim. Further, he adds, 'even if Amuse Travel provides certification to demonstrate that its employees are reliable. It can be hard for parents to entrust their children to others. I think that's fairly general around the world. Parents are more and more afraid of leaving their children in the hands of people they don't know.'

The challenge of COVID-19

The COVID-19 epidemic has adversely affected the global tourism industry and Amuse Travel, like many other travel and tourism companies worldwide, is experiencing its impact. According to Mr Kim, 'COVID-19 is freezing up the travel market, and fewer people are travelling. People are not spending money travelling and want to stay safe at home. The epidemic has restricted outdoor activities, and many people have suffered mentally.'

In the context of COVID-19, Amuse Travel realized that older people and people with disabilities could be at greater risk and may suffer particularly badly. They also felt that these people and their family members could be psychologically and physically challenged by the confinement associated with COVID-19 safety practices, more than others. Thus, in 2020, the company continued to offer its services, even extending the scope of its care trips – albeit with a much higher focus on safety and sanitary precautions. This service has had a positive response from users and has enabled the company to reach levels of sales similar to previous years.

Despite the COVID-19 uncertainty, Amuse Travel has observed an increase in demand for its childcare services. This is not surprising, as childcare service can relieve parents during a stressful period, while taking the children's attention off the hardship of the pandemic.

Customer development

While navigating challenges and opportunities, Amuse Travel continues its established relationships with sales channels and hopes to regain its trusting link with customers from accessible, senior and family tourism markets that were growing and have the potential to grow post-COVID-19.

Sales channels

In South Korea, direct channels to potential travellers (i.e. travellers with disabilities, senior travellers) are limited. Due to this, Amuse Travel maintains contact with various government and non-government organizations (e.g., social ventures, social enterprises, invest-

Continued

Case study: continued.

---

ment companies, intermediate support organizations). It is through such connections that Amuse Travel can reach potential customers with an intent to travel. In this regard, Mr Kim narrated, 'In the case of the [South Korean] disabled market, the B2G [business-to-government] market is more active than the B2C [business-to-consumer] market ... so we prefer indirect sales, such as providing brochures to each institution.'

Market growth and share

Although the tourism industry has come to a halt due to the COVID-19 situation, Amuse Travel is hopeful of gaining more market share, particularly in senior travel and family tourism. According to Amuse Travel, South Korea's ageing population and increasing cost of childcare services may positively impact the company. Mr Kim explained, 'The domestic elderly population rate is increasing, and so are the monthly costs for childcare.' He further elaborated, 'The ratio of small family trips to all trips has increased. Government funds for childcare are gradually increasing, but there are fewer beneficiaries due to the way families are classified according to their income. So many users are trying to find alternatives other than government childcare programmes. More than 60% of parents of elementary-school kids are using private enterprises for childcare services.'

To attract more potential customers, Amuse Travel plans to maximize on extensive use of social media and capitalize on the word-of-mouth reputation that has enhanced the company's image over the years.

The Future

Despite COVID-19-related challenges, Amuse Travel envisions a brighter future for the company. The company aims to provide quality services to its existing customer groups and extend its services nationally and internationally. Presenting this viewpoint, Mr Kim summarized the goals of the company as follows: 'We plan to provide pleasant trips not only for the disabled, but also for all members of the family including seniors, infants, and all other people. Our aim is to offer tour packages all around [South] Korea and also expand our business to other countries.'

Similarly, Mr Oh noted, 'We hope to grow into a travel platform for those who are older to offer an easy and convenient travel environment not only in [South] Korea but in Asia as well. I hope many more people will visit travel destinations, prompting the tourist sites to improve their infrastructure, including roads and facilities, in a way to provide easier access to the sites. With this mission in mind, we'll push to explore both [South] Korean and overseas markets, with the focus placed on Asia.'

References

Bouhalis, D. and Darcy, S. (2011) *Accessible Tourism: Concepts and Issues*. Channel View Publications, Bristol, UK.
Gillovic, B., McIntosh, A., Darcy, S. and Cockburn-Wootten, C. (2018) Enabling the language of accessible tourism. *Journal of Sustainable Tourism* 26(4), 615–630.
Iriarte, E.G., McConkey, R. and Gilligan, R. (eds) (2016) *Disability and Human Rights: Global Perspectives*. Palgrave Macmillan, London and New York.

Continued

> **Case study:** continued.
>
> Ministry of Health and Welfare (2011) Anti-Discrimination Against and Remedies for Persons with Disabilities Act (Act No. 10280). Available at: http://www.ilo.org/dyn/natlex/natlex4. detail?p_lang=en&p_isn=91249&p_country=KOR&p_count=145 (accessed 3 May 2021).
>
> NTG (Next Tourism Generation Alliance) (2021) Accessibility in tourism: challenges and op-portunities. Available at: https://nexttourismgeneration.eu/accessibility-in-tourism-chal-lenges-and-opportunities/ (accessed 28 June 2021).
>
> Shiraani, F. (2021) Navigating disability identity and language in research involving children and young people. Ethical research involving children case studies. Available at: https://childeth-ics.com/case-studies/navigating-disability-identity-and-language-in-research-involving-chil-dren-and-young-people-by-fathimath-shiraani/ (accessed 11 August 2021).
>
> Statutes of the Republic of Korea (2014) Act on Welfare of Persons with Disabilities. Available at: https://www.un.org/development/desa/disabilities/wp-content/uploads/sites/15/2019/11/Korea-Republic-of_The-Welfare-Law-for-Persons-with-Disabilities.pdf (accessed 3 May 2021).

Discussion Questions

1. Use the PESTEL framework to identify the opportunities in the macro-environment that contributed to the success of Amuse Travel.

2. Apply Porter's five forces framework to analyse the competitiveness of the industry in which Amuse Travel operates.

3. Conduct a SWOT analysis on Amuse Travel to analyse the strengths and weaknesses of the enterprise, and the opportunities and threats to the business.

4. What type of business strategy has Amuse Travel pursued to establish a competitive advantage? Explain the reasoning behind your answer.

References

Aguilar, F.J. (1967) *Scanning the Business Environment*. MacMillan, New York.

González-Rodríguez, M.R., Jiménez-Caballero, J.L., Martín-Samper, R.C., Köseoglu, M.A. and Okumus, F. (2018) Revisiting the link between business strategy and performance: evidence from hotels. *International Journal of Hospitality Management* 72, 21–31. DOI: 10.1016/j.ijhm.2017.11.008.

Helms, M.M and Nixon, J. (2010) Exploring SWOT analysis – where are we now? A review or academic research from the last decade. *Journal of Strategy and Management* 3(3), 215–251. DOI: 10.1108/17554251011064837.

Johnson, G., Whittington, R., Regner, P., Scholes, K. and Angwin, D. (2017) *Exploring Strategy*, 11th edn. Pearson Education, Harlow, UK.

Okumus, F., Altinay, L. and Chathoth, P. (2010) *Strategic Management in the International Hospitality and Tourism Industry*. Taylor and Francis Group.

Phadermrod, B., Crowder, R.M. and Wills, G.B. (2019) Importance-performance analysis based SWOT analysis. *International Journal of Information Management* 44, 194–203. DOI: 10.1016/j.ijinfomgt.2016.03.009.

Porter, M.E. (1980) *Competitive Strategy: Techniques for Analysing Industries and Competitors*. Free Press, New York.

Porter, M.E. (1991) Towards a dynamic theory of strategy. *Strategic Management Journal* 12, 95–117. DOI: 10.1002/smj.4250121008.

6 Human Capital and Human Resources

> HRM is a distinctive approach to employment management which seeks to achieve competitive advantage through the strategic deployment of a highly committed and capable workforce, using an integrated array of cultural, structural, and personnel techniques. (Storey, 1995)

Introduction

Entrepreneurship research often states that 'the small business firm is an extension of the individual who is in charge' and 'the individual entrepreneur is regarded as the firm' (Lumpkin and Dess, 1996, p. 138). Thus, small enterprises are built around entrepreneurs and the businesses' behaviours, and outcomes are linked with the founder's role in the enterprise (Cooper *et al.*, 1994). In many cases, entrepreneurs are often responsible for the process of determining and carrying out the actions of their enterprise (Cooper *et al.*, 1994). Following this reasoning, the level of the entrepreneur's knowledge and skills developed through education and training could determine their productivity and efficiency, which, in turn, can affect their firm's entrepreneurial behaviours and outcomes (Davidsson and Honig, 2003). These knowledge and skills are believed to originate from an entrepreneur's 'human capital' (Davidsson and Honig, 2003).

Human capital theory explains that humans are a form of capital which can be developed. Thus, investing in developing humans (i.e. through schooling and training) increases the productivity of the workforce (Nafukho *et al.*, 2004). A productive workforce, in turn, contributes to increased individual enterprise performance that, when put together, ultimately contributes to economic growth at a national level (Kenworthy and McMullan, 2010). The two critical investments in human capital that have been identified are education and training (Becker, 1994). Education and training provide individuals with more knowledge and skills, enabling them to be more productive. This, in turn, raises the earnings for the enterprise they work for and for themselves (Becker, 1994).

Learning Outcomes

After completing this chapter, you should be able to:

• Define what human resource management means
• Understand the recruitment and selection process, involving the preparation of a job description, shortlisting suitable candidates, and conducting interviews
• Identify the different ways employees can be trained
• Engage in the process of performance appraisal
• Identify the types and functions of rewarding employees
• Understand how to enact disciplinary procedures.

Human Capital

Human capital theory was developed in the 1960s when Schultz (1959) calculated the rate of economic growth in the United States and found that it was three times larger than the rate of increase in labour and capital. The perplexing puzzle because of this finding was that fewer resources were being spent to generate higher levels of income, which could not be accounted for by the factors of production identified at the time such as physical, capital, labour, land and management (Nafukho et al., 2004). Schultz (1959) theorized that this difference could be explained by considering the 'human capital' (represented by an individual's education and training levels) factor, which until then was not considered a valid form of capital. This concept was supported and illustrated by Becker (1994) who pointed out that countries such as Japan, Taiwan and other Asian economies were still able to grow rapidly by relying on a well-trained, educated, hard-working and conscientious labour force even if they lacked natural resources (i.e. they import almost all their energy sources).

Central to human capital theory is the assumption that individuals deliberately invest in education and training in preparation to join the workforce (Nafukho et al., 2004). This investment means individuals enter the workforce with a higher level of knowledge and skills, leading to economic pay-offs in the form of higher wages as compensation for their higher skillset (Kenworthy and McMullan, 2010). At the national level, Becker (1994) argued that the more scientific knowledge becomes essential to the production of goods and services in modern economies, the more the value of education and technical schooling, and on-the-job training, increases. Therefore, countries with highly educated workforces have greater supplies of scientists, scholars, technicians, managers, and other contributors of output who can apply their scientific and technical knowledge to increasing economic productivity.

Because of the belief that an individual's investment in his/her education and training increases their productivity, the effect of an entrepreneur's human capital on their enterprise's performance has been of significant interest to entrepreneurship researchers (Jo and Lee, 1996; Goedhuys and Sleuwaegen, 2000; Van Der Sluis *et al.*, 2005; 2008; West and Noel, 2009; Ganotakis, 2012). An entrepreneur's human capital is represented by, among other things, his/her level of formal education, experiences, practical learning and non-formal education (Davidsson and Honig, 2003). Research has shown that an entrepreneur's human capital is positively associated with their enterprise's business performance. Education in a similar field as the firm's products and services, and experience in a similar line of business, provides entrepreneurs with substantial prior understanding of the prospective product their start-up will offer as well as the market environment they are entering (Jo and Lee, 1996). In addition, as small-scale enterprises begin to increase the scale of their operations, entrepreneurs become more involved with managerial and administrative activities rather than activities related to production. Therefore, skills learnt through higher education such as how to successfully manage a firm, identify appropriate markets, and to better prepare applications for external funding, become more important to effectively grow the business (Goedhuys and Sleuwaegen, 2000; Ganotakis, 2012).

Human Resources

Baum (1995) notes that:

> In some geographical and sub-sector areas, tourism and hospitality provides an attractive, high-status working environment with competitive pay and conditions, which is in high demand in the labour force and benefits from low staff turnover.... The other side of the coin is one of poor conditions, low pay, high staff turnover, problems in recruiting skills in several key areas, a high level of labour drawn from socially disadvantaged groups, poor status, and the virtual absence of professionalism.

Baum's (1995) view demonstrates the perception of labour conditions within which tourism enterprises operate. Thus, managers need to take steps to ensure working conditions within tourism enterprises reflect the positive aspects of Baum's (1995) view (e.g., competitive pay and conditions, attractive working environment) while minimizing the opportunities for negative working conditions to arise (e.g., low pay, high staff turnover, absence of professionalism). To do this, the principles of human resource management need to be applied.

Human resource management has multiple definitions in academic literature.

Storey's (1995) definition of HRM (see above) is useful within the context of tourism, as many tourism products and services require an interaction between the customer and service provider for an exchange to occur. This means the 'human' element becomes a strategic resource that can determine the level of quality associated with a tourism firm's products and services. As such, HRM is a critical tool for tourism enterprises to:

- use an array of techniques to develop highly committed and capable employees;
- deploy employees in the most effective way;
- increase their ability to provide better quality products and services; and
- ultimately lead to a non-replicable competitive advantage.

Nickson (2013) considers the practice of HRM to be a continuous cycle. First, a tourism enterprise needs to attract an effective workforce by understanding labour markets, planning their labour needs, recruiting a suitable pool of candidates, and finally selecting the most appropriate hire. Next, managers need to maintain and retain employees they hire through techniques such as reward programmes, labour relations, and grievance and disciplinary procedures. Subsequently, employees who are maintained need to be developed into an effective workforce and continuously improved through training and development programmes and performance appraisals. Finally, employees will eventually leave the tourism enterprise, and the cycle begins anew (attract, maintain and develop, Figure 6.1). Thus, HRM can be thought of as a continuous loop.

Attracting an Effective Workforce

Recruitment and selection

If human resources are critical to tourism enterprises, how do we find the right people to hire? Recruitment is the process of generating a pool of candidates from which to select the appropriate person for a vacancy. Through this process, not only does the tourism enterprise seek to attract suitable candidates, but it is also an opportunity for the firm to present a positive image to potential applicants and the wider labour market.

While it is always desirable to have a rigorous recruitment and selection process that will always lead to the selection of the best candidate, it is important to also acknowledge that recruitment processes can vary in sophistication

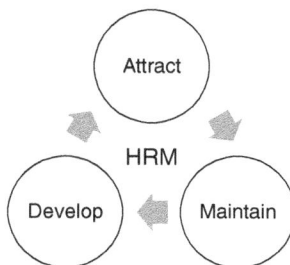

Figure 6.1. The HRM cycle. (Source: author developed.)

and complexity, and the outcome may not always lead to finding the perfect employee. For example, when selecting candidates for an international management trainee programme, many multinational hotel companies may employ a variety of sophisticated and time- and cost-intensive tools such as psychographic assessments, multiple interview rounds and/or group interviews. Conversely, when tour operators interview for part-time or seasonal work, a company may take less time to assess candidates, and instead conduct a perfunctory interview and rely on word-of-mouth to assess a candidate's credentials. Despite the variety of forms the recruitment and selection process can take, at the very least tourism enterprises should have mechanisms in place to enable a level of scrutiny for candidates for a vacant position. As a first step, recruitment involves creating a job description.

Job description

Heery and Noon (2008) define a job description as:

> A document that outlines the purposes of the job, the task involved, the duties and responsibilities, the performance of objectives, and the reporting relationships. It will give details of the terms and conditions, including the remuneration package and work hours.

Job descriptions should provide clear information to candidates about the organization and the job itself. In essence, it functions to offer applicants a preview of the job that they will be recruited for. Job descriptions should also act as a marketing document that seeks to make the job and the business look like an attractive place to work for potential applicants.

A conventional job description should advertise the essential and desirable criteria that the organization is looking for in the person they are seeking to hire. Essential criteria refer to the minimum standard expected for a given job, and these criteria will form the basis for the selection panel to potentially reject applicants. This can include criteria such as having a minimum completed educational requirement, a valid working visa, a driver's licence, etc. Desirable criteria refer to criteria which are over and above the minimum required and should provide the basis for selection. These can include criteria such as the ability to speak multiple languages, training certificates, years of work experience, etc. (Box 6.1).

Box 6.1. Criteria for a job description.

While there is no specific template that all job descriptions and advertisements should follow, the following information should be present:

- Details about the employing firm
- Role and duties of the job advertised
- Essential and desirable criteria for the role
- Training and development that will be provided
- Instructions on how to apply.

Shortlisting

Shortlisting refers to the process of systematically identifying the candidates you are interested in from your pool of applicants who best meet the essential and desirable criteria contained in the job description (Box 6.2). Shortlisted candidates then move on to the next stage of the recruitment process.

In cases where the number of applicants for a job opening is large, shortlisting can be a useful way to quickly eliminate unsuitable candidates from the applicant pool so that more time can be devoted to carefully choosing the best applicants. For example, if an essential criterion for a vacant position is for candidates to be within the country the business operates in when applying, any candidates applying from outside the country's borders can be automatically removed from consideration.

Interviewing

In the tourism industry, the most common step to assessing and selecting the ideal candidate is through the interview process. The employment interview is defined as:

> ...a personally interactive process of one or more people asking questions orally to another person and evaluating the answers for the purpose of determining the qualifications of that person in order to make employment decisions. (Levashina et al., 2014, p. 243).

Interviewing is the predominant method in assessing a candidate's suitability for a vacant position for tourism enterprises. While there is no standard structure as to how an employment interview should run, managers should be aware of certain principles to ensure the process is effective, fair and equitable.

- The interview process should focus on allowing the interviewee to speak. The interviewers should not be talking extensively.
- Questions should function to elicit information from the candidate, such as open-ended questions starting with 'what', 'why', 'when', 'which' and 'how'.

Box 6.2. The systematic process for shortlisting.

- Draw up the essential criteria to be shortlisted for the first round.
- Remove all applicants who do not meet the essential criteria.
- Set the number of candidates that an initial shortlist should contain (e.g., five candidates, eight candidates, etc.).
- Individual members on a selection panel produce their own individual list of candidates.
- The selection panel combines and reveals their lists.
- Where there are differences in the candidates selected between lists, panel members discuss why certain candidates were preferred while others were not. The final goal is to reach a consensus, through mutual agreement, negotiation, compromise, or a vote.
- The selection panel produces the final shortlist of candidates who will proceed to the next stage of the selection process.

- Interviewers need to be mindful of and reflect up on their personal biases to ensure that the effects from these are mitigated as much as possible. For example, interviewers may have prejudices related to gender, age and ethnicity. Interviewers also tend to relate easier to candidates with similar backgrounds to themselves.
- If conducting multiple interviews sequentially, interviewers need to be mindful of the contrast effect. This refers to allowing the experience of interviewing a previous candidate to influence the interview of the next candidate. As much as possible, each interview format should be similar and treated as separate cases.
- Both interviewers and interviewees are affected by physical cues. Interviewers need to avoid non-verbal cues associated with negative emotions, and instead adopt neutral expressions and body language. For example, crossing one's arms during an interview may indicate defensiveness, impatience or dissatisfaction.

Training

After employees are hired through the recruitment and selection process, they require training in order to understand and conform to the organization's culture and their job-related tasks. Training can be broadly categorized according to the desired outcomes of the training:

- *Induction and socialization*: This refers to training programmes designed to induct new employees into the organization (often referred to as on-boarding). It also functions to socialize new employees with current employees.
- *Development*: This refers to training programmes designed to develop and improve individuals within the organization. For example, preparing employees for promotion, up skilling, introduction of new processes and procedures, etc.
- *Disciplinary/remedial*: This refers to training programmes designed to improve the performance of employees who have fallen below the standards set by the firm.

Training can occur internally or external to the organization. These are broadly categorized as:

- *Internal, on-the-job training*: This type of training usually involves junior employees observing or shadowing senior employees when work takes place during working hours.
- *Internal, off-the-job training*: This type of training usually takes place within the organization, either outside the normal place of work (e.g., in dedicated training rooms in the back-of-house section instead of on the work site) or outside of work hours. There may also be a dedicated or specialized training department within the firm to facilitate this type of training.
- *External, off-the-job training*: This refers to training that takes place outside the organization and is usually associated with sending employees to be trained by external training providers.

Performance Appraisal

Performance appraisal refers to the process of evaluating the performance of employees to:

- ensure that expected standards of performance for an employee's role are being met;
- assess future training and development needs of the firms' workforce.

Within these two aims, managing performance can assist a tourism enterprise to:

- clarify minimum and/or expected performance standards required of employees;
- set future performance goals for employees or the enterprise;
- improve performance of employees by providing feedback (e.g., are they doing things the right or wrong way? How could they do things better?);
- identify future training and development needs;
- set and award pay and rewards;
- identify employees with high potential for career development and succession planning;
- increase employee motivation (e.g., from being able to set goals, provide rewards, etc.);
- solve job problems; and
- evaluate the effectiveness of the recruitment and selection process.

What needs to be appraised during the performance appraisal?

Generally, an employee's performance should be assessed on their ability to perform their job tasks, and their behaviour and attitude during work. These can be broadly categorized as task-based and personality-based performance.
Task-based performance includes an employee's:

- skill, ability and knowledge on the job;
- quality of work; this quality also needs to be assessed consistency over time; and
- volume of output.

Personality-based performance includes an employee's:

- attitude during work such as commitment, motivation, professionalism and enthusiasm;
- quality of interaction, encompassing:
  o their communication and ability to get along with colleagues, and other employees; and
  o their communication and professionalism during customer inter-actions.

Who should conduct performance appraisals?

Traditionally, the performance of employees is appraised by their direct superiors. However, relying on only one source of information can be less effective, for example if employees have had conflicts with their direct superiors in the past or if managers may be prejudiced against certain employees. Thus, several approaches can be used in tandem to measure the 'true' performance of employees using:

- *Self-evaluation*: In this method, employees self-assess their performance according to a specific set of criteria.
- *Peer-evaluation*: In this method, team members or colleagues (usually within the same department or work unit) assess all other individuals that they work with (except themselves).
- *Upward-evaluation*: In this method, the manager's performance is evaluated by their staff; and
- Customer-evaluation: In this method, the firm's customers may evaluate the performance of their staff through customer surveys, comments, observations, mystery shoppers, etc.

Rewards

Rewards for employees' work largely involves monetary compensation (i.e. pay). Pay plays a role for both employees and the employers.

Employees want and expect pay for their work to:

- achieve a level of purchasing power to maintain or attain their desired standard of living;
- perceive that they are being fairly treated (i.e. equal pay for equal work);
- perceive that they are being recognized for their work;
- obtain their rights as an employee. Since employees create wealth for the firm through their work, the expectation is that this wealth is, in turn, shared with them.

Employers pay employees for their work to:

- attract good candidates to work for the firm;
- retain high-performing employees within the firm;
- motivate employees to perform well in service to the firms' objectives;
- create change in the organization; for example, if employees are required to perform new tasks or different tasks, they may need to be compensated more for the increase in workload;
- maintain or enhance a firm's corporate reputation as a good place to work;
- determine the affordability of producing the firms' products and services, as labour costs factor into the prices a firm will charge to obtain a desired return on investment.

Other than pay, rewards offered to employees can also be non-monetary in nature, such as:

- promoting employees (while usually associated with higher levels of pay, this can also demonstrate recognition and value towards an employee);
- giving employees extra days off;
- offering recognitions of excellence (e.g., 'employee of the month' rewards, certificates of achievement, etc.);
- taking employees on activities or incentive trips;
- offering company health care and retirement plans.

Disciplinary Procedures

Conflict inevitably occurs within any firm. What is important is that firms should have policies and procedures in place to deal with conflict and mitigate any adverse situations that may arise. Sources of conflict can be broadly categorized into:

Environmental conflict: This refers to conflict arising due to adverse working conditions or the unacceptable nature of the work an employee performs. This encompasses the economic conditions of the job, the physical conditions of the job, and whether employees feel their workload is too much or too little.

Social substantive conflict: This refers to conflicts arising due to perceived disagreements of how decisions are made in the organization. This can be caused by actions from management or company policy that make employees perceive that decisions made or actions taken that impact on them are inequitable.

Social relational conflict: This refers to conflict arising from relationships between individuals and groups within the firm. For example, conflicts due to racism, sexism, differing personalities, etc.

Levels of conflict

Employees have the right to express and attempt to resolve dissatisfaction that they might have at work. The magnitude of the perceived conflict can be expressed according to different levels:

Dissatisfaction: This refers to anything that disturbs an employee's contentment with their job, whether this disturbance is expressed in words or internally.

Complaint: This refers to dissatisfaction which is brought to the attention of the manager or person responsible in words or in writing.

Grievance: This refers to a complaint that has been formally presented to a higher management representative, such as the human resources department or union official.

Procedures to report and deal with a grievance

Since employees have the right to express dissatisfaction and come to a resolution, a tourism enterprise should have steps for employees to lodge a formal grievance. These can include the following actions:

- Employees need to present the nature of the grievance formally in writing.
- The employer should hold a meeting to discuss the employee's grievance as soon as possible.
- The employee should be allowed to bring a support person to the meeting. This can be a co-worker, union representative, etc.
- Following the meeting, the employer should follow up by:
  o deciding on an appropriate action;
  o communicating in writing the decision to the employee, along with how the employer came to the decision;
  o explaining what the action involves, if action is taken;
  o detailing the timeframe for action to be taken.

Summary

This chapter discussed human capital theory and its implications for human resource management for tourism enterprises. An entrepreneur's human capital is represented by, among other things, their level of formal education, experiences, practical learning and non-formal education. Investing in education and training increases an entrepreneur's productivity, which, in turn, is associated with increased enterprise performance. Additionally, with tourism being a labour-intensive industry, the 'human' element becomes a strategic resource that can determine the level of quality associated with a tourism firms' products and services. Thus, HRM is a critical tool for tourism enterprises to use an array of techniques to develop highly committed and capable employees and to deploy employees in the most effective way, which increases their ability to provide better-quality products and services, ultimately leading to a non-replicable competitive advantage. The practice of HRM is a continuous cycle. Tourism enterprises need to attract an effective workforce through robust recruitment and selection procedures, and maintain, retain and develop employees through rewards, training and development programmes. Employees will eventually leave the tourism enterprise, and the cycle begins anew.

Review Questions

1. Draw up a job application for a hypothetical position in a tourism enterprise.
2. Come up with practical ways in which internal, on-the-job training can be conducted within a tourism enterprise.
3. What kind of training could be implemented to encourage teamwork within a tourism enterprise?
4. What types on non-monetary rewards can be used to reward teamwork within a tourism enterprise?

Case study: The social practice of care hotel vacations.

Care hotels with an adapted environment attract tourists with a mixture of care and/or medical services and facilities, linked to 24 hour personal care from physicians, nurses and other professionals, and regular tourist (health) amenities.

Author: Bertine Bargeman[1], Greg Richards[1] and Marleen van Charante-Stoffelen[2]

Affiliations: [1]NHTV University of Applied Sciences, Academy for Leisure, Breda, The Netherlands
          [2]Tilburg University, Department of Leisure Studies, The Netherlands

Origin: Vancouver Island University World Leisure Centre of Excellence

Background

The role of care hotels

According to Goodrich (1994), care hotels are essentially tourist facilities seeking to attract tourists with a blend of healthcare services and facilities and regular tourist amenities (Lee, 2010). Care hotels offer a combination of privacy, products, services and hospitality, linked to 24-hour personal care from physicians, nurses and other healthcare professionals (Han, 2013). Due to the increase in the number of elderly people and those seeking medical care, the hotel market with a blend of care and leisure experiences, is expected to grow in the future (Hui and Wan, 2009; Hume and DeMicco, 2007; Karuppan Karrupan, 2010; Laesser, 2011). 'Regular' hotels increasingly cater for guests who need a temporary replacement for care at home (respite care) and/or an adapted environment to go on vacation (Hofer *et al.*, 2012).

The role of care hotels as an intersection between the care and the tourism sectors makes a vacation in a care hotel an interesting social practice to study, because care hotels are confronted with the challenge of mixing professional care with a comfortable hotel environment including related services and leisure activities (Han, 2013). Nevertheless, the care hotel vacation has gained little attention from hospitality and tourism researchers, and thus has not been well studied as a facet of both the hotel industry and the care sector (Cook, 2010; Han, 2013). As these sectors have undergone a shift from supply-led to demand-led environments (Connell, 2013; Fottler *et al.*, 2000; Setterfield, 2002), it is increasingly important for them to provide high-quality service and positive guest experiences.

Research on interpersonal service encounters

In recent decades, service quality models have become very popular in hospitality, healthcare and tourism research to examine how customers assess (health) service quality (Bakan *et al.*, 2014; Duggirala *et al.*, 2008). While in the 1980s and 1990s the focus was on studying consumers' expectations of services related to service performance or perceived service to judge their satisfaction, in recent years, links with such concepts as loyalty, emotions, values, intentions and experiences of customers have been more frequently included to evaluate services or service encounters (see Dagger *et al.*, 2007; McColl-Kennedy *et al.*, 2012; Vargo and Lusch, 2004). According to Lemke *et al.* (2011), the contemporary consumer demands more than just competent services, and also seeks experiences which are engaging, robust, compelling and memorable. In articles on service-dominant logics, scholars study in a more holistic manner how customer experience quality is served through and co-created by

Continued

Case study: continued.

---

product/service usage and peer-to-peer interaction, and not just product and service quality (Karpen *et al.*, 2012).

Even though personal aspects nowadays play a more important role in service or experience quality research and supply-side and service encounters are studied more frequently in a hedonic manner (cf. concepts such as 'servicescapes', 'experiencescapes', 'services as destinations'), much research still focuses on the development of attributes or scales by using quantitative assessment measures (see Brand *et al.*, 1997). These studies also adopt either a customer or provider lens, even though the interaction between the two is vital in the contemporary 'co-creation' of experiences (Morgan *et al.*, 2010; Prahalad and Ramaswamy, 2004). We argue here that a practice approach can be an interesting tool to study complex interrelationships between demand and supply in care hotels as an adapted holiday environment. In the next sections we will present a multiple case study on the practices in care hotels using this theoretical approach.

The innovation: care hotels as an adapted environment for senior tourists

Case context

Care hotels with an adapted environment for senior tourists can be found in countries such as Norway, United Kingdom, Germany, Spain and The Netherlands. As already indicated by Goodrich (1994) and Han (2013), care hotels attract tourists with a mixture of care and/or medical services and facilities, linked to 24-hour personal care from physicians, nurses and other professionals, and regular tourist (health) amenities. Although care hotels focus both on (post-)care services and vacation experiences, they do not offer medical surgeries in general (Han, 2013).

These characteristics were also applicable to the five care hotels in The Netherlands we studied (Stoffelen, 2011). Because not all 14 officially recognized care hotels in our country agreed to participate, our study can be conceived as a multiple case study with a convenience sample. Besides care and hospitality facilities, the five care hotels offered both short and long stays, and had vacation guests as an important target group. The care hotels involved were similar in terms of services (5 stars) and price range (150–200 euros per night), although they had different locations (e.g. city centre, village) and sizes (number of rooms varies from 10 to 70). Our main intention was to generate a broader view of interactions between different stakeholders or actors in these care hotels, and not to compare the hotels based on their background characteristics or to generalize the results (cf. Gibbs, 2007).

Stakeholders involved

To study the encounters between different stakeholders or actors, face-to-face interviews were held with senior guests and managers of the five care hotels. Unfortunately, in three of the five hotels it was not possible to interview hospitality and care personnel, because the management teams 'did not want to disturb the services to the guests'. Therefore, we decided to interview only the managers as representatives of the supply side. Interviews with managers seemed an acceptable approach, because the five care hotels were small organizations in which the managers cooperated closely with the rest of the personnel, and were fully aware of what happens at the workplace.

Additionally, to obtain as complete and diverse a picture of the interactions in the five care hotels, 14 senior guests from the various care hotels participated in a face-

Continued

Case study: continued.

---

to-face interview, outside of the care hotel. Eight out of the 14 guests had physical or mental disabilities (e.g., need dialysis, physiotherapy, assistance because of wheelchair use), which, however, did not impair them in answering questions during the interview. The other six guests were accompanying the guest with disabilities. All interviewed guests visited the care hotel as an adapted environment to be on vacation and did not live near the hotel.

Two topic lists were established for interviewing purposes: one for the managers of the care hotels and one for the guests (see Bryman, 2008; Ritchie and Lewis, 2003). Voice recordings were used to register the information from the interviews. The recordings of the interviews were completely transcribed afterwards and functioned as the main data for this study. By constructing a data matrix, it became possible to detect connections and interrelationships and to compare the answers of the guests and hotel managers (cf. Bryman, 2008; Miles and Huberman, 1994).

Care hotel vacations: a social practices approach

Whereas service or experience quality studies tended to deal either with supply or demand, by using a social practices approach (SPA) the concrete interaction points between senior guests and personnel in the care hotel practices could be studied from a more holistic perspective. The SPA approach was developed by Spaargaren in 1997 and adopted from the structuration theory of Giddens (1979, 1984). The application of a practice theory approach is part of a general wave of renewed interest in practice theory in consumption studies, which aims to bridge the actor–structure dualism (see Schatzki *et al.*, 2001; Shove *et al.*, 2012; Spaargaren *et al.*, 2016; Warde, 2014). However, in recent years practice theory has already been successfully applied by academics in studying (leisure) practices (Bargeman *et al.*, 2016; Lamers and Pashkevich, 2015; Van der Poel and Bakker, 2016; Verbeek, 2009), but, to date, not in the healthcare tourism sector.

Practice theory centres on the social practices that people are engaged in during their everyday life (Røpke, 2009; Southerton, 2012; Warde, 2014). Social practices can be conceived as activities that are ordered across time and space, driven by routines and shared by groups of people (Reckwitz, 2002; Spaargaren, 1997). Because the SPA does not focus on the content of the interactions between demand and supply, the theory of Shove *et al.* (2012) has been used to study care hotel practices more extensively. According to this theory, social practices consist of three types of 'elements': meanings, materials and competences. (Symbolic) meanings refer to motivations, aspirations and ideas of the actors, for example the motives and aspirations of guests to perform leisure activities in the care hotel. The materials focus on tangible physical characteristics of the practice such as resources, tools and objects. Examples related to the care hotel practice were specially adapted facilities, leisure facilities and amenities in the physical environment of the care hotel. Understanding, skills and know-how can be conceived as 'competence' elements, which we related to the human resource capabilities and services provided by the care hotels. The interview items focused on an operationalization of the three elements of Shove *et al.* (2012) and helped us to study the crossing points or 'consumption junctions' (Spaargaren, 1997) in the care hotel practices. The interaction between demand and supply could either operate well, or difficulties could arise. An unsuccessful interaction suggested a 'poor fit' or 'misfit', resulting, potentially, in a negative outcome, while a successful interaction could be interpreted as a 'good fit' involving a positive outcome.

Continued

Case study: continued.

Findings

Competences and empathy of personnel

The interviews with guests indicated that the most important consumption junctions in the care hotels studied were the moments at which the guests met and communicated with the hospitality and care personnel. The hospitality personnel included receptionists, waitresses, cooks, hostesses, volunteers and housekeepers. The care personnel could be divided into carers and nurses. Important fits in the care practices are related to the competences and empathy of the personnel.

For instance, several respondents were pleased with the provision of 24-hour care and mentioned that they (and their family) felt very secure thanks to the idea of having a qualified caretaker nearby at all times (cf. Dagger *et al.*, 2007; Han, 2013). In addition, the guests interviewed pointed out that they received adequate and helpful assistance if they undertook leisure activities outside the care hotel environment. The majority of the hotel managers were keen on trying to assist guests to access these (leisure) activities in such a way that a successful experience was provided. If necessary, hostesses and volunteers are present to assist guests with a trip outside the care hotel environment, but also to have a conversation, play a game, shop for groceries or have a short walk with them. Referring to this, the guests indicated they were very pleased that hospitality employees are able to answer both care-related and hospitality-related questions, regardless of their function.

The interviews with the guests also identified situations in which empathy or individual attention played a crucial role in the experience:

> *What I liked so much, and also found very special, is that so many people entered our room to introduce themselves, and they were all, one by one, so nice and compassionate! It made me wonder, how did they get these employees?* – Guest

According to one care hotel manager, these aspects make care hotels different from 'regular hotels'. In addition, another manager highlighted that her care hotel focused on pampering its guests; they wanted to provide guests with a trouble-free vacation and meet their wishes as well as possible:

> *We just try to provide an amazing product in which the guest is centralized and regains control over his or her own life.* – Manager

Hence, to pamper their guests from time to time, the care hotels treated eating and drinking as a special experience or event. In one hotel a guest was selected to decide the menu for that evening, once a week. In the other hotels, for example, guests were invited to take a look in the kitchen and dine at the chef's table.

Materials: care and leisure facilities

Consumption junctions in the care hotels studied were positively facilitated by various material amenities. The interviewed guests were satisfied with the eating facilities provided in the care hotels, like a hotel bar and restaurant, which provided high-quality meals adapted to the wishes of the guests (including free room service). Many guests used words like 'outstanding', 'fabulous' and 'delicious'.

The care facilities were also highly appreciated. The hotel managers indicated that specially adapted care facilities have been provided (e.g., turning circles for wheelchairs, patient

Continued

Case study: continued.

lifters, lockers at eye level, kidney dialysis equipment) in order to reduce the guests' physical restrictions as much as possible. Most care hotels had chosen modern furniture, which was perceived by the interviewed guests as 'a warm homelike atmosphere with a hint of luxury' and which 'stimulated their healing process and vacation feeling' (cf. Fottler *et al.*, 2000). Some care facilities, such as hinged arm supports, shower chairs and toilet seat risers, were only installed in the room if the guest needed them. The underlying thought with regard to this policy was that guests needed to feel that they were in a hotel environment, and unnecessary care facilities might disturb their vacation experience.

Moreover, to offer a comfortable hotel environment, the care hotels studied provided many leisure facilities, such as sports, wellness (e.g. sauna, sunbed and whirlpool), health, beauty, media and entertainment facilities, and a small store near the front desk with souvenirs. The guests did not prefer lunch and dinner possibilities elsewhere, as they stayed in the care hotel on a full-board basis.

Meanings: motivations and aspirations of guests

The guests interviewed exhibited a mixture of care- and leisure-related motives for staying in a care hotel, such as the possibility to escape from everyday life, the availability of care facilities and services as a relief for informal carers, and the search for rest and individual attention. The guests noted that they particularly enjoyed relatively calm individual leisure activities during their stay, such as reading a book, listening to music and watching television in the common room, and taking a short walk in the garden. Sports facilities were generally only used by guests who needed them for physiotherapy. Both the respondents of the demand and supply side noted that the wellness facilities were rarely used. It seemed that the motives and aspirations of the current 'stereotypical' care hotel guest did not fit with the wellness facilities and services provided. In addition, one manager believed that using wellness facilities does not form an important part of the Dutch culture, as is the case in Germany for instance.

Implications and lessons learned

According to Yeoh *et al.* (2013), care hotels have to mix care and medical services with a comfortable hotel environment including leisure facilities to be attractive for a more diverse and growing group of elderly tourists who need an adapted holiday environment (see Han, 2013; Hui and Wan, 2009). We would argue that this mixture of care and leisure services, in combination with a focus on the practice of a care hotel vacation instead of a focus on either the guests or providers, requires a multidisciplinary and holistic research framework such as that offered by a practice approach. The theoretical framework used in this multiple case study, a combination of the SPA (Spaargaren, 1997) and the three elements derived from the theory of Shove *et al.* (2012), was found to be applicable in the care hotel context. The chosen theoretical framework, which was strongly linked to the interview topics, assisted us in understanding more comprehensively the specific consumption junctions that arose in the inter-sectorial context of the five Dutch care hotels.

Focusing on interactions between the interviewed personnel and guests allowed us to focus on various successful and less successful consumption junctions. The findings indicated that the successfulness of these consumption junctions was related to three types of elements which are strongly interlinked in the care hotel practice: materials (care and leisure facilities), competences (skills and empathy of the personnel) and meanings (motivations and aspirations of guests) (see Shove *et al.*, 2012). The most successful consumption junctions in the five care hotels were related to the element 'competences'. 'Fits' arose because

Continued

Case study: continued.

several guests were very pleased with the qualified care and adequate, friendly and helpful assistance of the care and hospitality personnel who provide them with a very positive holiday experience. The element 'competences' was strongly interlinked with the element 'materials' (see Shove *et al.*, 2012) because the well-evaluated care and assistance of employees in the five hotels studies were positively facilitated by various care and leisure facilities. In addition, successful consumption junctions were found related to the 'warm' and comfortable environment of the care hotels and the eating and care facilities which stimulated the guests' vacation feeling. The care hotels studied seemed to deal well with the different health conditions and dietary demands of guests. This flexibility had a good fit with the needs of different types of care hotel guests and the inter-sectorial character of care hotels (see Hofer *et al.*, 2012). A less successful practice was identified for wellness and sport facilities, because these facilities were rarely used by the guests interviewed. Because the care hotel industry is relatively new, particularly in The Netherlands compared to countries such as Germany, Dutch people are not familiar with the various care, leisure and wellness facilities of care hotels. Due to these factors, their motives and aspirations ('meanings') did not fit with the wellness facilities and services provided by the care hotels they visited.

It is clear that our multiple case study has some limitations. An important lesson learned or limitation is related to the fact that it was not possible to conduct face-to-face interviews with care personnel and to do participant observations, because of privacy issues of both guests and employees. As we stated before, particular participant observation is a very appropriate research method for analysing social practices. But what are the potential alternatives if we aim to study more privacy-related or intimate practices or rituals as in the case of care hotels (see Collins, 2004)? The development of new methods to collect such sensitive data would help to throw light on the nature of service encounters that are bounded by professional ethical concerns. Another limitation is that only Dutch care hotels have been studied, while a future study might include a wider variety of guests and personnel and more care hotels both in The Netherlands and abroad.

As Connell (2013) argues, more research in the emerging field of healthcare tourism is needed in order to understand how this sector operates, particularly as it is likely to grow due to the ageing of the baby-boom generation (e.g. Hofer *et al.*, 2012; Yeoh *et al.*, 2013). Additionally, it is likely that the healthcare industry and ancillary industries will grow even more in the future, and that care services will be increasingly integrated into hospitality environments. This will inevitably bring new challenges for the hospitality industry in adapting to the new consumption junctions that arise at the interface between health care and hospitality. A practice perspective could be helpful to analyse the elements which affect new interactions between guests and personnel and to disentangle the dynamics in existing consumption junctions.

References

Bakan, I., Buyukbese, T. and Ersahan, B. (2014) The impact of Total Quality Service (TQS) on healthcare and patient satisfaction: an empirical study on Turkish private and public hospitals. *The International Journal of Health Planning and Management* 29, 292–315. DOI: 10.1002/hpm.2169.

Bargeman, B., Richards, G. and Govers, E. (2016) Volunteer tourism impacts in Ghana: a practice approach. *Current Issues in Tourism*. DOI:10.1080/13683500.2015.1137277.

Continued

Case study: continued.

Brand, R.R., Cronin, J.J. and Routledge, J.B. (1997) Marketing to older patients: perceptions of service quality. *Health Marketing Quarterly* 15(2), 1–31. DOI: pdf/10.1300/J026v15n02_01.

Bryman, A. (2008) *Social Research Methods.* Oxford University Press Oxford, UK.

Connell, J. (2013) Contemporary medical tourism: conceptualisation, culture and commodification. *Tourism Management* 34, 1–13. DOI: 10.1016/j.tourman.2012.05.009.

Cook, P.S. (2010) Constructions and experiences of authenticity in medical tourism: the performances of places, spaces, practices, objects and bodies. *Tourist Studies* 10, 135–153. DOI: 10.1177/1468797611403048.

Dagger, T.S., Sweeney, J.C. and Johnson, L.W. (2007) A hierarchical model of health service quality: scale development and investigation of an integrated model. *Journal of Service Research* 10(2), 123–142. DOI: 10.1177/1094670507309594.

Duggirala, M., Rajendran, C. and Anantharaman, R.N. (2008) Patient-perceived dimensions of total quality service in healthcare. *Benchmark International Journal* 15(5), 560–583. DOI: 10.1108/14635770810903150.

Fottler, M.D., Ford, R.C., Roberts, V. and Ford, E.W. (2000) Creating a healing environment: the importance of the service setting in the new consumer-oriented healthcare system. *Journal of Healthcare Management* 45(2), 91–106. (accessed 14 November 2022).

Gibbs, G.R. (2007) *Analyzing Qualitative Data*. Sage, London.

Giddens, A. (1979) *Central Problems in Social Theory: Action, Structure and Contradiction in Social Analysis*. University of California Press Berkeley, California.

Giddens, A. (1984) *The Constitution of Society: Outline of the Theory of Structuration*. Polity Press Cambridge, UK.

Goodrich, J. (1994) Health tourism: a new positioning strategy for tourist destinations. *Journal of International Consumer Marketing* 63, 227–238. DOI: 10.1300/J046v06n03_12.

Han, H. (2013) The healthcare hotel: distinctive attributes for international medical travelers. *Tourism Management* 36, 257–268. DOI: 10.1016/j.tourman.2012.11.016.

Hofer, S., Honegger, F. and Hubeli, J. (2012) Health tourism: definition focused on the Swiss market and conceptualization of the health(i)ness. *Journal of Health Organization and Management* 26(1), 60–80. doi: 10.1108/14777261211211098.

Hui, T.-K. and Wan, D. (2009. Health-care in Singapore. *Advances in Hospitality and Leisure* 5, 109–123. DOI: 10.1108/S1745-3542(2009)0000005010.

Hume, L.F., and DeMicco, F.J. (2007) Bringing hotels to healthcare: a Rx for success. *Journal of Quality Assurance in Hospitality & Tourism* 8(1), 75–84. DOI: 10.1300/J162v08n01_04.

Karpen, I.O., Bove, L.L. and Lukas, B.A. (2012) Linking service-dominant logic and strategic business practice: a conceptual model of a service-dominant orientation. *Journal of Service Research* 15(1), 21–38. DOI: 10.1177/1094670511425697.

Karuppan, C.M. and Karuppan, M. (2010) Changing trends in health care tourism. *The Health Care Manager* 29(4), 349–358. DOI: 10.1097/HCM.0b013e3181fa05f9.

Laesser, C. (2011) Health travel motivation and activities: insights from a mature market – Switzerland. *Tourism Review* 66(1/2), 83–89. DOI: 10.1108/16605371111127251.

Lamers, M. and Pashkevich, A. (2015) Short-circuting cruise tourism practices along the Russian Barents Sea coast? The case of Arkhangelsk. *Current Issues in Tourism*. DOI: 10.1080/13683500.2015.1092947.

Lee, C.G. (2010) Health care and tourism: evidence from Singapore. *Tourism Management* 31, 486–488. DOI: 10.1016/j.tourman.2009.05.002.

Continued

Case study: continued.

Lemke, F., Clark, M. and Wilson, H. (2011) Customer experience quality: an exploration in business and consumer contexts using repertory grid technique. *Journal of the Academy of Marketing Science* 39, 846–869. DOI: 10.1007/s11747-010-0219-0.

McColl-Kennedy, J.R., Vargo, S.L., Dagger, T.S., Sweeney, J.C. and van Kasteren, J. (2012) Health care customer value cocreation practice styles. *Journal of Service Research* 15(4), 370–389. DOI: 10.1177/1094670512442806.

Miles, M.B. and Huberman, M. (1994) *Qualitative Data Analysis: An Expanded Sourcebook*. Sage, Thousand Oaks, California.

Morgan, M., Lugosi, P. and Ritchie, B.J.R. (2010) *The Tourism and Leisure Experience: Consumer and Managerial Perspectives*. Channel View Publications, Clevedon, UK.

Prahalad, C.K. and Ramaswamy, V. (2004) Co-creation experiences: the next practice in value creation. *Journal of Interactive Marketing* 18(3), 5–14. DOI: 10.1002/dir.20015.

Reckwitz, A. (2002) Toward a theory of social practices: a development in culturalist theorizing. *European Journal of Social Theory* 5, 243–263. DOI: 10.1177/13684310222225432.

Ritchie, J. and Lewis, J. (2003) *Qualitative Research Practice: A Guide for Social Science Students and Researchers*. Sage, London.

Røpke, I. (2009) Theories of practice: new inspiration for ecological economic studies on consumption. *Ecological Economics* 68, 2490–2497. DOI: 10.1016/j.ecolecon.2009.05.015.

Schatzki, T. R., Knorr-Cetina, K. and von Savigny, E. (2001) *The Practice Return in Contemporary Theory*. Routledge, London and New York.

Setterfield, M. (2002) *The Economics of Demand-led Growth: Challenging the Supply-side Vision of the Long Run*. Edward Elgar, Cheltenham, UK.

Shove, E., Pantzar, M. and Watson, M. (2012) *The Dynamics of Social Practice: Everyday Life and How It Changes*. Sage, Los Angeles, California.

Southerton, D. (2012) Habits, routines and temporalities of consumption: from individual behaviours to the reproduction of everyday practices. *Time & Society* 22(3), 335–355. DOI: 10.1177/0961463X12464228.

Spaargaren, G. (1997) The ecological modernization of production and consumption: essays in environmental sociology (doctoral dissertation). Wageningen University, The Netherlands.

Spaargaren, G., Weenink, D., and Lamers, M. (2016) Introduction: using practice theory to research social life. In: G. Spaargaren, D. Weenink and M. Lamers (eds) *Practice Theory and Research: Exploring the Dynamics of Social Life*. Routledge, Abingdon, UK, pp. 3–27.

Stoffelen, M. (2011) Vacation in a care hotel: a qualitative study towards the practice of a vacation in a care hotel. Unpublished Master's thesis, Tilburg University, The Netherlands.

Van der Poel, H., and Bakker, S. (2016) Grounding the practice: material elements in the constitution of tennis practices. In: G. Spaargaren, D. Weenink and M. Lamers (eds) *Practice Theory and Research: Exploring the Dynamics of Social Life* Routledge, Abingdon, UK, pp. 131–150.

Vargo, S.L. and Lusch, R.F. (2004) Evolving to a new dominant logic of marketing. *Journal of Marketing* 68, 1–17. DOI: 10.1509/jmkg.68.1.1.24036.

Verbeek, D. (2009) Sustainable tourism mobilities: A practice approach. Doctoral dissertation, Tilburg University, The Netherlands.

Continued

Case study: continued.

Warde, A. (2014) After taste: culture, consumption and theories of practice. *Journal of Consumer Culture* 14(3), 279–303. DOI: 10.1177/1469540514547828.
Yeoh, E., Othman, K., and Ahmad, H. (2013) Understanding medical tourists: word-of-mouth and viral marketing as potent marketing tools. *Tourism Management* 34, 196–201. DOI: 10.1016/j.tourman.2012.04.010.

Discussion Questions

1. The case study highlighted how the competences and empathy of hospitality personnel played a crucial role in creating a good experience for the guest. One guest went so far as to say: 'What I liked so much, and also found very special, is that so many people entered our room to introduce themselves, and they were all, one by one, so nice and compassionate! It made me wonder, how did they get these employees?'. Discuss how a recruitment and selection process can attempt to identify and hire employees who have the level of competence and empathy as described in the case study.

2. In the case study, guests were very pleased that hospitality employees were able to answer both care-related and hospitality-related questions, regardless of their function. Discuss how hospitality managers could train their employees to ensure that they are equipped with the appropriate knowledge to cope with dynamic situations such as those described in the case study.

3. Being able to provide such a high level of service, as described in the case study, requires additional time and effort on the part of employees to perform in a highly professional manner. Come up with non-monetary reward strategies that could encourage staff in the case study to maintain their high levels of service excellence.

References

Baum, T. (1995) *Managing Human Resources in the European Hospitality and Tourism Industry: A Strategic Approach*. Chapman and Hall, London.
Becker, G.S. (1994) *Human Capital: A Theoretical and Empirical Analysis, with Special Reference to Education*, University of Chicago Press, Chicago, Ilinois.
Cooper, A.C., Gimeno-Gascon, F.J. and Woo, C.Y. (1994) Initial human and financial capital as predictors of new venture performance. *Journal of Business Venturing* 9(5), 371–395. DOI: 10.1016/0883-9026(94)90013-2.
Davidsson, P. and Honig, B. (2003) The role of social and human capital among nascent entrepreneurs. *Journal of Business Venturing* 18(3), 301–331. DOI: 10.1016/S0883-9026(02)00097-6.
Ganotakis, P. (2012) Founder's human capital and the performance of UK new technology based firms. *Small Business Economics* 39(2), 465–515. DOI: 10.1007/s11187-010-9309-0.
Goedhuys, M. and Sleuwaegen, L. (2000) Entrepreneurship and growth of entrepreneurial firms in Cote d'Ivoire. *The Journal of Development Studies* 36(3), 123–145. DOI: 10.1080/00220380008422631.

Heery, E. and Noon, M. (2008) *A Dictionary of Human Resource Management*, 2nd edn. Oxford University Press, Oxford, UK.

Jo, H. and Lee, J. (1996) The relationship between an entrepreneur's background and performance in a new venture. *Technovation* 16(4), 161–171. DOI: 10.1016/0166-4972(96)89124-3.

Kenworthy, T.P. and McMullan, W.E. (2010) Theory morphing vs. theory testing: human capital in entrepreneurship. International Council for Small Business (ICSB), World Conference Proceedings, Washington, DC, pp. 1–36.

Levashina, J., Hartwell, C.J., Morgeson, F.P. and Campion, M.A. (2014) The structured employment interview: narrative and quantitative review of the research literature. *Personnel Psychology* 67, 241–293. DOI: 10.1111/peps.12052.

Lumpkin, G.T. and Dess, G.G. (1996) Clarifying the entrepreneurial orientation construct and linking it to performance. *The Academy of Management Review* 21(1), 135–172. DOI: 10.2307/258632.

Nafukho, F.M., Hairston, N. and Brooks, K. (2004) Human capital theory: implications for human resource development. *Human Resource Development International* 7(4), 545–551. DOI: 10.1080/1367886042000299843.

Nickson, D. (2013) *Human Resource Management in Hospitality, Tourism and Events*, 2nd edn. Taylor and Francis, New York.

Schultz, T.W. (1959) Investment in man: an economist's view. *Social Service Review* 33(2), 109–117.

Storey, J. (1995) Human resource management: still marching on, or marching out? In: Storey, J. (ed.) *Human Resource Management: A Critical Text*. Routledge, London, pp. 3–32.

Van Der Sluis, J., Van Praag, M. and Vijverberg, W. (2005) Entrepreneurship selection and performance: a meta-analysis of the impact of education in developing economies. *The World Bank Economic Review* 19(2), 225–261. DOI: 10.1093/wber/lhi013.

Van Der Sluis, J., Van Praag, M. and Vijverberg, W. (2008) Education and entrepreneurship selection and performance: a review of the empirical literature. *Journal of Economic Surveys* 22(5), 795–841. DOI: 10.1111/j.1467-6419.2008.00550.x.

West, G.P. and Noel, T.W. (2009) The impact of knowledge resources on new venture performance. *Journal of Small Business Management* 47(1), 1–22. DOI: 10.1111/j.1540-627X.2008.00259.x.

7 Leadership for Tourism Enterprises

> Leadership is important for motivating followers and mobilizing resources towards the fulfilment of the organization's mission; it is also essential for organizational innovation, adaptation, and performance. (Antonakis and House, 2014, p. 746)

Introduction

Tourism firms operate in a highly competitive and dynamic business environment. The success of these organizations requires entrepreneurs to be effective leaders, capable of creating and managing high-performance teams that deliver quality service experiences. Tourism employees operate on the front line, with day-to-day interactions with customers, therefore effective leadership is important in influencing service quality, customer satisfaction, and employee performance and loyalty (Chang *et al.*, 2020). Leaders in tourism enterprises must recognize the challenges and stresses experienced by their staff; these include irregular hours of work, emotional labour and uncertainty about their career progression. Thus, effective leadership practices that support and motivate employees are important for enterprise performance. Leadership is also critical during times of crises, as was evident during COVID-19 with its impacts on global tourism. Innovation in tourism business model transformation, such as restaurants shifting to online delivery of grocery items, event organizers shifting to virtual conferences, and tourism hotels transforming into medi-hotels or housing the homeless during lockdowns, are examples of leadership during COVID-19.

A focus on leadership in organizations has been slow to emerge within tourism entrepreneurship research. This chapter explores the concept of leadership in the context of small and medium tourism enterprises. It reviews the different styles of leadership, and their diverse effects on employee engagement

© Rob Hallak and Craig Lee 2023. *Managing Tourism Enterprises: Start-up, Growth and Resilience* (R. Hallak and C. Lee)
DOI: 10.1079/9781789249446.0007

and performance outcomes (Huertas-Valdivia *et al.*, 2019). The chapter will also present 'entrepreneurial leadership', a leadership style that is essential for successful entrepreneurship but remains under explored in tourism.

Learning Outcomes

After completing this chapter, you should be able to:

- Recognize the critical role of high-performance leadership in tourism enterprises
- Understand the different styles of leadership, including transformational leadership, servant leadership, authentic leadership, etc.
- Evaluate how different leadership styles create different outcomes on performance
- Understand the concept of 'entrepreneurial leadership' and how this can be applied in tourism enterprises.

Leadership in Tourism Firms

Leadership is defined as 'the process, not a person, of influencing others in a manner that enhances their contribution to the realization of group goals' (Platow et al., 2015, p. 20). Leadership extends beyond control and direction; a successful leader delegates, stimulates, motivates, mobilizes and influences others in order to achieve specific objectives (Nanjundeswaraswamy and Swamy 2014).

The tourism industry centres around services and experiences; thus, the competitiveness and performance of tourism and hospitality firms is heavily dependent on employee attitudes and behaviours and their interactions with tourists/customers/guests (Weber and Ladkin, 2010). Unfortunately, however, employees in the tourism industry frequently experience emotional exhaustion, a lack of appreciation, low pay, stress and uncertainty in their career progression (Huertas-Valdivia *et al.*, 2019). Therefore, leaders within this space need to understand and adapt their leadership styles to effectively motivate employees' positive behaviours and improve their job performance (Fu *et al.*, 2020). Tourism business owners/managers need to understand their own leadership styles and develop their abilities in leading employees and organizations.

Differences between Leadership and Management

Leadership and management are both important for organizational success. While there are common characteristics, there are certain nuances that should be recognized (Algahtani, 2014). The *Harvard Business Review* highlights that leadership and management can differ, as in Table 7.1.

Table 7.1. A comparison between leadership and management.

Criteria	Leadership	Management
Definition	The ability to influence, motivate and empower others to contribute toward the effectiveness and success of organizations	Involves directing and controlling a group of people for the purpose of coordinating and harmonizing that group towards achieving organizational goals
Orientation	• Long-term-oriented • People-oriented	• Short-term-oriented • Task-oriented
Styles	• Participative, consultative and transformational	• Authoritative, autocratic, dictatorial and transactional
Behavioural	• Create vision • Has followers • Asks questions • Shows how to do • Change agent, i.e., leaders create and drive change • Establishes principles and guidelines • Defines a sense of purpose	• Manage vision • Has subordinates • Gives directions • Tells what to do • Maintains the status quo but may sometimes reacts to change • Develop procedures and policies • Supports sense of purpose
Decision-making role	• Facilitates decision making	• Involved in decision making
Skills	• Creativity • Strategic thinking • Succession planning and organizing • Communication • Delegation • Motivation • Ability to challenge status quo • Emotional intelligence	• Planning and organizing operations • Tactical thinking • Communication • Delegation • Problem solving • Coordinating and controlling
Power	• Influence and charisma (come from personal relationships)	• Authoritative (comes from position in organization)
Risk	• Risk taker	• Risk-averse (control risk)
Accountability	• Has no well-defined accountability	• Accountable to organizations management
Outcome	• Achievement orientation	• Results orientation

Source: author created, adapted from https://www.forbes.com/sites/williamarruda/2016/11/15/9-differences-between-being-a-leader-and-a-manager/?sh=2f6b6fb64609 (accessed 8 July 2022); https://hbr.org/2013/08/tests-of-a-leadership-transiti (accessed 14 November 2022); https://online.hbs.edu/blog/post/leadership-skills (accessed 14 November 2022)

Research on leadership in tourism has focused on leadership characteristics (Box 7.1) and leadership outcomes. Clearly, leaders of tourism enterprises need to be passionate about the tourism industry and be committed to providing customers/tourists with quality service experience.

Effective leadership creates positive outcomes for the tourism enterprise. The ability to establish goals, motivate and empower staff can help to achieve the goals given in Box 7.2.

Leadership Styles

Leadership is not a one-size-fits-all. Different contextual factors, including the size of the organization, industry characteristics, employee backgrounds and behaviours, cultural factors, etc., impact upon the types of leadership required to support the performance of the organization. There are several different leaderships styles that business operators can adopt. Box 7.3 presents a description of some leadership styles that are important for the tourism industry.

Authentic Leadership: A type of leadership that focuses on providing employees with a work environment that is realistic and genuine. Leadership involves understanding oneself, as well as adopting a 'value-based mission' toward those who follow. Authentic leaders take on the responsibility of making staff feel safe and supported. They focus on building trust, helping to strengthen the psychological growth and self-development of the employees (Chang *et al.*, 2020).

Box 7.1. Leadership characteristics.

The characteristics of high-performance leadership in tourism enterprises include:

- High energy and determination
- Ability to learn from others
- Ability to learn from mistakes and past experience
- Being open-minded and self-reflective
- Strong communication skills and an ability to influence others
- Competent in building relationships
- Ability to learn from failures
- Ability to recognize personal weaknesses
- Develops and communicates a strategic vision for the enterprise
- Competent in operations management.

(Source: authors' own compilation, drawing on Weber and Ladkin (2010); Cong and Thu (2020).)

Box 7.2. Outcomes of effective leadership.

- Improved service quality and customer satisfaction
- Strengthened competitiveness of the tourism SME
- The SME becomes more innovative
- Employee engagement and loyalty is enhanced
- Employee creative performance.

(Source: authors' own compilation, derived from Fu *et al.* (2020); Khan *et al.* (2020).)

Authentic leaders use positive modelling to establish the organizational culture. They aim to create a team environment that is rewarding rather than authoritarian. There is a focus on employee vitality, learning and having a positive mindset (Avolio and Gardner, 2005). Building employee satisfaction extends to positive interactions between staff and customers in tourism organizations, supporting service quality.

Transformational Leadership: Transformational leadership is defined as a 'style of leadership that transforms followers to rise above their self-interest by altering their morale, ideals, interests, and values, motivating them to perform better than initially expected' (Pieterse *et al.*, 2010, p. 610). Transformational leaders 'have the ability to transform organizations through their vision for the future, and by clarifying their vision, they can empower the employees to take responsibility for achieving that vision' (Kim, 2014, p. 398). Transformational leaders work on mentoring their followers in developing their capability for innovativeness, becoming creative, and developing optimism and enthusiasm in the workplace (Box 7.4). Specifically, enthusiasm and optimism, in pursuit of organizational goals, are central to transformational leadership as well as monitoring and mitigating employee frustrations (Rabiul and Yean, 2021).

Idealized influence refers to 'charisma', and modelling ethical and moral behaviours. *Inspirational motivation* refers to establishing and communicating the organizational vision, and inspiring followers to contribute to achieving the vision. *Intellectual stimulation* involves keeping employees engaged and encouraging creativity and problem solving. *Individualized consideration* involves a focus on the needs of the followers; providing coaching, mentoring and career growth (Buil *et al.*, 2019).

Transformational leadership affects tourism and hospitality employees' work engagement and job performance, as well as their organizational citizenship behaviour (Buil *et al.*, 2019). Thus, tourism business owners should adopt transformation leadership practices by focusing on the practices given in Box 7.5.

Box 7.3. Leadership styles.

- Authentic leadership
- Transformational leadership
- Servant leadership
- Empowerment leadership
- Wisdom leadership
- Entrepreneurial leadership.

Box 7.4. Transformational leaders display four key behaviours:

1. Idealized influence
2. Inspirational motivation
3. Intellectual stimulation
4. Individualized consideration (Bass, 1990).

Wisdom Leadership: Elbaz and Haddoud (2017) examined the extent to which different leadership styles influence employee satisfaction and team performance in a tourism industry context. In addition, they focused on the leadership style of 'wisdom leadership' and its role in relation to performance.

Wisdom leadership is defined as the individual's 'awareness of one's workplace surroundings and the ability to anticipate consequences within the dynamic of the workplace...the ability to understand organizational dynamics and connect reasonable outcomes based upon the environmental cues that they read' (McCann *et al.*, 2014, p. 29).

Elbaz and Haddoud (2017) argue that the leadership styles of transformational leadership and visionary leadership enable the development of 'wisdom' in leadership (Box 7.6). Based on data collected from 505 travel agents in Egypt, their research discovered that different leadership styles have varying effects on performance; however, when leadership styles shape a leader's level of 'wisdom', this 'wisdom leadership' contributes directly to supporting employee satisfaction in tourism.

Wise leaders have a greater level of awareness of themselves and the changing environment.

Servant Leadership: Servant leadership is defined as an:

'(1) other-oriented approach to leadership, (2) manifested through one-on-one prioritizing of follower individual needs and interests, (3) and outward reorienting of their concern for self towards concern for others within the organization and the larger community' (Eva *et al.* 2019, p.114).

In its essence, servant leaders focus on the psychological needs and wellbeing of their followers. Leaders engage followers in multiple dimensions and emphasize humility, spirituality, ethics and justice (Figure 7.1).

Box 7.5. Transformational leadership practices for tourism firms.

- Establishing and reinforcing the vision, mission and goals of the tourism firm
- Acting as role model for expected behaviours
- Being attentive to the needs of the employees
- Using active listening
- Mentoring employees to build their capabilities in creativity and problem solving
- Supporting employees in achieving their personal goals.

Box 7.6. Characteristics of wise leaders.

- Ability to relate to people different from themselves
- Able to inspire others
- Able to be supportive and helpful to others
- Confident in what they know (and are aware of what they don't know)
- Prepared to deal with uncertainty in various situations.

(Source: authors' compilation derived from Parco-Tropicales and de Guzman (2014); Elbaz and Haddoud (2017).)

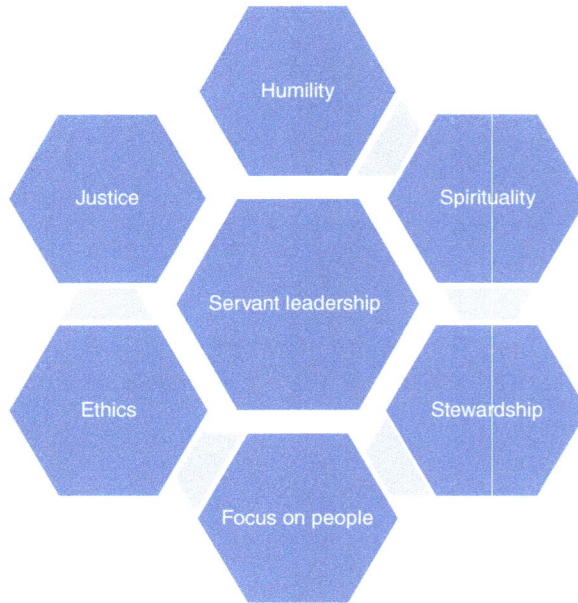

Figure 7.1. Servant leadership. (Source: author created.)

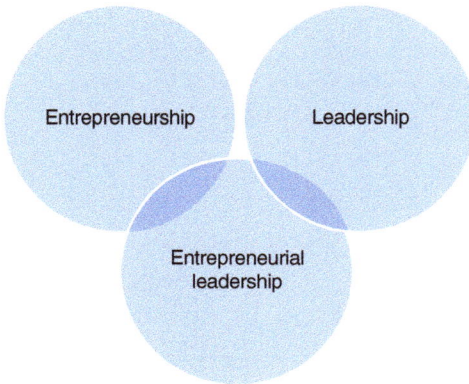

Figure 7.2. Entrepreneurial leadership. (Source: author created.)

Building relationships through these approaches, the leader aims to empower the employee, enabling them to grow and increase their potential and capabilities (Mayer *et al.*, 2008; Eva *et al.*, 2019).

Servant leadership distinguishes itself from traditional performance-related types of leadership. The immediate priority is on 'people' and long-term sustainability. Servant leaders are motivated by a sense of conviction to serve and make a positive difference in people's lives. Therefore, servant leadership extends beyond mentoring but incorporates stewardship (Eva *et al.*, 2019).

Evidence from the tourism and hospitality industry suggests servant leadership as the 'next step in leadership evolution' (Huertas-Valdivia *et al.*, 2019).

Employees in tourism and hospitality enterprises experience many challenges associated with emotional labour, therefore servant leadership increases their self-determination, self-efficacy, and conviction to grow and perform well (Huertas-Valdivia *et al.*, 2019). Through empowering tourism employees and building their capabilities, this leads to better interactions between staff and customers, improving service quality and tourism enterprise performance.

Empowerment leadership: Empowerment leadership is another type of positive leadership that emphasizes managers giving their employees more power, freedom and autonomy in decision making. Employees develop greater confidence and leadership responsibilities. Leaders focus on creating an environment of inclusivity and distribution of power, reducing bureaucratic constraints (Huertas-Valdivia *et al.*, 2019).

Empowerment leadership creates psychological empowerment of employees. In tourism and hospitality enterprises, this empowerment enables front-line staff to make decisions and take actions in service delivery and service recovery. Staff are given authority to act in pursuit of achieving customer satisfaction and retention.

A recent study of leadership behaviours in hotel businesses identified the positive outcomes of empowerment leadership. Huertas-Valdivia *et al.* (2019) examined the effects of different leadership styles on maximizing the potential of hotel workers. Data collected from 340 employees in Spanish hotels revealed that empowerment leadership has a positive effect on employees' psychological empowerment, and this, in turn, has a positive effect on employee engagement. Huertas-Valdivia *et al.* (2019) argue that empowerment leadership is a key leadership style for hotel businesses as it supports the capabilities and performance of the front-line and customer-contact staff, creating positive outcomes for guest satisfaction and hotel business performance.

Entrepreneurial leadership: Entrepreneurial leadership (Figure 7.2) is at the interface between entrepreneurship and leadership. Leadership is an important element of entrepreneurship. Entrepreneurs require competencies in leading people, resources and processes required for value creation (Reid *et al.*, 2018). Effective leadership is also required for start-ups and new entrepreneurial ventures as the systems, operations, procedures, business model and organizational structures require sound development (Hmieleski and Ensley, 2007). Employees look toward leaders to design and start the entrepreneurial engine of the new firm.

Both leaders and entrepreneurs share common attributes including (Renko *et al.*, 2015; Reid *et al.*, 2018):

- Articulating a vision
- Setting goals
- Inspiring employees/followers
- Competencies in planning and operations
- Motivating staff to perform
- Having technical expertise
- Being creative
- Achievement orientation
- Risk-taking
- Influencing and directing a team
- Tolerance of ambiguity

- Self-confidence
- Internal locus of control
- Patience
- Persistence
- Being able to lead in dynamic environments.

While there are shared attributes between entrepreneurship and leadership, entrepreneurial leadership is distinct from traditional types of leadership. Specifically, entrepreneurial leadership involves a focus on achieving entrepreneurial goals of recognizing and exploiting entrepreneurial opportunities. Thus, entrepreneurial leaders motivate and direct their team toward the goals of opportunity recognition. Employees at all levels of the enterprise are encouraged to adopt entrepreneurial behaviours and attitudes, thus creating an entrepreneurial culture in the organization that is focused on innovation and new opportunities (Renko *et al.*, 2015).

Entrepreneurial leadership does share some similarities with transformational leadership, although there are nuances. For example, a transformational leader will utilize charisma to inspire followers into action, as well as to build respect, admiration and loyalty among followers. An entrepreneurial leader, on the other hand, may not necessarily be 'charismatic' *per se*, but acts as a role model in entrepreneurial behaviour to inspire employees to follow suit. By mentoring staff to become entrepreneurial, creative and opportunity focused, the leader's role extends beyond processes and the business model to developing an entrepreneurial organization (Renko *et al.*, 2015).

An effective entrepreneurial leader needs to set the example and energize staff to pursue an opportunity-focused vision; this in contrast to HRM practices that focus on rewards and punishments. Staff should be encouraged to challenge the status quo, to develop and experiment with new ideas and new ways of doing things, thus the leaders and staff begin to share the entrepreneurial mindset and vision for the tourism enterprise.

A summary of the leadership styles is given in Table 7.2.

Summary

This chapter has reviewed the role of leadership in tourism enterprises, as well as presenting insights into the different leadership styles including authentic leadership, transformational leadership, servant leadership, wisdom leadership, empowerment leadership, and entrepreneurial leadership. Effective leadership is required at all stages of the tourism enterprise life cycle from start-up, to growth, to maturity. At the early stage of the tourism venture, leadership is necessary to establish the business model, processes and organizational structures. However, once established, it is imperative that entrepreneurs motivate and understand the needs of their staff to ensure employee engagement and performance. Entrepreneurs can use different leadership approaches, depending on the needs of the employees and general context. In tourism organizations with high levels of interaction between customers and front-line staff, evidence suggests that empowerment leadership enables staff to develop their psychological empowerment and self-determination, enabling high levels of service quality, customer

Table 7.2. Summary of leadership styles.

Leadership style	Characteristics	Leadership focus
Authentic leadership	Creates a team environment that is rewarding, rather than authoritarian	Providing employees with a work environment that is realistic and genuine Employee vitality, learning and having a positive mindset.
Transformational leadership	Acts as a role model Enthusiasm, optimism, motivation	Mentoring employees to build their capabilities in creativity and problem solving Establishing and reinforcing the vision, mission and goals of the tourism firm
Wisdom leadership	Aware of oneself and the changing environment Teaches and inspires others	Focus on employee satisfaction Creating an environment for team performance
Servant leadership	Stewardship Humility Cares for people's wellbeing	Prioritizing of follower individual needs and interests Focusing on the psychological wellbeing of staff Empowering employees to grow and reach their potential
Empowerment leadership	Gives employees power, freedom and autonomy	Focusing on supporting psychological empowerment of employees Positive outcomes on employee engagement
Entrepreneurial leadership	The interface between entrepreneurship and leadership Leadership in dynamic environments Energizes staff to pursue an opportunity-focused vision	Focused on achieving entrepreneurial goals of recognizing and exploiting entrepreneurial opportunities Creating an entrepreneurial culture that focuses on innovation

Source: author created.

satisfaction and retention. Servant leadership can assist staff with their psychological wellbeing, supporting their ability to manage stress and emotional labour.

At the cross roads of entrepreneurship and leadership lies 'entrepreneurial leadership'. This leadership approach inspires employees to think and behave in an entrepreneurial manner, focusing on creativity, innovation and pursuit of opportunities. Leadership that inspires and energizes employees to become entrepreneurial will create an entrepreneurial culture in the organization and will lead the tourism enterprise to being an entrepreneurial firm that adds value through creativity and innovation.

Review Questions

1. Consider how leadership in tourism enterprises may different from leadership in other types of organizations, for example manufacturing.

2. How does leadership of employees in tourism enterprises affect service quality and enterprise performance?

3. Explain how entrepreneurial leadership is distinct from other types of leadership such as servant leadership, authentic leadership, etc.

4. Do some research and find examples of different leadership behaviours in tourism firms.

5. Imagine that you are in the process of launching your own tourism enterprise. Discuss what leadership approach you would adopt and provide reasons.

Case study: Nazy's battle to change the image of the Pankisi Valley through tourism.

Nazy's Guest House is located in the Pankisi Valley, a valley in the east of Georgia. The guest house welcomes regular clientele and encourages female entrepreneurship in the valley.

Authors: Katie Seabolt, Alizée Couttet and Marine Jeannon

Affiliation: Skema Business School

Origin: Written on the basis of material provided by Nazy Dakishvili of Nazy's Guest House.

© CAB International 2021

Background and Context

Destinations with negative reputations

There are destinations around the world that have struggled with their image. Among them, cities such as Marseille (France) and Belfast (Northern Ireland), and countries such as Croatia, following the break-up of Yugoslavia; and Cambodia and Columbia, at the height of the drug wars. No matter the reason for their negative image, whether it be civil strife, gang violence, drug warfare or anything else, many have turned to tourism to change their destination image and spark their economy. The Pankisi Valley in Georgia is no different. It has seen success through the determination and perseverance of its residents, in particular Nazy Dakishvili who returned to her Pankisi Valley home to open a guest house. This case study recounts her experience.

Tourism in Georgia

Georgia is a relatively small country (69,700 sq. km) at the junction of eastern Europe and western Asia. Annual tourism reports, provided by the Georgian National Tourism Administration, indicate that in 2019 Georgia saw 7.7 million international tourist trips, of which 43.5% were for recreational or leisure purposes; 73.8% were repeat trips, indicating that many international visitors may have strong links to Georgia, including family connections. Two thirds of these trips included an overnight stay, and the remainder were day trips. The most visited region of Georgia (with 54.6% of annual visitors in 2019) is the capital, the Tbilisi region, located in the eastern part of the country. The Pankisi Valley, in the Kakheti region, east of Tbilisi, only represents 6.5% of total international visits (GNTA, 2019).

The Pankisi Valley

The Pankisi Valley, sometimes referred to as the Pankisi Gorge, is home to a small community of Kists (people who have origins in lower Chechnya), known for their tight family

Continued

Case study: continued.

bonds, values of hospitality and unique Muslim beliefs. The Kist people have preserved their culture and traditions throughout history and continue to uphold their values of friendship, family, respect and hospitality.

The Pankisi Valley consists of mountainous countryside, with peaks rising up on either side of the steep valley. At its heart is the dramatic Pankisi Gorge. On the rough slopes of the valley, there are hamlets where people previously survived through subsistence farming and some still raise crops and livestock. It can be desolate in winter, but cool and pleasant even in the hottest summers.

Although the Kists bring a unique culture to the Pankisi Valley, for many years the valley has been linked to jihadist extremism. Once known as the Valley of Terror, this valley was considered by outsiders to be a centre of crime and violent extremism. This perception began with the Chechen crisis and war with Russia, causing hundreds of thousands of Chechen refugees to flee to their southern neighbour, Georgia. Many of these refugees settled in the Pankisi Valley. From there, in the early 2000s, this area was linked to Al-Qaeda and ISIS extremism, causing the 'Pankisi Gorge Crisis', a political and military crisis between the Georgian government, the Russian and US governments, and the region. These links to Islamic extremism have painted a negative picture of the valley that has lasted until recent years.

A photojournalist piece published in July 2018 states that 'most villagers dissociate themselves from radical beliefs', and insist that negative coverage was often because 'journalists had typically stayed for a very short time'. In the same piece, the photographers explained that 'with a deep interest in people and enough time, trust develops on both sides', and a new image of the valley has had space to emerge (Clifford, 2018).

Journalism and the Pankisi Valley

The Pankisi Valley has, in other words, struggled with destination image, much of it perpetuated by journalism on the area. For example, Wikipedia – often an unreliable source – has only one paragraph on the region (as of 2 March 2021) and much of it focuses on its past relationship with 'Chechen rebels and Islamic militants, including foreign fighters', adding that 'others allege that it is more peaceful now, although there are still many Chechen refugees living there'. Even the rare positive coverage can be two-edged: in a photojournalism piece titled 'Inside Pankisi: Life in Georgia's Troubled Muslim Enclave', published in August 2019, an attempt to present a more positive image of the valley is undermined by the very title, with negative language and connotations used throughout.

After many years of what one local describes as 'disappointing coverage by journalists' in an article entitled 'Georgia's Pankisi Gorge fights "terrorism" stereotypes', some more recent articles and travel blogs are beginning to focus on a new image of the valley as 'a wonderful, off-beat destination to visit in Georgia' where 'crime in the gorge is unheard of – not virtually, but literally' (Lush, 2020). Much of this is due to the work of Nazy Dakishvili, as this case will show.

The female experience in the Pankisi Valley

In an article written in 2012, the female experience for women in the Pankisi Valley is described as one where the 'lack of career and educational options' disproportionately affect

Continued

Case study: continued.

---

women more than men. It also states that the women of the valley are 'watched closely and judged severely by family members and neighbors...They are judged mostly in terms of whether they act as upstanding wives and mothers. Little attention is paid to their own psychological needs. Little thought is given to self-fulfillment.' (Mielnikiewicz, 2012).

According to Nazy Dakishvili, this description of the female experience in the valley is outdated and far from the reality:

> Women in the Pankisi Valley do not have restrictions or limitations imposed on them and receive support from their families, male relatives and wider community to pursue educational or business goals. Local tourism is almost exclusively managed and developed by females in Pankisi Valley.

> Furthermore, she adds: 'Due to their [women's] strengths, intelligence, principles and independence, they take a lead in various community and business initiatives.'

Nazy's Guest House

Nazy's story

Eight years ago, in an effort to use tourism to improve the destination image of the Pankisi Valley and to share its unique culture, a Pankisi local, Nazy Dakishvili, gave up her law practice in Tbilisi to return home and open a guest house to inspire change. The aim of Nazy's Guest House, a family-owned business, is to bring sustainable tourism to the Pankisi Valley by providing guests with an authentic experience. Guests can benefit from traditional accommodation and food and have an immersive experience in the local lifestyle. Guests also come to enjoy cultural tours and trekking activities throughout the valley. The host families are Kist, who have lived in Jokolo for five generations.

Nazy's Guest House received the Best Community Based Tourism Award as a guest house in Georgia in 2018. It is featured in the Lonely Planet travel guidebook for *Georgia, Armenia and Azerbaijan* (6th edn, June 2020) as well as various other European-language travel guidebooks. Many articles have also been written about Nazy's Guest House and Nazy's mission to challenge and change the negative stereotypes associated with Pankisi. Many Georgian TV programmes have also interviewed Nazy over recent years as her business and reputation in the tourism industry grows, inciting regional and national media coverage.

This journey to success was not an easy path: 'I had no previous knowledge, skills, or experience in starting and managing a small business, nor had any access to funding prior to 2012, which meant I started from scratch.' Nazy took steps to educate herself on the ins and outs of owning a small business in the tourism sector. Nazy described this experience saying:

> I quickly learned how to employ marketing and promotion methods using online social media platforms (Facebook, Instagram, Booking.com, Airbnb.com, Tripadvisor.com, Google Business) and created my own dedicated business website. I conducted my own research into sustainable rural tourism, guest houses and services by traveling to Tusheti and other regions in Kakheti.

This was only the first battle. It is one thing to understand how marketing and managing a small business works, but a whole different thing to put it into practice. The next tasks

Continued

Case study: continued.

'...included identifying and applying for NGO funding, renovating my home, buying furniture, and developing services'. At the beginning, Nazy was 'fortunate to get the support of private investors (tourists that visited in 2012 and 2018) from the UK and New Zealand. This support was crucial and accelerated progress'.

After achieving success in running her own guest house, Nazy used her influence in the community to encourage other local women to open their own homes to visitors. Nazy also created the Pankisi Valley Tourism and Development Association, which, for now, includes about nine guest houses in the valley, which share resources and buy locally. Thanks to other women like Nazy, 'The women in the community are very active. The men help, but the women are empowered to be entrepreneurs and be active. Men and women also work together and especially around eco-tourism. There is always something going on in the valley.'

In Nazy's Guest House, and in other guest houses in the region, all guests are asked to respect the traditional rules of the host families, such as no alcohol or smoking, as these guest houses and the community want to provide a healthy, safe, friendly and immersive environment for the guests.

Although the local guest houses in the Pankisi Valley now work together, at the beginning of this tourism journey, a part of the community was understandably a bit suspicious. People were not sure if it was even possible to get tourists into the valley after such negative media coverage. Some members of the community found it hard to trust outsiders, as journalists who had visited the valley in the past had used the words of the locals against them and published articles that gave an inaccurate image of the valley.

Not only were locals skeptical in the beginning, but so also was the Georgian government: 'I started to contact NGOs [...], but they were suspicious from the beginning.' When guests arrived at her guest house, they revealed to Nazy that the Tourist Office 'told them that [they] should not go' to the Pankisi Valley. She recalled an instance in which she designed, printed and delivered leaflets to promote the Pankisi Valley at the National Tourist Office. After dropping them off with the receptionist, she asked if they would display them. The receptionist replied 'yes' and laid them out on the desk. Nazy left and ten minutes later returned to the desk to see her leaflets in the garbage. The receptionist then told her that she could do nothing about it. The National Tourism Administration has first to approve it.

'It took me four years chasing the National Tourism Administration to bring them here [to visit].' Finally, after four years of constant chasing, Nazy was able to get the National Tourism Administration to visit the Pankisi Valley and write a description of the region on their website. When Nazy asked why it had taken them so long, they replied, 'to be honest, we were not sure, and we were afraid.' The National Tourism Office is now supportive and helps to provide resources for improving tourism to the valley. Nazy also recently

...initiated a collaborative project between the Pankisi Valley Tourism & Development Association in Georgia and students from Ostrava and Charles University in the Czech Republic, to promote awareness of the Kists and the Pankisi Valley to leaders, policymakers, institutions, academics, professionals, media and the public, in order to foster better understanding, relations and peace. The first exhibition was hosted at

Continued

Case study: continued.

the Assembly Hall at Ostrava University in November 2018, then at the Great Meeting Room at the Institute of International Relations (IIR) in Prague in April 2019. Plans to host this photodocumentary exhibition at the Czech Embassy in Tbilisi in 2019 were thwarted due to the emergence of the COVID pandemic. I aim to launch the exhibition in Tbilisi at several embassies as soon as the opportunity allows. A dedicated website and book are also planned.

Community sceptics also came round, as they started to realize that tourists were coming to the valley with a deep interest in and respect for the culture.

Ten years ago, 'there was not much going on in the valley', with a lack of job opportunities. Locals felt that the rest of the world was steadfast in their stereotypes about the valley and so they did not have hope. Also, 'they were suspicious, because they had bad experiences with journalists'. After two years, the community has seen that people are interested in their culture, and they have both hope and desire to start their own businesses. Present day, many people in the community are now involved in tourism, as it is now one of the most viable and profitable industries in the valley.

Who are the guests at Nazy's Guest House?

Nazy's Guest House hosts international guests, many from Poland and Germany. These guests are almost exclusively young Europeans and families interested in the Kist culture. Many guests are also interested in the religion of the Kist people, as it is a unique Sufi branch of Islam, and some visitors come to particularly see these traditions, for example the Zikr Ritual, an ecstatic prayer performed by women, including pleas for peace, and poetry. There are also 'a few foreigners who visit Pankisi Valley to conduct academic research or offer charitable support or funding to vulnerable people and families'.

The guest house is also open to domestic tourists and has seen an increase in domestic visits during the COVID-19 pandemic, as international travel has become limited.

Many of the guests visit Nazy's Guest House and the Pankisi Valley mostly due to the efforts of Nazy herself. 'I actively promote the Kists, their culture, the Pankisi Valley, local attractions and Nazy's Guest House and its services on different online platforms', including the Nazy's Guest House website, social media, reputable travel guides (including Lonely Planet) and online booking platforms such as Booking.com and AirBnb. Nazy also explained that she has 'developed good relationships with ambassadors of many foreign embassies based in Tbilisi. They have visited the Pankisi Valley and stayed at Nazy's Guest House.' These efforts have helped visitors 'easily find out about Nazy's Guest House and make informed decisions to book their accommodation and treks'.

Other Guest Houses in the Area

The Pankisi Valley Tourism and Development Association, an association started by Nazy Dakishvili, plays an important role in the tourism development of the valley. The association has the mission of 'forging strong partnerships with leaders and professionals from the tourism industry, NGOs and governments to bring new ideas, opportunities, and funding to help Pankisi Valley realize its potential as a special place in Georgia.'

Continued

Case study: continued.

As of now, there are nine guest houses in the valley, three of which are very popular and operate well throughout the year. According to Nazy:

All the guest houses in the area have good relationships with each other. They are aware of the importance of working and cooperating together and sharing resources...The wider community is aware of the importance of developing and sustaining local tourism which provides economic and social benefits. People are aware tourism is the only industry with potential in the valley and is the only way to change the negative perceptions and improve the image of the community.

Supporting Tourism and Women's Engagement

Support from the Georgian government

Georgia is a country that has the potential to be a 'four seasons' destination thanks to its diversity: natural beauty, varied topography, pleasant climate, rich culture and history. It can also offer many different types of tourism activities such as wine, medical, entertainment, sports and other sorts of tourism.

To facilitate its development, the Georgian government eased the visa regime, limited tax incentives for tour operators and expanded its road rehabilitations. 'Check-In Georgia' is an example of a project from the government to encourage Georgia to become a regional cultural and entertainment centre. The government is developing regions like Batumi, and even ski resorts in Gudauri, Bakuriani, Goderdzi and Mestia. Although Check-In Georgia is not involved yet in helping to develop the Pankisi Valley, the Georgian National Tourism Administration is supporting development of tourism in the valley. For the moment, Nazy's Guest House is the only guest house from the valley featured on their website, but they have 'also created marked trails and information boards about the Pankisi Valley'.

Support for small businesses and women entrepreneurs

As for financial support,

NGO support has been very important in developing tourism in the Pankisi Valley. Organizations active in the Pankisi Valley like USAID, Elkana, CSRDG, GCSD, CENN etc. provide funding and offer training on a range of aspects from starting small businesses, managing finances, writing business plans, marketing and funding applications, as well as supporting and promoting cultural activities and events. The involvement and support offered by NGOs provide significant incentives and motivation to small businesses.

Women entrepreneurs in Georgia also receive support thanks to the United Nations Women organization. UN Women is dedicated to women's empowerment and to gender equity. 'A global champion for women and girls, UN Women was established to accelerate progress on meeting their needs worldwide'. At the current stage, Nazy's Guest House has not had any involvement with UN Women, but Nazy plans to reach out for assistance following the COVID-19 pandemic.

Continued

Case study: continued.

Tourism to Overcome Prejudice

When asked what the most important thing was that Nazy wanted people to take away from her story, she responded:

> The biggest challenge that I faced from the beginning in 2013 when I started my guest house business and subsequent years was learning to deal with institutional and public racism and discrimination, which is deeply ingrained in Georgian society, due to the persistent negative media coverage and political abuse regarding the Kists and Pankisi Valley. Through understanding this problem carefully and taking a stand to challenge the media and political powers, I was able to counteract and address these negativities by highlighting the positive aspects.

> Negative stereotypes about ethnic and religious minority groups in Georgia, especially towards Muslim Kists, is prevalent and presents major barriers to open and free communication, cooperation and peace, preventing social cohesion. Therefore, it was important for me to develop and implement a range of strategies using tourism as the most suitable vehicle for changing perceptions and attitudes.

> I would say from my personal experience it is important to be focused, determined and persistent in pursuing your goals and ambitions, and to do your best regardless of how daunting the challenge is or any setbacks suffered.

References

Clifford, E. (2018) An alternative view of life in Georgia's Pankisi Valley. *Huck Magazine*. Available at: https://www.huckmag.com/art-and-culture/photography-2/what-is-life-really-like-in-europes-valley-of-terror/ (accessed 8 April 2021).

GNTA (2019) Research and Planning Department, Tbilisi, Georgia: Georgian National Tourism Administration.

Lush, E. (2020) Pankisi Gorge: a unique homestay experience in Georgia. *Wander Lush*. Available at: https://wander-lush.org/pankisi-gorge-nazys-homestay-georgia/#content (accessed 8 April 2021).

Mielnikiewicz, J. (2012) Georgia: in a valley of tradition, women struggle to build independent lives. *Eurasianet*. Available at: https://eurasianet.org/georgia-in-a-valley-of-tradition-women-struggle-to-build-independent-lives (accessed 15 April 2021).

Questions

1. How would you describe Nazy's leadership approach in her community?
2. How has her leadership empowered women in her country?
3. What are the challenges that Nazy faces in being a business leader in her community?

References

Algahtani, A. (2014) Are leadership and management different? A review. *Journal of Management Policies and Practices* 2(3), 71–82.

Antonakis, J. and House, R.J. (2014) Instrumental leadership: measurement and extension of transformational–transactional leadership theory. *The Leadership Quarterly* 25(4), 746–771.

Avolio, B.J. and Gardner, W.L. (2005) Authentic leadership development: getting to the root of positive forms of leadership. *The Leadership Quarterly* 16(3), 315–338.

Bass, B.M. (1990) From transactional to transformational leadership: learning to share the vision. *Organizational Dynamics* 18(3), 19–31.

Buil, I., Martínez, E. and Matute, J. (2019) Transformational leadership and employee performance: the role of identification, engagement and proactive personality. *International Journal of Hospitality Management* 77, 64–75.

Chang, W., Busser, J. and Liu, A. (2020) Authentic leadership and career satisfaction: the mediating role of thriving and conditional effect of psychological contract fulfillment. *International Journal of Contemporary Hospitality Management* 32(6), 2117–2136.

Cong, L.C. and Thu, D.A. (2021) The competitiveness of small and medium enterprises (SMEs) in the tourism sector: the role of leadership competencies. *Journal of Economics and Development* 23(3), 299–316. DOI: 10.1108/JED-06-2020-0080.

Elbaz, A.M. and Haddoud, M.Y. (2017) The role of wisdom leadership in increasing job performance: evidence from the Egyptian tourism sector. *Tourism Management* 63, 66–76.

Eva, N., Robin, M., Sendjaya, S., Van Dierendonck, D. and Liden, R.C. (2019) Servant leadership: a systematic review and call for future research. *The Leadership Quarterly* 30(1), 111–132.

Fu, H., Ye, B.H. and Xu, X. (2020) The cross-level effect of shared leadership on tourism employee proactive behavior and adaptive performance. *Sustainability* 12(15), 6173.

Hmieleski, K.M. and Ensley, M.D. (2007) A contextual examination of new venture performance: entrepreneur leadership behavior, top management team heterogeneity, and environmental dynamism. *Journal of Organizational Behavior* 28(7), 865–889. Available at: https://doi.org/10.1002/job.479 (accessed 15 November 2022).

Huertas-Valdivia, I., Gallego-Burín, A.R. and Lloréns-Montes, F.J. (2019) Effects of different leadership styles on hospitality workers. *Tourism Management* 71, 402–420.

Khan, A., Bibi, S., Lyu, J., Garavelli, A.C., Pontrandolfo, P. and Perez Sanchez, M.D.A. (2020) Uncovering innovativeness in Spanish tourism firms: the role of transformational leadership, OCB, firm size, and age. *Sustainability* 12(10), 3989.

Kim, H. (2014) Transformational leadership, organizational clan culture, organizational affective commitment, and organizational citizenship behavior: a case of South Korea's public sector. *Public Organization Review* 14(3), 397–417.

Mayer, D.M., Bardes, M. and Piccolo, R.F. (2008) Do servant-leaders help satisfy follower needs? An organizational justice perspective. *European Journal of Work and Organizational Psychology* 17(2), 180–197.

McCann, J.T., Graves, D. and Cox, L. (2014) Servant leadership, employee satisfaction, and organizational performance in rural community hospitals. *International Journal of Business and Management* 9(10), 28.

Nanjundeswaraswamy, T.S. and Swamy, D.R. (2014) Leadership styles. *Advances in Management* 7(2), 57.

Parco-Tropicales, M. and de Guzman, A.B. (2014) A structural equation model (SEM) of the impact of transformational, visionary, charismatic and ethical leadership styles on the development of wise leadership among Filipino private secondary school principals. *Asia Pacific Education Review* 15(4), 547–559.

Pieterse, A.N., Van Knippenberg, D., Schippers, M. and Stam, D. (2010) Transformational and transactional leadership and innovative behavior: the moderating role of psychological empowerment. *Journal of Organizational Behavior* 31(4), 609–623.

Platow, M.J., Haslam, S.A., Reicher, S.D. and Steffens, N.K. (2015) There is no leadership if no-one follows: why leadership is necessarily a group process. *International Coaching Psychology Review* 10(1), 20–37.

Rabiul, M.K. and Yean, T.F. (2021) Leadership styles, motivating language, and work engagement: an empirical investigation of the hotel industry. *International Journal of Hospitality Management* 92, 102712.

Reid, S.W., Anglin, A.H., Baur, J.E., Short, J.C. and Buckley, M.R. (2018) Blazing new trails or opportunity lost? Evaluating research at the intersection of leadership and entrepreneurship. *The Leadership Quarterly* 29(1), 150–164.

Renko, M., El Tarabishy, A., Carsrud, A.L. and Brännback, M. (2015) Understanding and measuring entrepreneurial leadership style. *Journal of Small Business Management* 53(1), 54–74.

Weber, K. and Ladkin, A. (2010) Developing effective tourism leadership. *Journal of China Tourism Research* 6(4), 410–427.

8 Sources of Financial Capital

Introduction

Establishing and operating a tourism enterprise requires the investment of financial resources. The amount of resource required, at different stages of the business's life cycle, depends heavily on the type of business, the scale of operations, as well as the objectives and aspirations of the business owner(s). For example, the amount of capital required for setting up a boutique wine tour operator, owner-operated with two tour vans, is different from setting up a 40-room hotel, which is, again, different from setting up a café or restaurant. This chapter focuses on the finance requirements for tourism enterprises, with insights into different requirements at various stages of the business life cycle. The chapter illustrates that although most small tourism businesses are funded by the owners' personal assets, the business will reach a stage where the these assets are exhausted and further financing through either debt (i.e. bank loans) or equity (e.g., investors), or combinations of sources of funding, will be required for the sustainability and growth of the business. The chapter will discuss and evaluate the different financing options available to business owners, as well as the challenges the business will face in successfully obtaining funding. The chapter also covers alternative sources of financing such as government grants, matching-funds schemes for seed funding, and crowdsourcing and crowdfunding opportunities.

Learning Outcomes

After completing this chapter, you should be able to:

- Understand the financing requirements for tourism businesses at different stages of the business life cycle
- Understand the different sources of finance for tourism firms

© Rob Hallak and Craig Lee 2023. *Managing Tourism Enterprises: Start-up, Growth and Resilience* (R. Hallak and C. Lee)
DOI: 10.1079/9781789249446.0008

- Identify the challenges experienced by tourism firms in acquiring finance
- Understand the differences between debt and equity finance
- Recognize the different types of debt finance
- Recognize the different types of equity finance
- Understand new types of finance including crowdfunding, tourism investment funds and government grants.

Why and When a Business Needs Finance

Start-up capital for the majority of new businesses comes from the three 3Fs – founder, friends and family. These may be in the form of debt (a loan) or equity (shares/ownership) in the business. In addition to funding for start-ups, tourism businesses require access to finance for a wide range of purposes including:

- Managing cash flows
- Seasonality and fluctuations in sales revenues
- Purchase or lease of property, vehicles equipment
- Purchase of inventory and accounts payables
- Covering its expenses, including overheads and staff wages
- Marketing costs
- Research and development.

Finance is also required throughout different stages of the business life cycle including its growth and maturity, as well as for survival during times of crisis (see Chapter 11). Many tourism businesses will have seasonal fluctuations in their revenues, while incurring fixed costs and expenses such as loans, leases, overheads, etc. Tourism businesses will need to be financially prepared to manage adverse economic cycles, changing environments and events beyond their control (Liu *et al.*, 2021). Thus, businesses will need access to financing as a means to managing cashflow deficits.

A tourism business's financing options for managing cashflows include:

1. overdraft facility;
2. line of credit;
3. factoring;
4. trade credit from suppliers;
5. invoice financing; and
6. lease agreements.

Bank overdraft facility: A finance arrangement where a bank/lender allows a business to withdraw more than the balance of an account. Bank overdrafts are often used by small businesses for their working capital. A set limit is determined and interest payments on a bank overdraft can be tax-deductible in certain countries. Interest on an overdrafts is considerably high; for example. in Australia in 2022, the cash rate is around 0.1% as determined by the Research Bank of Australia; however, the interest rate of a bank overdraft can be around 12%.

Line of credit: An agreement between the lender and borrower that allows a borrower to withdraw money from an account, exceeding the current available balance. When a business sets up a line of credit with a bank it can access funds to be drawn up to an approved limit. The funds can be drawn any time as long as they do not exceed the limit.

Factoring: Also known as 'debtor's finance' and 'accounts receivable' finance. This is where a *factor* organization buys a business's outstanding invoices at a discount price. The factor organization then chases the debtors. Factoring is a way to get quick access to cash but can be quite expensive compared to traditional financing options.

Trade credit from suppliers: This is financing available from the business's suppliers. The business purchases and receives goods/stock before payment is made. The business then has a term of perhaps 30–55 days to make payment. The extended time to pay for stock provides a business with short-term cash-flow contributions to working capital.

Invoice finance: Finance based on the strength of a business's accounts receivable. This form of financing is similar to factoring except that the invoices or accounts receivable remain with the business.

Leases: This form of financing does not explicitly provide money into a business but it does allow a business to access assets such as equipment, motor vehicles, land or premises without having to pay the full cost. Leases offer minimal up-front costs and there may be benefits to the business's financial position as lease repayments can be categorized as an 'expense' in the profit-and-loss statement.

Types of Finance

The financial requirements of tourism organizations change as the business grows and matures. New start-up businesses face challenges in securing bank loans in the start-up stage due to the banks perceiving the business to be high-risk and with little certainty of continuity. Thus, start-ups will depend on insider financing from the business founder, or family and friends. Loans from banks and financial institutions can become accessible once a business has a track record, a steady cash-flow, and a balance sheet that is asset-rich, which allows the use of assets as collateral (Cumming *et al.*, 2019). Both new and existing businesses need to obtain both equity and debt financing to have a sound financial foundation.

Types of financing for small enterprises can be classified into three main categories:

1. debt financing;
2. equity financing; or
3. a combination of debt and equity.

Debt financing

Most hospitality and tourism enterprises are small and medium-sized ventures with limited sources of internal funding (Liu *et al.*, 2021). There will come a time where the business needs to borrow money (access debt) as the business owner will find that their own funds are insufficient for meeting business needs, whether it is paying business expenses, or plans to grow. Thus, debt financing refers to money borrowed from an external source which becomes a liability/loan to the business. The debt needs to be reimbursed/repaid within specific time-frames and repayment conditions. The most common source of debt financing for small businesses comes from commercial banks in the form of bank loans or business loans. Bank loans and business loans can vary in terms of their amount, loan terms, interest rate, type of interest rate, whether fixed or variable, fees and security. To be approved for a loan, a business will need to disclose its financial information including a business plan, main financials for the last three years, if available, financial forecast ratio calculations (discussed in Chapter 9).

Business loans can be unsecured or secured (borrowing against an asset, e.g., property, inventory). Unsecured business loans usually have a maximum 12-month term, with regular (weekly or fortnightly) repayments. Interest rates of unsecured loans are usually high as they are seen by lenders to be a higher risk. Applications for unsecured loans consider the cashflow or financial health of the business as security. Secured loans for small and medium enterprises can be secured by either the business assets or the personal assets of the business owner; for example, the equity owned by the applicants from their personal property and other assets. Business loans can vary in duration and can be considered short-term (12 months or less) or longer-term (1–5 years). Short-term debt is used for working capital and repaid out of sales revenues. Longer-term borrowings can be used for working capital and/or to finance property or equipment.

Tourism businesses seeking financing through bank loans will encounter several challenges:

1. Banks perceive loans for business start-ups as a high risk as the business has a weak asset base and is yet to establish a credit reliability.
2. The tourism business owner is unable to provide sufficient security to meet the bank's risk requirements.
3. There is a discrepancy between the term to repay the loan expected by the bank and the loan duration requested by the applicant.
4. Tourism businesses, specifically, are considered to have high operational risk and high probability of failure. For example, data from the China Tourism Association (2020) indicated that 70% of China's hospitality and tourism businesses had difficulties in obtaining financial capital (Liu *et al.*, 2021).

Equity financing

Equity finance is distinct from debt finance as it involves shares/ownership in the business. Money that is invested in the business results in a new ownership structure for the enterprise. Typically, for new/start-up small businesses, the funding comes from the business owner – this may be from his/her personal savings, sale of assets such as shares, or drawing funds from personal assets such as property. When a business owner invests personal funds, this reduces reliance on external debt and loans, and avoids interest repayments. Profits from the business's operations, i.e. retained earnings, can be reinvested in the business as a source of funding. If the owner's personal finances are insufficient to sustain the business, whether through start-up or growth, the owner can raise equity finance by attracting partners or investors into the business – essentially selling a share of the business to investors. A new venture will have difficulty obtaining short-term or longer-term bank debt without a cushion of equity financing (Spinelli and Adams, 2016). The question of debt vs. equity is not either/or, but often businesses will secure combinations of both. For example, a business may have maximized its capacity to borrow any further money from the bank, in which case the business can look for equity/investment. Tourism business owners need to consider how they are leveraging their business. Leverage refers to 'the degree to which a business uses borrowed money; what the debt-to-equity ratio measures' (Schaper *et al.*, 2014, p. 244). Entrepreneurs have a high incentive to retain their equity in the business and may be reluctant to give up ownership through equity finance. However, a business that is highly leveraged through debt becomes at risk of bankruptcy if it fails to meet its debt obligations, for example if there is a drop in sales or revenues or experiences a financial crisis.

Financing through equity has both advantages and disadvantages. For the business owner, it is important to recognize that you are not only sharing the profits and giving away part of the current business, but also that you are giving up part of the future wealth of the business. In addition to giving away part of its wealth, selling ownership of the business also involves giving up full control over decision making. If the original founder's share in the business is less than 50%, they can lose control in decision making and management of the operations. This is why business founders seeking equity investors must be very careful (Box 8.1).

Equity financing has several distinct advantages over debt finance. For example, although the business founder will forgo part of the profits, these new investors will share in the risks and expenses and consequently reduce the founder's exposure to financial loss. Although equity financing may be expensive, it may still be less than the cost of debt financing that incurs high interest repayments. Perhaps a major advantage of equity financing is that it potentially brings new expertise to the business. In fact, business owners should look for investors that add value well beyond purely financial value. This includes investors with key skills, capabilities, experience and industry networks. For example, a restaurant business looking to expand into digital marketing and

---

Box 8.1. Important questions to consider before bringing in investors.

1. Who do you invite as investors?
2. How much share of the business are you willing to sell?
3. How much control of the business are you willing to forgo?
4. How much return on their investment are the investors expecting?

distribution could seek investors with key digital skills and networks. This will empower the business to expand its operations and access new market opportunities as a result of the value-added investment

Equity financing can be accessed through two main sources:

1. Angels and informal investors;
2. Venture capital and institutional investors.

Angel investors: Business 'angels' are 'high net worth individuals who usually invest their own private wealth, mostly between US$10,000 and US$250,000, in ventures that are, typically, local, unlisted, and without a family connection to the business angels' (Cumming and Groh, 2018, p. 551). They are among the greatest sources of seed and start-up capital for entrepreneurial ventures. Business angels provide cash in exchange for share of ownership/equity, with an agreed-upon rate of return on their investment. Investment usually occurs in the early stage of the business or during growth/expansion. Their goal is to grow the business and hence share in the capital gains from when the venture raises its next round of finance.

An advantage of business angels is that, as part-owners of the business, they are motivated to help the business and owner succeed. Thus, they bring expertise in entrepreneurship, business and industry, networks, and business acumen. They can play a mentoring role, helping business owners to build business capital and to identify and pursue profitable opportunities. As business angels may be portfolio investors, they may be satisfied with remaining as silent partners; however, they often want to take an active role in the business to protect their investment and ensure the business's future success. Business angels may also be part of business angel networks and can therefore provide access to further investment from other angels.

Venture capital: Venture capital firms are institutional investors that use syndicated managed funds to invest in high-growth entrepreneurial ventures (Schaper *et al.*, 2014). Investments are usually greater than US$1 million with the goal of growing the business, but with a longer-term intention of exiting the business with a return on their investment. Thus, 'venture capitalists buy a stake in an entrepreneur's idea, nurture it for a period of time and then sell their investment' (Schaper *et al.*, 2014, p. 251). Unlike business angels, VCs may not be interested in managerial input in the firm but will require representation on the firm's board of directors.

Venture capitalists typically demand that financing to the firm be made in the form of a combination of debt and equity ownership. It is common for venture capitalists to demand that as much as half of their investment be in the form of a long-term loan at a high interest rate, as much as 20%. In addition to the cost of interest on the loan, venture capitalists typically expect 30–70% ownership of the equity capital provided. Thus, a founder who accepts venture capital funding often gives up half or more of the ownership of the business and is faced with a large demand on cash to meet loan payments.

The ability of a business to access equity financing is influenced by several factors as determined by the investors. These include: (i) the business's (and owners') past and current performance; (ii) investor's perceived risk of investing in the business; (iii) investors' valuation of the business; (iv) the perceived risk attaching to the industry in which the business operates; (v) the growth (or decline) of the industry in which the business operates; (vi) the business's potential for growth and expansion; (vii) the investors' required rate of return; (viii) amount of capital required; (ix) the business owners' goals regarding growth, control and liquidity; and (x) the relative bargaining position of the business owner (Spinelli and Adams, 2016). Statistics from Zero2IPO, the leading database of China's entrepreneurship and investment industry, show that VC investment in China's hospitality and tourism industry reached US$37.6 billion by 2019 (Liu *et al.*, 2021).

Once a business has outside investors it will have legal and ethical requirements to keep accurate records and to make regular disclosures of the operations and financial position of the business. Having outside investors may require establishing formal lines of authority and reporting within the business's management structure. Outside investors may require that the founder steps down from as chief executive, concentrating instead on his/her area of greatest experience and ability.

Venture capitalists assess the investment opportunity according to several key criteria:

Team: Capabilities and experience of the entrepreneurs and the team involved in the business

Business model and technology: The business they are investing in needs to have a significant competitive advantage

Market opportunity: VCs evaluate the opportunity in the market, size of the market, growth potential, profitability, etc.

Industry: VCs like to invest in industries where they have experience, knowledge and networks

Exit: VCs will consider the timing of the exit (e.g., 3–7 years), as well as the exit strategies available, including initial public offering, management buy-out, or selling to another company. (Source: adapted from Schaper *et al.*, 2014)

Alternative types of finance: crowdfunding and government grants

In addition to conventional debt and equity financing, there are increasing opportunities for tourism businesses to access finance through government investment schemes as well as crowdfunding. 'Crowdfunding' is an internet-based funding practice which involves collecting capital from external sources, represented by a large community (Cumming and Groh, 2018). Thus, crowdfunding centres around businesses (and nascent entrepreneurs) raising funds through a crowd (i.e. via online social networks). Crowdfunding occurs in several forms and is based on agreements between the funder and the business. These crowdfunding models include:

1. Reward-based crowdfunding
2. Equity crowdfunding
3. Peer-to-peer lending (crowdlending)
4. Donation-based crowdfunding
5. Fundraising
6. Experiment crowdfunding (Cichy and Gradon, 2016).

Reward-based crowdfunding is traditionally the most common model of crowdfunding. Entrepreneurs seek funding for a new idea or unique concept with the objective of using these collected funds for commercialization of the idea, and bringing the product service into fruition. Individuals who contribute funds, therefore, can be among the first recipients/users of the product or service. Thus, the business receives immediate financing and create a guaranteed, pre-paid order backlog. In case the business does not achieve the required funding amount to commercialize the project, the entrepreneur can either refund all contributions (all-or-nothing model), reduce the scale of the project, or keep the funds for the purpose of acquiring other sources of capital (keep-it-all model) (Cichy and Gradon, 2016).

Equity-based crowdfunding, also referred to as crowd-investing, offers the opportunity for contributors to become equity shareholders in the company. In this model, the initiator of the business project specifies the price and amount of shares allocated, as well as the investors' return on investment.

Crowdlending is an alternative to traditional debt financing. Businesses use online crowdfunding platforms to acquire debt financing through a peer-to-peer network, with specified interest rates and repayment terms.

Donation-based crowdfunding seeks donations through online communities in order to support social entrepreneurship or charitable causes. This is deemed to be purely a donation with no debt or equity share in the business.

Experiment crowdfunding is designed to raise funds to support research and scientific experiments.

Crowdfunding enables tourism businesses to promote the business concept and access debt or equity financing from a global audience (Box 8.2).

The challenge of crowdfunding is that as these online platforms, such as Kickstarter, Indiegogo, Circle Up, etc., rise in popularity, there is increasing competition among businesses that are crowdfunding their ideas. The competition for crowdfunding means that there is no guarantee that the funding campaign will reach its funding goals in the required timeframe. For entrepreneurial ideas that do become secured through crowdfunding, there is the expectation that the business will deliver on its promises and meet customer and investor expectations (Business.gov.au).

Government grants and investment schemes

The creation and success of tourism enterprises is the foundation of a successful tourism industry. Government support for tourism enterprises takes form

---

Box 8.2. Advantages of crowdfunding.

1. Testing the market for customer and investor interest in your product
2. Opportunity to engage directly with customers and potential investors
3. Adapt and develop your products and services based on customer feedback
4. Word-of-mouth marketing and international promotion of your product through crowdfunding platforms – customers and investors become followers.

through various mechanisms such as seed funding grants, co-investment grants, low (or no) interest loans, and funding and relief packages to support the economic development of the tourism industry. Tourism is an economic priority for many destinations and government funding schemes are designed to boost business start-up and entrepreneurship, encourage innovation and capabilities, as well as support businesses through times of crisis. The schemes target key priority areas for destinations, for example the South Australian government launched the Nature-Based Tourism Co-investment Fund, providing matching funding for entrepreneurial ventures that offer nature-based, 'ecologically sensitive' tourism experiences (business.gov.au).

Support packages for tourism businesses proliferated throughout the COVID-19 pandemic as many businesses required a lifeline from their government in order to maintain operations. Government investment in tourism has broader economic, environmental and social outcomes. For example, the Indigenous Tourism Fund launched by the Australian government provides direct funding for tourism businesses and communities for investment in new products, equipment, business planning and marketing in the tourism sector. This AU$40 million-dollar investment provides up to AU$50,000 in support for privately owned tourism businesses (National Indigenous Australian Agency, 2022).

In July 2020, the UK government launched their first round of support packages to business through the £10 million 'Kick-starting Tourism Package', offering small businesses in tourism destination, up to £5000 in order to innovate and adapt their businesses following the pandemic (gov.uk). With evolving variants of COVID causing new waves of outbreaks in 2021 and 2022, the Scottish government launched the Omicron Business Support Fund where eligible businesses in sectors such as coach operators, day tour operators, hostels, inbound tour operators and visitor attractions could apply for cash payments of up to £6800 (gov.scot).

In addition, government funding organizations such as the European Union and UNWTO offer various funding schemes in their efforts to support tourism development. For example, the UNWTO, as part of its innovation programmes, runs the UNWTO Start-up Competitions that support entrepreneurial ideas and ventures that transform the travel industry and help to achieve the sustainable development goals. The UNWTO holds two types of competitions: (i) generic, and (ii) thematic. Generic competitions look at innovative ideas that have broader contributions throughout the tourism value chain, whereas specific competitions focus on priority sectors such as gastronomy tourism or rural tourism (UNWTO, 2022). The competition winners can receive support in the form of mentoring by UNWTO and partner organizations, investment opportunities, networking and business promotion.

Finance requirement through different stages of the business life cycle

Businesses at various stages of their life cycle will require access to funding for different objectives. Funds are needed for commercialization of the concept and bringing the idea into fruition. As the business is established and begins trading, it will expand its customer base and outputs, requiring investment to expand production, delivery of service and meeting customer demand.

The stages at which a business will require financing can be categorized as 'early-stage financing' and 'expansion financing' (Schaper *et al.*, 2014).

Early-stage finance focuses on the business's conception and early periods of its trading. This is categorized into the following: (i) seed financing, (ii) start-up financing, and (iii) first-stage financing (Schaper *et al.*, 2014).

Seed funding is the money that is needed to begin product development or testing a concept before moving toward commercialization. Funds are required for research and development, testing the market and developing a business plan. Seed funding usually comes from the owner(s) of the business, while the concept is in its infancy stage and still to be developed. Government can also provide seed funding of new entrepreneurial ventures through grants and innovation funds. Government seed-funding grants schemes look toward supporting new business concepts that can generate significant economic and social benefits, and export and employment opportunities for the local population. Seed funding can take the form of grants funding, or a matching funds scheme, e.g. AU$2 from the government for every AU$1 investment by the applicant. An example of government support is the 'Seed-Start' (2021) initiative launched by the government of South Australia. This programme provides opportunities for financial support for early-stage businesses that are deemed to have high growth potential (https://business.gov.au/grants-and-programs/Research-Commercialisation-and-Startup-Fund-SA, accessed 16 November 2022).

Start-up financing is what the owner requires to get the business established for trading. At this stage the business's products or concept has been tested. Start-up funds are required for the business model to initiate and the business to begin trading. Funding for start-up is most likely to come from the owner (or 3Fs). Some debt financing may be used, such as bank loans, but the owner will be required to provide security (personal assets) in order to obtain debt/loans from banks.

First-stage financing: At this stage the business is operating, but has exhausted its initial capital and requires funding to reach full production, e.g., investment in marketing, inventory and new equipment. First-stage funding can come from multiple sources; as the business is operating with a track record of sales, customer base, assets and profitability, it can now seek debt financing or attract angel investors.

Expansion financing refers to the stage of the business life cycle where it has moved beyond the start-up phase and has become established in terms of its customer base and its position in the market. The objective of expansion financing is on business growth, innovation and pursuit of new opportunities. The business may look at launching new product lines, expanding into new markets, setting up new branches, etc. For example, a restaurant business that becomes established may look at expansion through setting up branches in new locations. A resort may expand by increasing its facilities or offering more accommodation space. A wine tour operator may expand by moving operations into new regions, or by acquiring more tour vans to cater for more tourists (Schaper and Volery, 2014).

Conclusion

A tourism business owner's ability to access and raise finance is one of the biggest challenges it will face. This chapter has explored the different types of finance available for tourism businesses including debt, equity and government grants/support. Businesses require funding at various stages of their life cycle.

Start-up businesses are commonly financed by the founder as they face challenges in securing bank loans in the start-up stage due to the banks perceiving the business to be high-risk, and because they have little certainty of continuity. Investors are also wary of start-up firms as they want to see a track record of performance before they invest.

Tourism business owners need to evaluate the advantages and disadvantages of different types of funding. While this chapter distinguishes between debt and equity as separate sources of funding, the reality for entrepreneurial ventures is that they will require a combination of both, especially as the business moves into the expansion phase.

The proliferation of online communities also provides several options for crowdfunding as a source of capital. However, as these crowdfunding platforms grow in popularity, there is increased competition among businesses seeking funding. Tourism business owners therefore need to be resourceful and strategic in how they identify and access different types of capital throughout the stages of the business life cycle. These decisions need careful evaluation as they can have long-term impacts on the direction, management and performance of the tourism enterprise.

Study Questions

1. Why is it so difficult for start-up businesses in tourism to obtain debt financing?

2. Discuss a scenario where a small tourism-business owner would benefit from obtaining equity finance (e.g., through business angels) rather than debt financing through loans.

3. What are the risks associated with obtaining financing through investments from family and friends?

4. Discuss an example where an established and profitable business would require expansion financing.

5. Provide examples of how the government in your country provides financial support for tourism enterprises.

References

Business.gov.au (2022) Nature-based tourism co-investment fund SA. Available at: https://business.gov.au/grants-and-programs/NatureBased-Tourism-Coinvestment-Fund-SA (accessed 21 March 2022).

China Tourism Association (2020) 'Ten dilemmas' faced by venture investment and financing in culture and tourism industry. Available at: http://www.tsingyanresearch.com/?p=4375 (accessed 7 January 2021).

Cichy, J. and Gradon, W. (2016) Crowdfunding as mechanism for enhancing small and medium-sized enterprises. *E-Finanse – Financial Internet Quarterly* 12(3), 38–48.

Cumming, D. and Groh, A.P. (2018) Entrepreneurial finance: unifying themes and future directions. *Journal of Corporate Finance* 50, 538–555.

Cumming, D., Deloof, M., Manigart, S. and Wright, M. (2019) New directions in entrepreneurial finance. *Journal of Banking & Finance* 100, 252–260.

Gov.uk (2020) 'Government announces £10 million for small businesses to kickstart tourism'. Available at: https://www.gov.uk/government/news/government-announces-10-million-for-small-businesses-to-kickstart-tourism (accessed 20 March 2022).

Gov.scot (2022) Coronavirus (COVID-19): funding for businesses affected by Omicron control measures. Available at: https://www.gov.scot/publications/coronavirus-covid-19-business-funding/travel-sector/outbound-travel-support-fund/ (accessed 20 March 2022).

Liu, B., Luo, C., Meng, F. and Jiang, H. (2021) Modeling venture capital networks in hospitality and tourism entrepreneurial equity financing: an exponential random graph models approach. *International Journal of Hospitality Management* 95, 102936.

National Indigenous Australian Agency (2022) Indigenous Tourism Fund. Available at: https://www.niaa.gov.au/indigenous-affairs/economic-development/indigenous-tourism-fund (accessed 20 March 2022).

Schaper, M., Volery, T., Weber, P. and Gibson, B. (2014) *Entrepreneurship and Small Business*. 4th Asia Pacific edn. Wiley, Queensland Australia.

Seed-Start SA (2021) Available at: https://business.gov.au/grants-and-programs/Research-Commercialisation-and-Startup-Fund-SA (accessed 10 January 2021).

Spinelli, S. and Adams, R.J. (2016) *New Venture Creation: Entrepreneurship for the 21st Century*. 10th edn. McGraw Hill Education, New York.

UNWTO (2022) UNWTO tourism start-up competitions. Available at: https://www.unwto.org/unwto-startup-competition (accessed 20 March 2022).

9 Managing Financial Performance

Introduction

In a dynamic environment shaped by fierce competition and scarcity of resources, entrepreneurs must attain the competencies required to accumulate and allocate resources in an efficient manner. Successfully managing one important resource that could lead to making or breaking the business is financial resource. It requires efficient planning, execution and periodic monitoring. A business's inability to develop workable strategies to earn profits from the best utilization of financial resources could lead to business failure. It is essential to implement a proper financial management system to not only assist the entrepreneur in understanding the financial details in an easy-to-read format on a timely basis, but also identify why and how the business is performing from a financial standpoint. For many small-business operators, understanding and monitoring the financial performance of their business continues to be a major challenge. For example, almost 23% of North American small-business owners lack sufficient financial literacy and almost 75% fail to understand the importance of the financial details of their businesses (Klein, 2011; Sage, 2012).

For independently owned tourism enterprises, financial management and reporting assists the entrepreneur in identifying the financial health of the business, identifying opportunities to reduce costs, and improving efficiencies and profitability. The objective of this chapter is to illustrate the fundamentals of finance for independently owned tourism enterprises, utilizing the Barossa Boutique Hotel as a working example (see Box 9.1).

© Rob Hallak and Craig Lee 2023. *Managing Tourism Enterprises: Start-up, Growth and Resilience* (R. Hallak and C. Lee)
DOI: 10.1079/9781789249446.0009

Box 9.1. Case study: Barossa Boutique Hotel.

In 2018, Donald Burke bought the ownership of Barossa Boutique Hotel, a boutique hotel with 20 rooms and a well-known restaurant and café, located at the scenic Barossa Valley in South Australia. Donald saw an opportunity to acquire the business at a good price, and intends on implementing new innovative strategies to grow the business. Since purchasing the hotel, Donald has been running its operations as efficiently as possible. He believes that, with some further investment, Barossa Boutique has the potential to grow into a 50-room capacity resort with the possibility of running events such as corporate functions, weddings, conferences, etc. This growth strategy requires major capital investment, and to implement clear financial strategies.

Learning Outcomes

After completing this chapter, you should:

- Understand the importance of financial management for tourism organizations
- Have learnt about determining costs and calculating break-even analysis
- Have learnt to develop and understand the main financial statements – balance sheet, income statement (profit and loss), cash budget
- Have developed a working knowledge of capital budgeting for tourism businesses
- Be confident with assessing the financial performance of an organization through the use of financial ratios.

Understanding Costs and Break-even Analysis

Operating a business will incur associated costs. In a typical hospitality business with hotel and/or food services, a major portion of sales revenue is consumed by costs, running up to 80–90% of the total sales revenues (Jagels, 2006). If Donald wants to make his Barossa Boutique venture a success, one of the first factors he will need to focus on is to ensure that his costs are controlled within a predetermined budgeted level. A practical approach to cost management is to understand the contribution of each cost (expense) component to net income and make changes accordingly.

Different types of costs

Two of the most common accounting costs associated with the operations of a business are *direct* and *indirect* costs. Direct costs can be traceable and generally move in direct correlation to changes in sales. Some examples of these direct costs include the cost of sales for food and beverages, wages and salaries, and laundry costs for hotels. On the other hand, indirect costs are those that cannot be identified with and are untraceable to a particular division, and therefore cannot be allocated to any specific department. They are often referred to as overhead costs. An example of an indirect cost could be general building maintenance costs that cannot be charged to any specific hotel department such as rooms, food or beverage.

Another grouping of important costs for consideration is fixed and variable costs. Fixed costs can be identified as those that are expected to remain fixed for short-term operations and do not vary with the changes in sales figures. While these fixed costs may change in the long run, they are not expected to do so in the short term. For example, management salaries, rent payable on a square-foot basis or expenses committed to a particular advertising campaign are not expected to change in the short term, and are considered fixed costs. In comparison, variable costs change in direct proportion to any changes in sales revenue levels. For a hotel operation, the cost of sales of food and beverages fits that definition.

Break-even analysis

The breakdown of costs into variable and fixed costs can be used for the break-even analysis, which is also known as the cost–volume–profit (CVP) analysis. For a small business, the break-even point refers to the level of 'breaking even' by sales revenue equalling expenses. Donald can use the break-even analysis to identify the minimum level of sales revenue required on a monthly or yearly basis to break even; exceeding that point would produce a profit while operating below it would lead to suffering net loss. Understanding the break-even helps small-business operators like Donald to identify the target operations level, but also it is widely used by lenders and investors to evaluate the earning potential of the business.

The break-even point can be identified by using a simplified quantitative equation but requires identification of fixed and variable costs beforehand. For Donald, fixed costs could be expenses such as depreciation expense, insurance, or loan payments that do not fluctuate with changing sales levels. In contrast, variable costs for Barossa Boutique could be wages and salaries and cost of food and beverages sold, as they fluctuate with the changing sales revenue levels. After identifying these different costs, Donald can complete the following steps for a break-even analysis:

> *Forecasting and categorizing expenses*: Based on past observations and using budgeting tools (to be discussed in the later parts of this chapter), Donald can estimate the sales revenue, cost of sales and other expenses for his desired period (monthly, quarterly, half-yearly or annually). To work with the break-even equation, Donald should classify those expenses into variable and fixed costs.
>
> *Computing the ratio of variable costs to net sales*: Based on the estimated variable costs, the ratio of variable costs to net sales can be calculated. Donald needs to then estimate the contribution margin to cover fixed costs and make a profit, by deducting the previously calculated variable costs to net sales ratio from 1.
>
> *Using the break-even point equation*: Use the data calculated in the previous steps in the following equation:

$$Break - Even\ Sales(\$) = \frac{Fixed\ Costs(\$)}{Contribution\ Margin(\%)} = \frac{Fixed\ Costs(\$)}{1 - Variable\ Costs(\%\ of\ Sales)}$$

Let's assume that Barossa Boutique Hotel had a net sales revenue of $632,800 in the last financial year. Its total expenses for the year were $504,000, out of which approximately $220,000 were fixed costs and the remaining $284,000 were variable in nature. To use the break-even equation, first we will need to identify the ratio of variable costs to net sales:

$$\text{Variable costs to net sales} = \frac{\$284,000}{\$632,800} = 0.4488 = 44.88\%.$$

Therefore, the contribution margin will be $(1 - 0.4488) = 0.5512$. Now we can use these inputs into the break-even sales equation:

$$\text{Break-even sales}(\$) = \frac{\$220,000}{0.5512} = \$399,129.$$

Thus, Barossa Boutique will break even if it can hit yearly sales of $399,129. At this level, the sales revenue generated will be enough to cover total fixed and variable expenses, thereby earning no profits yet incurring no losses. This helps Donald to set a minimum target sales revenue, as higher revenue will generate profits for the year. Moreover, if Donald wants to incorporate a reasonable level of profit (before taxes) into identifying the break-even sales point, he can do that with the following modification to the equation:

$$\begin{aligned}\text{Desired sales}(\$) &= \frac{\text{Fixed costs}(\$) + \text{target net income}(\$)}{\text{Contribution margin}(\%)}\\ &= \frac{\text{Fixed costs}(\$) + \text{target net income}(\$)}{1 - \text{variable costs}(\% \text{ of sales})}\end{aligned}$$

As an example, if Donald's target net income is $75,000 before taxes, Barossa Boutique Hotel must generate $535,196 in sales revenue, as evident from the following calculation:

$$\text{Target sales}(\$) = \frac{\$220,000 + \$75,000}{0.5512} = \$535,196.$$

A break-even analysis acts as a simple planning tool for small-business owners, particularly when they are approaching potential lenders and investors for funds to fuel future growth. For aspiring entrepreneurs, a break-even analysis can act as a preliminary screening tool to justify set-up decisions, and is commonly used in start-up pitches to potential investors. However, entrepreneurs do need to consider the limitations to this analysis as well. While it is a great tool in the initial stages, it ignores the importance of cashflows, considering all revenues and expenses without factoring in how much of it is actually happening on a cash basis. Some of the underlying assumptions in a break-even analysis, such as constant fixed expenses across all levels of sales volume and variable costs fluctuating in direct proportion to sales volume changes, are not entirely realistic for some business set-ups.

Break-even analysis: modifications for industry requirements

Considering Barossa Boutique is in the hospitality sector, depending on changing industry factors, Donald can consider modifying the break-even analysis equation. In this section, we consider some of those factors.

From time to time, hotel owners may need to increase their existing levels of fixed costs to facilitate planned growth in operations. For example, if Donald plans on increasing the advertising expenses, then he might want to identify how much additional room sales revenue will be needed to finance this investment. In that case, the equation can be modified into the following manner:

$$\text{Required sales revenue}(\$) = \frac{\text{Old fixed costs}(\$) + \text{New fixed costs} + \text{Target net income}(\$)}{\text{Contribution margin}(\%)}$$
$$= \frac{\text{Old fixed costs}(\$) + \text{New fixed costs} + \text{Desired net income}(\$)}{1 - \text{Variable costs}(\% \text{of sales})}$$

In the case of Barossa Boutique Hotel, if its advertising expense is expected to increase by \$40,000 and it retains it target net income level of \$75,000 before taxes, then its required sales revenue should be:

$$\text{Required sales revenue}(\$) = \frac{\$220,000 + \$40,000 + \$75,000}{0.5512} = \$607,765.$$

This shows that Barossa Boutique's sales revenue should be \$607,765 to facilitate this added fixed cost. If the average room rate is \$125, then we can find the number of additional rooms needed to be sold by dividing the difference in sales revenues needed by the average room rate:

$$\text{Number of additional rooms to sell} = \frac{\text{New required revenue} - \text{Old required revenue}}{\text{Average room rate}}$$
$$= \frac{\$607,765 - \$535,196}{\$125} = 581 \text{ rooms}.$$

In general, the break-even analysis for the short-term period should adjust for the cyclical nature of the hospitality industry. This sector has a number of cyclical sales revenue cycles, starting with a daily operating cycle is applied to the restaurant side of operations with sales varying with meal periods. Secondly, the weekly cycle affects the hotel side of operations, where business travellers are more likely to occupy rooms on weekdays while domestic tourists mostly come for weekend stays. Moreover, monthly cycles also apply, with a higher level of sales and general business operations expected during summer months. It would be wise for Donald to consider such cyclical variations in the break-even analysis and focus on a shorter period analysis instead of analysing for yearly break-even points.

Understanding Financial Statements

Proper financial management does not imply that an entrepreneur should know how to prepare financial statements. It is possible to prepare the financial

statements with the aid of a professional accountant or even through accounting software such as Xero. It is generally advisable for small-business owners to
set up the business accounting system using any popular computerized account
program with the help of an accountant, and later have an employee or a book-
keeping service enter transactions and manage regular record-keeping tasks.
However, an entrepreneur should be able to interpret the inputs and figures
on those statements, to identify where potential cost savings can be made and
how to improve the financial aspect of the business. In this section, the major
financial statements will be explained from Barossa Boutique Hotel.

The balance sheet

The balance sheet is characterized by the fundamental accounting equation
where the value of assets equals the combined values of liabilities and owner's
equity. The term 'balance sheet' hails from the fact that any changes on one side
of the accounting equation must be offset by the same change on the other side
of the equation. At any given date, the balance sheet provides a snapshot of the
business's financial position, usually prepared on the last day of a month or a
financial year. Users of the balance sheet can identify the assets the business
owns, and the claims held by its lenders and owners against those assets (i.e.
liabilities). These figures are valued at cost, not on actual market values. Both
sides of the balance sheet are usually organized based on their maturities, with
assets and liabilities with shorter term to maturity and easier to liquidate coming
up first, followed by those that have longer terms and are less liquid in nature.
    The first section on the left-hand side of the balance sheet records the assets
owned by the business. *Current assets* include cash and assets that can be converted to cash within a year such as accounts receivables and inventories. They
are followed by *non-current or fixed assets,* which are usually acquired for
use in the long term and are not expected to be converted to cash in one year.
Examples of non-current assets include intangible assets such as trademarks
and copyrights and tangible assets like buildings and properties. The value of
tangible assets can be ascertained by their physical use, but accounting rules
must be used to determine the value of intangible assets. On the right-hand side
of the balance sheet exists the business's liabilities and owner's equity. *Current
liabilities* are shown first, as they are creditors' claims that are to be paid back
within a year. They are followed by *long-term liabilities,* which are due to be
paid to the creditors after one year, i.e. mortgage and long-term loan payables.
The balancing factor in a balance sheet is the *owner's equity,* which represents
the owner's equity contributions to the business in addition to all accumulated
retained earnings not yet being distributed out to the owner(s).
    Barossa Boutique's balance sheet in Table 9.1 demonstrates one that is
typical for a small business in the hospitality sector. Because Donald must
take bookings for hotel reservations via credit card, Barossa Boutique's current assets include credit card receivables. Their food and beverage operations
would lead to having a sizeable inventory held for standard operations, which
might fluctuate depending on the business cycle. The location and setting of

Table 9.1. Barossa Boutique Hotel – balance sheet (for the year ending on 31 December 2017).

Assets			Liabilities and shareholders' equity		
Current assets			**Current liabilities**		
Cash		$30,000.00	Trade payables		$10,000.00
Credit card receivables		$12,150.00	Accrued expenses		$1,750.00
Accounts receivables		$21,500.00	Income tax payable		$14,000.00
Inventory – food & beverage	$12,400.00		Deposit and credit balances		$8,500.00
Inventory – supplies	$10,000.00		Current portion, long-term mortgage payable		$25,000.00
Prepaid expenses	$3,200.00	$25,600.00	**Total current liabilities**		**$59,250.00**
Total current assets		**$89,250.00**			
			Long-term liabilities		
Non-current assets			Mortgage payable – net of current portion payable	$500,000.00	
Land (at cost)		$250,000.00	Long-term bank loan payable	$200,000.00	$700,000.00
Building (net of depreciation)		$800,000.00	**Total liabilities**		**$759,250.00**
Equipment (net of depreciation)		$60,000.00	**Owner's equity**		
Furniture (net of depreciation)		$70,000.00	Equity capital	$450,000.00	
Total non-current assets		**$1,180,000.00**	Retained earnings	$60,000.00	$510,000.00
Total assets		**$1,269,250.00**	**Total liabilities and owner's equity**		**$1,269,250.00**

Barossa Boutique's operation would mean that it is going to have a sizeable level of non-current assets in the form of land, building, furniture along with kitchen equipment. Building carries the most value in their asset side of the balance sheet, as it is expected to cost them the most during the construction and subsequent renovations over time. On their liabilities side, typical hotel operations incur trade and income tax payables along with deposit and credit balances, which arise when Donald takes in room deposits of $100–200 per room on the guests' credit cards, which are subsequently refunded within a week. As commonly seen in standard hospitality operations, Barossa Boutique's non-current liabilities constitute the largest portion on the left-hand side of the balance sheet, with substantial values of mortgage and bank loans payable over a long-time horizon. The remaining portion, acting as the balancing factor in the balance sheet, is the owner's equity, which includes the owner's invested equity capital and retained profits not being distributed to the owners.

Income statements

While the balance sheet records the business's assets and liabilities, it does not present the earnings and expenses. We look at income statements for that information, which documents the changes occurring in a firm's position because of its operation over a specific period. Known frequently as a profit-and-loss statement, this financial statement compares expenses against revenue over a certain period to demonstrate the business's net income or loss. While income statements can be prepared on a monthly or quarterly basis, typically they are prepared on a yearly basis that reports the bottom line over the fiscal or calendar year. In the tourism and hospitality sector, because their operations may be departmentalized (e.g. revenues from accommodation, food and beverage, banqueting), income statements are often prepared to show the operating results of each department along with that of the whole business. Table 9.2 demonstrates the example of a departmental income statement in the form of Barossa Boutique's food and beverage department, followed by the complete income statement in Table 9.3.

Generally, income statements begin with the reporting of the *sales revenues,* which refers to the asset inflows received in exchange of the goods or services provided. For Barossa Boutique, sales revenue is earned from rooms and sale of food and beverage from its restaurant operations. Due to the nature of the business, it is expected that Barossa Boutique will have separate *departmental income statements* for its hotel and food and beverage operations. They might also have *miscellaneous incomes* from other sources ranging from transport, gift shops and venue bookings. Against these revenues, there will be *cost of sales* or cost of goods sold – that represents the total cost of goods and services sold during that accounting period. Income statements will also record *additional operating and related expenses* that need to be subtracted from the sales revenues. The *departmental contributory incomes or losses* calculated, as per Table 9.2, need to be consolidated with the other departmental contributions in the complete income statement. As demonstrated in Table 9.3, from

Table 9.2. Barossa Boutique Hotel – departmental income statement.

Hotel – income (loss) from food & beverage department for the year ending 31 December 2018		
Sales revenue		
Eatery restaurant & bar	$ 245,000.00	
Café	$ 105,000.00	
Banquets	$ 130,000.00	
Room service	$ 75,000.00	
Total sales revenue		$ 555,000.00
Cost of sales		
Cost of sales – food	$ 135,000.00	
Less: employee meals	$ (12,000.00)	
Net cost of sales – food		$ (123,000.00)
Net cost of sales – beverage		$ (55,000.00)
Total net cost of sales		$ (178,000.00)
Gross profit margin		$ 377,000.00
Departmental operating expenses		
Salaries and wages	$ (175,000.00)	
Employee benefits	$ (28,500.00)	
Total payroll and related expenses	$ (203,500.00)	
Glassware and silverware	$ (5,000.00)	
Cleaning supplies	$ (8,900.00)	
Decorations	$ (2,500.00)	
Laundry	$ (4,000.00)	
Licences	$ (8,000.00)	
Menu	$ (1,600.00)	
Linen and miscellaneous	$ (3,500.00)	
Uniforms	$ (2,000.00)	
Utensils	$ (3,000.00)	
Total operating expenses		$ (242,000.00)
Departmental contributory income (loss)		$ 135,000.00

those contributory incomes, all *undistributed operating expenses* that cannot be directly allocated to these departments, such as advertising, property maintenance and administrative expenses, must be deducted to find the *income before fixed charges*. Subsequently, deductions of fixed charges, i.e. property taxes, insurance, depreciations and income taxes, lead to the business's *net income* for the period.

Cash budget

While not considered a financial statement by itself, cash budgets are useful tools in cash management for small businesses. To remain financially solvent, a cash budget helps to ensure that there are minimum instances of cash shortages in paying the necessary bills, assisting in maintaining an optimum level of cash balance is kept at all times. Maintaining a tight control over the cash receipts

Table 9.3. Barossa Boutique Hotel – income statement for the year ending 31 December 2018.

Hotel – income (loss) from departments		
Rooms		$ 490,000.00
Food & beverage		$ 135,000.00
Miscellaneous income		$ 7,800.00
Total departmental income		$ 632,800.00
Undistributed operating expenses		
Administrative and general	$ (140,000.00)	
Marketing and promotions	$ (60,000.00)	
Property operations and maintenance	$ (155,000.00)	
Utility bills	$ (36,000.00)	$ (391,000.00)
Income before fixed charges		$ 241,800.00
Fixed charges		
Property taxes	$ (38,000.00)	
Insurance	$ (25,000.00)	
Interest	$ (15,000.00)	
Depreciation	$ (35,000.00)	$ (113,000.00)
Operating income before tax		$ 128,800.00
Income tax		$ (65,000.00)
Net income		$ 63,800.00

and disbursements is particularly important since the net income reported by a business in its income statement does not necessarily indicate the amount of cash held in hand. For example, Donald could be forced to pay for certain rare wines for Barossa Boutique's restaurant in cash. However, a large wedding function to be held in the banquet hall could be paid for in credit with only a 10% deposit paid in cash. In such instances, although accounting profits reported could be high, there might be a cash shortage until all the wedding function bills are settled after a month. Therefore, Donald would need to keep a tight control over the planned cashflows to ensure that his business is running in a cash-positive state.

Table 9.4 illustrates a quarterly cash budget for Barossa Boutique, demonstrating the forecasted cash inflows and outflows over the natural business operations. In practice, cash budgets can be maintained even further down to a weekly or monthly basis to maintain tighter control. Because it is a budget in nature, cash budgets are usually forecasted cash receipts and disbursements, based on past and anticipated transactions. After the estimated cash receipts and disbursements are documented, the end-of-period cash balance is calculated as follows:

End-of-period/closing cash balance = Beginning cash balance + receipts – disbursements.

With the aid of this cash budget, business owners can predict when they might have surplus funds to plan for further investments or larger disbursements

Table 9.4. Cash budget.

Barossa Boutique – cash budget based on sales forecast				
	Q1	Q2	Q3	Q4
Cash receipts				
Cash sales	$ 62,000.00	$ 35,000.00	$ 28,000.00	$ 78,000.00
Credit sales collected	$ 70,000.00	$ 45,000.00	$ 35,000.00	$ 35,000.00
Other cash receipts	$ 750.00	$ 380.00	$ 400.00	$ 270.00
Total cash receipts	$ 132,750.00	$ 80,380.00	$ 63,400.00	$ 113,270.00
Cash disbursements				
Purchases	$ (35,000.00)	$ (18,000.00)	$ (15,000.00)	$ (29,000.00)
Loan payments	$ (6,000.00)	$ (6,000.00)	$ (6,000.00)	$ (6,000.00)
Utilities bill	$ (2,000.00)	$ (1,400.00)	$ (1,350.00)	$ (1,750.00)
Capital additions	$ –	$ –	$ (750.00)	$ (500.00)
Wages and salaries	$ (60,000.00)	$ (45,000.00)	$ (45,000.00)	$ (60,000.00)
Insurance	$ (1,200.00)	$ (1,200.00)	$ (1,200.00)	$ (1,200.00)
Advertising	$ (5,000.00)	$ (4,000.00)	$ (4,000.00)	$ (5,000.00)
Miscellaneous	$ (750.00)	$ (500.00)	$ (500.00)	$ (1,000.00)
Total cash disbursements	$ (109,950.00)	$ (76,100.00)	$ (73,800.00)	$ (104,450.00)
End-of-quarter balance				
Beginning cash balance	$ 4,500.00	$ 27,300.00	$ 31,580.00	$ 21,180.00
Add: cash receipts	$ 132,750.00	$ 80,380.00	$ 63,400.00	$ 113,270.00
Less: cash disbursements	$ (109,950.00)	$ (76,100.00)	$ (73,800.00)	$ (104,450.00)
End-of-quarter cash balance	$ 27,300.00	$ 31,580.00	$ 21,180.00	$ 30,000.00

in advance. However, it is not always expected that the cash balance at the end of the period would be positive. In cases of negative cash balance, management can prepare beforehand by having short-term lending or other sources prepared to mitigate the cash shortage (see Chapter 8).

Capital Budgeting

From a regular business operations perspective, it is essential to make regular investments on capital projects, which include assets with relatively long life. While regular decision making regarding day-to-day items such as inventory do not typically have much long-term effect, the same cannot be said for capital assets. For example, if Donald invests $45,000 in an upgrade of the kitchen and bar facilities, and it turns out that the wrong equipment has been purchased, this decision cannot be altered or modified easily. The supplier may be unlikely to accept a return of the equipment. Therefore, it is essential that these capital decisions are made with sound analysis. From a financial point of view, analysing the value-addition potential of long-term capital assets is known as capital budgeting. In this section, we will discuss some commonly used capital budgeting tools to make sound investment decisions.

Fundamentals of capital budgeting

Entrepreneurs can make plans for capital expenditures through capital budgeting. Usually, the capital budgeting process has the following steps (Fig. 9.1):

Identify the potential opportunities: Business owners need to conduct a proper identification of all potential investment opportunities. For example, if Donald is planning to attract more customers to the restaurant department, he might analyse the customer patterns to identify scope to draw in customers for barista quality freshly brewed coffee or by offering local beers. In this regard, he can consider investing in procuring a new coffee machine or installing a modern beer tap system.

Estimate operating costs: After identifying the potential assets, the next step would be to identify all costs that are relevant to the particular capital investment. In this case, attention must be drawn to identify only the cashflows that are relevant to the project, and not cashflows that have already been incurred or are unrelated to the implementation of the actual project.

Estimate cashflows: Once the costs are identified, the next step would be to look at the data on either past similar projects or by drawing up new ones to specify what would be the expected cashflows generated by the investment. In some instances, instead of generating cashflows, benefits can be gained through cost savings. For example, by renovating the restaurant dining room, Barossa Boutique can either save costs on utilities and maintenance or earn more through increased seating capacity.

Assess risk: At this stage, all risks associated with the project such as potential losses or failure to produce anticipated results must be identified. Given the level of risks involved, an appropriate discount rate needs to be considered.

Implementation and feedback loop: After all the analysis, if the project is deemed to be value-adding, then it should be implemented. The implementation plan must consider key project deadlines and cost tracking. After and during implementation, a periodic feedback loop must be enforced to gain useful data while measuring the project's success or failure.

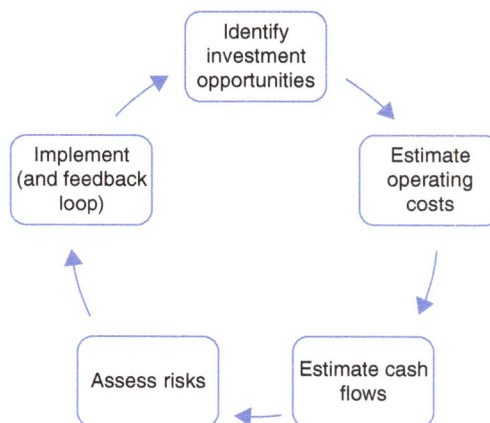

Figure 9.1. Capital Budgeting Process. (Source: author developed.)

Independent vs. mutually exclusive projects

Business owners need to consider whether the project is independent or mutually exclusive. If potential projects share common resources, then they are considered mutually exclusive, and only the project with the highest value addition may be considered for implementation. However, if they do not share common resources and the implementation of one does not impact on the other, then they are considered as independent projects. In such cases, both projects can be considered as long as they add value to the business. For example, let us assume that Donald is considering the acquisition of vacant land adjacent to the Barossa Boutique Hotel, to develop this site for either a conference centre or for luxury cabins. If the land space is sufficient only to accommodate one of these projects, then they would be considered mutually exclusive since the acceptance of one means the other will be rejected. However, if there is adequate land space for both, then they are to be considered as independent projects, and both may be undertaken given that they are adding value to the hotel.

Capital budgeting techniques – net present value (NPV)

There are a number of capital budgeting techniques used by decision makers across different industries. The payback period, accounting rate of return, profitability index and internal rate of return are some of them. Among these methods, one of the most commonly used is the net present value (NPV) method (Table 9.5). This is based on the time-value of money concept of finance, which is set up on the premise that a dollar today is worth more than a dollar in the future. Depending on the business's risks associated with the uncertainties of the cashflows, the expected future cashflows of the project are discounted to today's terms by determining their present values. The net of these present values of cashflows from the initial investment outlay is considered to be the NPV of the project, with a positive figure signifying value addition to the business while negative values indicate value deduction from the project. The formula to calculate the NPV, assuming the project has t years of useful life and a discount rate of r, is:

Table 9.5. Capital budgeting using the net present value (NPV) method.

Year	New coffee machine	New beer tap system
0	$ (20,000.00)	$ (45,000.00)
1	$ 3,500.00	$ 17,500.00
2	$ 5,000.00	$ 13,000.00
3	$ 9,800.00	$ 10,000.00
4	$ 6,500.00	$ 10,000.00
5	$ 5,500.00	$ 9,000.00
NPV	$ 6,379.77	$ 8,021.54
Cost of capital	4.5%	4.50%

$$\text{NPV} = -CF_0 + \sum_{t=1}^{n} \frac{CF_n}{(1+r)^n}.$$

After estimating the cost of capital as the discount rate, it is possible to use spreadsheet software like Microsoft Excel or financial calculators to calculate the present value of the cashflows and subtract them from the initial investment outlay to find the NPV of the project. For example, if Donald is considering the implementation of a new coffee machine or a beer tap system for the restaurant, based on the estimated cashflows, it is possible to use the =NPV function to calculate the NPV for both projects. If Barossa Boutique's cost of capital is 4.5%, then the NPV for these two projects would be $6,379.77 and $8,021.54, respectively. Since both the projects have positive NPV, Donald can consider undertaking either one of them if these are independent projects, or implement the beer tap system since its NPV is higher for mutually exclusive projects.

Performance Measurement

With the help of the financial statements, an entrepreneur can get a robust assessment of a firm's financial position at a given point in time, and its performance over the past period. However, to reap the most benefit from financial statements, one must analyse them in assessing the business's financial position, trends in liquidity, profitability and solvency, and use them as a starting point in planning for the future. To that end, financial ratios assist in evaluating a business entity's financial and economic performance over a given accounting period. In this section, the use of financial ratios along with recent developments in measuring a business's sustainable performance will be discussed.

Financial ratio analysis

Financial ratios guide the business owner in comparing the relative efficiency and productivity of a business's performance with respect to a particular benchmark. There is no single ratio that judges how well a business is performing. Instead, ratios are calculated across a variety of dimensions to measure the business's composite financial performance. Moreover, for a ratio to have meaning, it must be compared with a standard or an established base ratio. Typically, such ratios are compared against industry averages or with a similar competitive business, to evaluate how its operations are faring against set benchmarks. In addition, ratios of several years are calculated to provide a trend analysis, which helps the user of the financial statements to identify how the business has performed over time.

Commonly used ratios for tourism organizations include:

- **Liquidity ratios:** Evaluate the business's level of liquid assets held against short-term debt obligations
- **Activity ratios:** Measure how efficiently the different assets are utilized for business operations

- **Profitability ratios:** Demonstrate the business's profitability in comparison to the financing and revenue earned
- **Long-term solvency ratios:** Evaluate the business's ability to repay its long-term debt obligations.

Table 9.6 explores the formulas used to calculate some financial ratios across these different dimensions along with their interpretations.

Sustainability performance measures

In addition to measures on financial performance, tourism businesses are embracing other measures of performance related to sustainability. With increasing stakeholder demands for businesses to be more accountable and transparent, businesses are expected to conduct their operations in a manner that is both good for their business and satisfies stakeholder concerns (Keeble *et al.*, 2003). Research has shown that since 2016, consumer searches for sustainable goods have increased by almost 71%, with investors looking at a business's compliance with Environmental, Social, and Corporate Governance (ESG) requirements with increased importance (Florman *et al.*, 2016). While in Australia reporting on sustainability compliance is not mandatory, public companies are advised to disclose whether their operations carry environmental and social risk implications. Therefore, it is appropriate for an entrepreneur like Donald to consider measuring the sustainability performance of his business in preparation for future investments from investors. Here, some popular sustainability performance measures are discussed (Fig. 9.2):

- *Life cycle assessment (LCA)*: This measure evaluates the environmental, social and economic negative impacts and benefits in the decision-making processes towards developing more sustainable products in its typical life cycle (Finkbeiner *et al.*, 2010). Using LCA spreadsheets, available globally, an entrepreneur inputs data and other project information, i.e. project costs, energy savings and operations costs into the model. Based on the data entered, the model calculates a stream of cashflow and produces a range of economic evaluation information, i.e. net present value of cashflows and debt coverage ratios. This method helps to understand and address the impacts of products along their life cycle, and has been stimulated by a growing global awareness of the importance of protecting the environment.
- *Triple bottom line (TBL) performance measures*: This represents the spectrum of important organizational values – economic, environmental and social, and encourages expanding traditional financial reporting frameworks with the inclusion of these values. In addition to the financial performance measures, TBL includes the business's outcomes focused on its people as human capital, and plant as natural capital. Entrepreneurs can select the most appropriate set of TBL indicators applicable for their business from the set of indicators published by the Global Reporting Initiative (GRI).

Table 9.6. Financial ratios as performance measurement tools.

Ratio	Formula	Calculation	Interpretation
		Liquidity ratios	
Current ratio	$\text{Current ratio} = \dfrac{\text{Current assets}}{\text{Current liabilities}}$	$\text{Current ratio} = \dfrac{\$89,250}{\$59,250} = 1.51$	Demonstrates whether the business has adequate capacity to pay short-term debt without considering liquidity of current assets.
Quick ratio	$\text{Quick ratio} = \dfrac{\text{Cash} + \text{Credit card and accounts receivables} + \text{Marketable securities}}{\text{Current liabilities}}$	$\text{Quick ratio} = \dfrac{\$63,650}{\$59,250} = 1.07$	Demonstrates whether the business has adequate cash or other liquid assets to meet its short-term debt obligations.
Accounts receivables turnover	$\text{Accounts receivable turnover ratio} = \dfrac{\text{Total accounts receivable}}{\text{Average accounts receivable}}$	Assuming that for Barossa Boutique, the average accounts receivables equal $2,500 — Accounts receivable turnover ratio $= \dfrac{\$21,500}{\$2,500} = 8.6 \text{ times}$	Measures how quickly the receivables are being turned over in a year. Higher values of this ratio indicate better productivity with the receivables.
Receivable average collection period	$\text{Receivable average collection period} = \dfrac{365 \text{ days}}{\text{Accounts receivable turnover ratio}}$	Receivable average collection period $= \dfrac{365}{8.6} = 42.44 \text{ days}$	Measures the average number of days it takes to collect its outstanding receivables. A lower ratio is better as it demonstrates faster recovery of the receivables.
		Activity ratios	
Inventory turnover	$\text{Inventory turnover} = \dfrac{\text{Cost of sales during the period}}{\text{Average inventory during the period}}$	Assuming Barossa Boutique's average inventory is $30,000 — Inventory turnover $= \dfrac{\$178,000}{\$30,000} = 5.9 \text{ times}$	Demonstrates the liquidity of the business's inventories. Higher ratio figures show better inventory productivity.

| Working capital turnover | Working capital turnover $= \dfrac{\text{Total sales revenue}}{\text{Average working capital}}$ | Assuming Barossa Boutique's average working capital is $25,000 – Working Capital Turnover $= \dfrac{\$632,800}{\$25,000} = 25.31 \text{ times}$ | Measures the relative efficiency of utilizing the business's working capital in generating sales revenue. |
| Fixed asset turnover | Fixed asset turnover $= \dfrac{\text{Total sales revenue}}{\text{Total average fixed assets}}$ | Assuming Barossa Boutique's average fixed asset is $500,000– Fixed asset turnover $= \dfrac{\$632,800}{\$500,000} = 1.27 \text{ times}$ | Measures the relative efficiency of utilizing the business's fixed assets in generating sales revenue. Higher turnover figures imply more productive use of fixed assets. |

Profitability ratios

Return on assets	Return on assets $= \dfrac{\text{Income before interest and income tax}}{\text{Total assets}}$	Return on assets $= \dfrac{\$241,800}{\$1,269,250} = 19.05\%$	Demonstrates how well the business's assets are being employed. Higher figures imply better profitability on the total assets.
Return on owner's equity	Return on owner's equity $= \dfrac{\text{Net income after income tax}}{\text{Owner's equity}}$	Return on owner's equity $= \dfrac{\$63,800}{\$510,000} = 12.51\%$	Demonstrates how well the business owner's equity capital is being employed. Higher figures demonstrate greater profitability for the owner's equity invested.
Profit margin	Profit Margin $= \dfrac{\text{Net income}}{\text{Total sales revenue}}$	Profit margin $= \dfrac{\$63,800}{\$632,800} = 10.08\%$	Illustrates the business's operating efficiency in turning sales revenue into profits. Higher figures imply efficiency in turning sales revenues into profits.

Continued

Table 9.6. Continued.

Ratio	Formula	Calculation	Interpretation
Long-term solvency ratios			
Total liabilities to total assets	Total liabilities to total assets $= \dfrac{\text{Total liabilities}}{\text{Total assets}}$	Total liabilities to total assets $= \dfrac{\$759{,}250}{\$1{,}269{,}250} = 0.60$	Measures the portion of the business's assets financed by liability.
Total liabilities to total equity	Total liabilities to total equity $= \dfrac{\text{Total liabilities}}{\text{Total equity}}$	Total liabilities to total equity $= \dfrac{\$759{,}250}{\$510{,}000} = 1.49$	Measures the level of liabilities carried by the business compared to the owner's equity capital.
Times interest earned ratio	Times interest earned ratio $= \dfrac{\text{Income before interest and income taxes}}{\text{Interest expense}}$	Times interest earned ratio $= \dfrac{\$128{,}800 + \$15000}{\$15{,}000} = 9.59 \text{ times}$	Demonstrates the level of business's earnings to meet its debt obligations. Higher figures demonstrate better ability to repay interest expenses and solvency.
Operating and hospitality – sector-specific ratios			
Labour cost percentage	Labour cost percentage $= \dfrac{\text{Salaries and wages} + \text{Employee benefits}}{\text{Total sales revenue}}$	Labour cost percentage $= \dfrac{\$175{,}000 + \$28{,}500}{\$555{,}000} = 36.67\%$	For hospitality sector, this ratio demonstrates the portion of sales revenue spend on employee salaries.
Revenue per available room	Revenue per available room = Occupancy percentage × Average room rate	Revenue per available room = 75% × \$125 = \$93.75	Demonstrates the hotel's applicable revenue per available room after accounting for the level of room occupancy.
Percentage of beverage sales revenue to food sales revenue	Percentage of beverage sales revenue to food sales revenue $= \dfrac{\text{Beverage sales revenue}}{\text{Food sales revenue}}$	Assuming Barossa Boutique's total monthly sales revenue was \$83,250, out of which food was \$61,000 and beverages were \$22,250 – Percentage of beverage sales to food sales $= \dfrac{\$22{,}250}{\$61{,}000} = 36.48\%$	Demonstrates how profitable beverage sales revenue is compared to food sales.

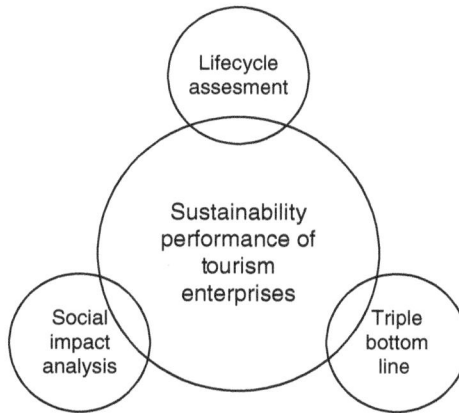

Figure 9.2. Measures of Sustainability Performance. (Source: author developed.)

- *Social impact analysis*: There are several social impact analysis methods used all around the world, but, commonly, they all seek to address the intended and unintended positive and negative social consequences derived from business interventions. For example, the social return on investment (SROI) method looks at analysing the data on a cost–benefit perspective, by assigning monetary values to the social impacts created by a project and assessing it against the cost spent. SROI figures equal or greater than one indicate that the project has generated a social return greater than the cost, with higher figures considered better with respect to social outcomes.

Summary

This chapter presented some of the key financial concepts, statements and calculations that are important for assessing and monitoring the financial health of a tourism organization. Tourism business operators need to have financial literacy, and make data-driven decisions based on the financial information. This is needed to protect business assets, increase revenues, control expenditure and improve profitability to support business growth. Moreover, as modern businesses increase in their complexity, they need to track not only income sales and expenses but also their short- and long- term liabilities, working capital and return on investments. Cash budgets help businesses keep track of cash needs arising from operations. Working capital management helps in understanding the amount of excess current assets in hand against the current liabilities, needed in smoothly conducting sales revenue generation. While current assets, i.e. cash, credit cards and accounts receivables and inventories are the resources necessary in the production of sales revenue for the next operating cycle, current liabilities, i.e. accounts, wages, salaries, interest and taxes payable, represent the operating costs incurred in credit to pay for the production of goods to be sold in the next operating period. Therefore, entrepreneurs need to be on top of the working capital needs to ensure smooth operations without facing short-term solvency issues. Entrepreneurs need to be mindful of meeting the regular debt payments, as failure to meet liability obligations can lead to the business becoming insolvent.

In the hospitality sector, in addition to the use of financial tools to forecast potential sales revenue and costs, entrepreneurs need to control the variances from those forecasted figures in real time. After making forecasts in potential revenues and costs, it is essential for the entrepreneurs to regularly monitor how actual figures are deviating from the forecasts. These variances can be computed in either nominal dollars or on a percentage basis, and corrective actions must be undertaken to prevent undesirable situations from occurring. With these measures in place, an entrepreneur can look into establishing financial stability in their business venture.

Exercises

1. After attending a National Hospitality Industry Expo, Donald learned about key benchmarks of industry average ratios for similar types of hotels. He is keen to examine how Barossa Boutique is performing in comparison to industry averages. Based on the information in Table 9.7, analyse and evaluate how Barossa Boutique is performing financially.

2. Beautiful summer weather has witnessed a large increase in the number domestic visitors to The Café at Barossa Boutique. However, existing coffee machines at The Café are outdated and new equipment is required to cater for the demand. Donald is considering purchasing and installing new coffee machine equipment. He has come across two options with different levels of serving capacity but with the same useful life of four years. Based on capital budgeting analysis using the net present value (NPV) method, identify which of these machines Donald should purchase, given that the loan to buy this machine has a cost of 5% and the expected incremental cashflows from these two options are given in Table 9.8.

3. Donald has decided to install a new beer tap system in the bar of the hotel, to allow for showcasing new local beers and bringing in new customers. The machine has a yearly fixed running cost of $20,000 with around 40% of variable costs for each dollar of sales revenue. Donald wants to know exactly at which sales level will this investment in the beer tap system break even. (a) Identify the break-even sales level in dollar terms. (b) If Donald wants this

Table 9.7. Barossa Boutique's performance against industry averages.

Ratio	Barossa Boutique	Industry average
Current ratio	1.51	1.32
Receivable average collection period	42.44 days	38.60 days
Profit margin	10.08%	10.95%
Labour cost percentage	36.67%	32.45%

Table 9.8. Expected incremental cashflows from two coffee machines.

Year	Machine A	Machine B
0	−$75,000	−$45,000
1	16,000	11,000
2	25,000	14,000
3	28,000	15,000
4	18,000	12,000

beer tap system to bring in $12,000 in additional net income, what should be the desired beer sales in dollar terms?

Solutions

1. Table 9.9 outlines the evaluation of Barossa Boutique's financial performance.

2. Using Microsoft Excel's =NPV function, we find machine A, and B's NPV to be $1818.98 and $956.76, respectively. If the alternatives are independent, then choosing both the machines would be value-adding, as their NPVs are positive. However, because of the resource constraints, Donald can only consider purchasing the best alternative, making it a mutually exclusive decision. In that case, only the best option can be undertaken, which in this case is machine A.

3. Since the variable costs to net sales is 40%, the contribution margin will be $(1 − 0.4) = 60\%$.

Table 9.9. Barossa Boutique's financial performance.

Ratio	Evaluation
Current ratio	Barossa Boutique has higher than industry average current ratio, which means it has more than enough current assets to meet any current liabilities. However, having too high a current ratio is not necessarily a good thing, as Barossa Boutique might have too much productive current assets lying around.
Receivable average collection period	Barossa Boutique's average receivables collection period is longer than the industry average, which means it is slower than normal in collecting its receivables. It is not a good indicator, and Donald must ensure that efficient collection of receivables is in action to ensure quick cash recovery.
Profit margin	There is not much difference in the profit margin figures, indicating that Barossa Boutique is in line with the industry with regards to its ability to convert sales revenues into profits.
Labour cost percentage	In the hospitality industry, labour cost is a crucial element that requires constant control. Barossa Boutique's labour costs are higher than the industry benchmarks, indicating that it requires more control in keeping labour costs in check.

$$\text{Break even sales}(\$) = \frac{\text{Fixed costs}(\$)}{\text{Contribution margin}(\%)} = \frac{\$20,000}{0.60} = \$33,333$$

$$\text{Desired sales}(\$) = \frac{\text{Fixed costs}(\$) + \text{Target net income}(\$)}{\text{Contribution margin}(\%)}$$
$$= \frac{\$20,000 + \$12,000}{0.60} = \$53,333.$$

References

Finkbeiner, M., Schau, E.M., Lehmann, A. and Traverso, M. (2010) Towards life cycle sustainability assessment. *Sustainability* 2(10), 3309–3322.

Florman, M., Klingler-Vidra, R. and Facada, M.J. (2016) A critical evaluation of social impact assessment methodologies and a call to measure economic and social impact holistically through the External Rate of Return platform. *LSE Enterprise Working Paper* 1602.

Jagels, M.G. (2006) *Hospitality Management Accounting* 9th edn. John Wiley, Hoboken, New Jersey.

Keeble, J.J., Topiol, S. and Berkeley, S. (2003) Using indicators to measure sustainability performance at a corporate and project level. *Journal of Business Ethics* 44(2) 149–158.

Klein, K.E. (2011) Building a business vs. making a living. *Bloomberg Business Week*. Available at: https://www.bloomberg.com/news/articles/2011-06-10/building-a-business-vs-dot-making-a-living (accessed 17 November 2022).

Sage (2012) *Sage Canadian Small Business Financial Literacy Survey*. Available at: https://www.sage.com/na/~/media/site/sagena/documents/surveys/Sage-Canadian-Small-Business-Financial-Literacy-Survey (accessed 17 November 2022).

10 Social Capital and Business Networks

Integrating entrepreneurs in the relationship networks that afford them access to certain resources is clearly a key factor in their business's future. It is, therefore, important that entrepreneurs evaluate what type of relationships they should maintain, consolidate, or invest in to obtain the required resources and capabilities. (Hernández-Carrión et al., 2017, pp. 82–83)

Introduction

Tourism enterprises do not operate in a vacuum. Day-to-day business requires the enterprise to interact with multiple stakeholders such as suppliers, customers, workers, government, trade associations, and even family. The extent to which a tourism enterprise has relationships with other parties is known as 'social capital'. This is because these social connections are a form of capital that can be used to extract resources that the business needs, such as supplies, financing, information and manpower. Social relationships that are leveraged for business purposes are known as business networks made up of personal networks (e.g., family and friends), professional networks (e.g., business partners, suppliers, staff), associative networks (e.g., trade associations, chambers of commerce) and institutional networks (e.g., local government, banks). In today's business environment, these networks can be developed through two main mediums: face-to-face and online connections. Traditionally, businesses would establish relationships through in-person meetings. However, contemporary methods include building online networks through social media platforms such as Facebook, LinkedIn and Twitter.

© Rob Hallak and Craig Lee 2023. *Managing Tourism Enterprises: Start-up, Growth and Resilience* (R. Hallak and C. Lee)
DOI: 10.1079/9781789249446.0010

Learning Outcomes

After completing this chapter, you should be able to:

- Define what social capital is and identify different types of social capital
- Identify four different types of business networks, and the types of resources that can be obtained from these networks
- Understand how online social networks can be used to build social capital.

Social Capital

Social capital is defined as the actual and potential resources available through an individual's network of relationships with others (Stam *et al.*, 2014). These 'others' refer to people an individual knows or who are known by the people that an individual knows (Greve and Salaff, 2003). These connections can serve as resources/assets to help achieve certain objectives (Burt, 1992, 2000).

Social capital is an important resource for tourism enterprises as it provides access to financial resources, labour, skills and information (Greve and Salaff, 2003). Research on business networks finds that social capital supports an enterprise's efforts in opportunity recognition (Anderson and Miller, 2003), building of inter-firm alliances (BarNir and Smith, 2002), access to sources of funding (Honig, 1998), access to potential employees (Bosma *et al.*, 2004), obtaining business advice (Zhou *et al.*, 2007) and creating ideas for innovation (Hughes *et al.*, 2007).

Social capital has been classified in several ways. One classification is to divide the concept into 'bonding' and 'bridging' social capital (Adler and Kwon, 2002; Davidsson and Honig, 2003). Bonding social capital refers to the relationships between individuals that know each other well (e.g., family and friends), allowing exchanges of resources based on trust and reciprocity (Davidsson and Honig, 2003). In an enterprise context, this refers to linkages among individuals and groups within an enterprise (e.g., between staff, between departments, between firms under the same organization, etc.) (Adler and Kwon, 2002). Bridging social capital refers to relationships between individuals from diverse groups or backgrounds (e.g., between a firm and trade organizations), which facilitate the attainment of information otherwise unavailable within an individual's familiar group (i.e. bonding social capital) (Davidsson and Honig, 2003). In an enterprise context, this refers to the extent to which an enterprise has external connections with actors outside the organization (Adler and Kwon, 2002).

Another framework to distinguish types of social capital is provided by Granovetter (1973) through the concept of 'strong' and 'weak' ties. The strength (i.e. strong or weak) of a tie refers to the combination of the amount of time, emotional intensity, intimacy (mutual confiding) and reciprocal services that characterizes the tie. Strong ties refer to ties derived from strong relationships such as family bonds that provide consistent access to resources. Strongly connected individuals are more often in contact, are usually like each other, and are more likely to exchange similar information. While this results in quicker and easier access to resources, the downside is that strong ties can be barriers to change since no new information is shared between the two parties in the relationship (Atterton, 2007). Weak ties represent loose relationships between individuals to obtain resources that are otherwise unavailable. Weak ties may be formed with a wider range of dispersed and less familiar individuals, be shorter in duration, have lower frequency of contact and trust, and are broken more easily (Atterton, 2007). The benefits of weak ties are that weak ties offset the tendencies of introversion present within strong ties by providing access to wider sources of information and expertise.

Finally, bridging social capital and weak ties also relates to the concept of 'structural holes' (Burt, 1992), where weak connections between groups create 'holes' in the social structure. These holes allow an individual to derive a competitive advantage by becoming a 'broker' who spans the hole, brokering the flow of information between individuals across holes, thus controlling the processes in-between.

Business Networks

In a tourism enterprise context, social relationships that are leveraged to extract resources for the enterprise are known as business networks. Business networks can be classified into four categories: personal, professional, associative and institutional (Hernández-Carrión *et al.*, 2017), as shown in Figure 10.1.

- Personal networks are relationships with people in an individual's private circle, such as family, relatives and friends that share common characteristics and interests. These are related to the concepts of bonding social capital or strong ties. For example, a tourism entrepreneur can seek investments from their relatives to provide seed funding for their start-up.

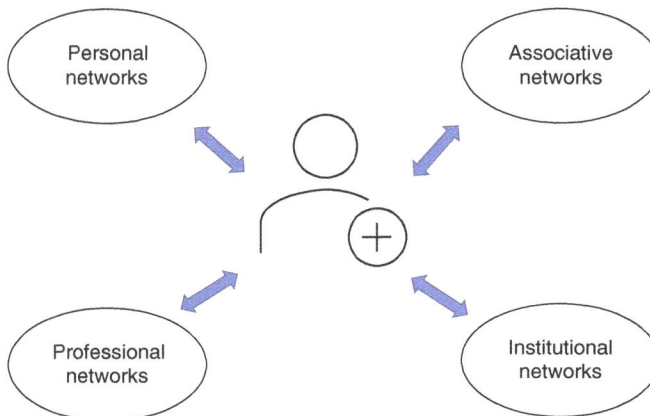

Figure 10.1. Types of business networks. (Source: author developed.)

- Professional networks are relationships with partners, workers, suppliers, customers and colleagues. These can be related to the concepts of bonding social capital or strong ties for relationships within an enterprise, or are related to the concepts of bridging social capital or weak ties for relationships between the enterprise and external parties (e.g., suppliers, customers). For example, a tourism entrepreneur can ask their supplier if there are any new supplies being introduced to market that can be used to enhance current products and services.
- Associative networks are relationships with associations an individual belongs to, e.g., business, trade, professional, political, sports or volunteer associations. These relationships can be formal in nature, especially when these groups operate according to rules that regulate membership entry and behaviour, but can also involve informal interactions (such as religious and sporting associations). Thus, these relationships can involve both bonding and bridging social capital or strong and weak ties. For example, a tourism entrepreneur can consult with their local chamber of commerce to find staffing recommendations.
- Institutional networks are relationships with people within public or private institutions (such as local, regional or national governments, large firms and banks). These relationships are usually not voluntary in nature and are highly regulated. For example, a tourism entrepreneur can negotiate with their bank to establish a new line of credit.

Benefits of Business Networks

Establishing business networks allows tourism enterprises to access resources in several key areas such as:

Financial resources: Funds obtained to finance the enterprise. These can include loans (whether personal or from a bank) as well as credit or subsidies and public aid.

Technology and innovation: Technologies the enterprise uses (e.g., IT tools, machinery, exploitation of patents, etc.) and/or knowledge for new business ideas and to develop innovations.

Market information: Information about the enterprise's customers, suppliers and competitors that can be used to satisfy current customers and attract new customers.

Quality management capabilities: The enterprise's ability to design products and services, to access suppliers providing high-quality raw materials, to train employees, or to introduce quality management systems (e.g., ISO norms, etc.).

Human resources: The employee's professional quality and qualifications as well as the enterprise's ability to manage these human resources (i.e. attract, retain and motivate workers).

Management capabilities: The owner's/manager's ability to coordinate all the previous resources (e.g., human, quality, sales, technological and financial resources) so the enterprise is successful and generates value. This includes information to enhance the owner's/manager's management skills, help the enterprise adapt to change, and the management of information and communication systems, whether they are managed directly or externally (e.g., consultancy, advice).

Online Social Networks

Developing social capital is context-specific; the rules that govern interactions, access to resources and entrepreneurial business practices are influenced by historical, cultural and business contexts (Kristiansen, 2004; Foley and O'Connor, 2013). In the contemporary business environment, the growing use of technology in everyday work has created a platform for enterprise managers to build online networks through social media platforms such as LinkedIn, Facebook and Twitter.

The utilization of online networking platforms to build and maintain relationships is significantly different to in-person interactions (Baym, 2010). In online settings, time and space is compressed, the speed of communication is rapid, and accessibility to individuals in increased (Baym, 2010). This can allow a wide-reaching social network to be built quickly but can also lead to several drawbacks.

Social networking sites may enable entrepreneurs to find others with similar interests, assess the content of networks they may wish to join, and make social judgements about potential connections. This helps individuals broaden their networks, which can be hard, time-consuming or socially awkward through face-to-face interaction (Smith *et al.*, 2017). In addition, with the vast availability of information through social networking sites, entrepreneurs could use this opportunity to make calculative connections that may not be possible in real-world settings (Smith *et al.*, 2017). Entrepreneurs can convert weak ties to stronger ties by leveraging common ground and shared attributes through social networking site profiles, which are difficult to determine offline (Smith *et al.*, 2017).

Several studies have sought to investigate the effectiveness of several of the most popular social networking sites in helping entrepreneurs build their social networks. Fischer and Reuber (2011) examine how the use of Twitter may enhance the effectuation process in entrepreneurs. Through interviewing 12 entrepreneurs, their findings suggest that moderate online social interaction through Twitter allows entrepreneurs to gain new insights into the resources available to them and how they can be used to achieve a set of goals. However, if one invests too heavily in social media interaction, they may continuously loop between gaining new information about resources and reassessing their set of means and potential goals, without using their means to pursue a goal.

Quinton and Wilson (2016) focus on the business networking platform LinkedIn to examine the nature of business relationships developed through this platform in wine networks. Their study identified multiple tensions between actual networking behaviours and business relationship theory. LinkedIn facilitates sharing industry insights, but this goes against competitive strategy. Also, the immediacy of obtaining information about other actors allows emergent relationships to form by chance, as opposed to rational and strategic relationship development. In addition, membership in social media networks acts as heuristics to determine an actor's trustworthiness, reducing the time required to assess this trait over a prolonged period of interactions.

Summary

This chapter has reviewed the role of social capital and business networks in tourism enterprises. Social capital is the actual and potential resources available through an actor's network of relationships with other people. These relationships vary in strength, referring to the combination of the amount of time, emotional intensity, intimacy (mutual confiding) and reciprocal services which characterize the tie. Strong or bonding ties are relationships established with close or similar individuals, while weak or bridging ties are relationships established with less-known individuals or parties external to a firm. Business networks are relationships leveraged to extract resources for the firm and can be classified into four categories: personal, professional, associative and institutional. These networks provide access to financial resources, technology and innovation, market information, quality management capabilities, human resources, and management capabilities among others. Social capital can also be established through online social networks, such as LinkedIn, Facebook and Twitter. Establishing connections in this way has both benefits and drawbacks. Social networking sites enable entrepreneurs to find others with similar interests, assess the content of networks they may wish to join, and make social judgements about potential connections, aiding network-broadening behaviours that may be hard, time-consuming or socially awkward for face-to-face interaction. However, by their nature, social networks function to share information, which is against competitive strategy. Additionally, there can be a tendency for individuals to be presented with or use information on social media to seek out others who share similar interests and profiles as themselves, meaning it can reinforce the build-up of strong ties at the expense of weak ties.

Review Questions

1. Consider whether different types of business networks (i.e. personal, professional, associative and institutional) may provide access to different types of resources.
2. What kind of online platforms may be useful for tourism enterprises to build online social networks?

CABI case study: Utah farm-chef-fork: linking rural growers with urban chefs.

A programme that brings together chefs and local producers, through workshops and food events, has served as a catalyst for smarter marketing by growers and increasing use of local food in Utah's restaurants.

Authors: Kynda R. Curtis[1] and Roslynn Brain[2]

Affiliations: [1]College of Agriculture and Applied Sciences, Utah State University, Logan, Utah, USA [2]College of Natural Resources, Utah State University, Moab, Utah, USA

Origin: Adapted from Chapter 14: Utah farm-chef-fork: linking rural growers with urban chefs to enhance local food sourcing. In: Slocum, S.L. and Kline, C. (eds) *Linking Urban and Rural Tourism*. CAB International, Wallingford, UK, pp. 202–215.

© CAB International 2017

Growth in Food Tourism and Demand for Local Foods

The rise in consumer demand for local foods in the US is demonstrated by a number of measures, including the 185% increase in farmers' markets from 2000 to 2014, the 275% increase in community supported agriculture (CSA) programmes from 2004 to 2014 and the 288% increase in regional food hubs from 2007 to 2014 (Low *et al.*, 2015). In 2012, 7.8% of US farms sold US$6.1 billion in food through local direct-marketing channels, which included intermediate sales of local food to grocers, restaurants, institutions and food service (USDA-ERS, 2008). The National Grocers Association 2014 Consumer Survey Report found that the availability of local foods was a major influence on grocery shopping decisions, as 87.2% of respondents rated the availability of local food as 'very or somewhat important' and 44.2% rated it as 'very important' when choosing a grocery store (National Grocers Association, 2014). Locally grown food availability was the second most desired improvement among surveyed grocery shoppers. In fact, 32% of respondents said they would consider purchasing their groceries elsewhere if their preferred store did not carry locally sourced foods. While only 15% of the respondents indicated they shop at national supermarket chains, Walmart and Kroger have incorporated local food sourcing into their long-term growth strategies (Rushing, 2013).

This trend towards local food is also illustrated by the growing emphasis on food-related tourism. The US Travel Association reports that 27 million travellers (17% of American travellers) engaged in gastronomic activities while travelling, across a three-year period (Sohn and Yuan, 2013). Food tourism is the practice of exploration through food consumption, in which individuals eat unfamiliar food or participate in foreign food customs in order to learn about or understand other cultures (Ryan and Brown, 2011). Food tourism examples include farm stays, beer and wine festivals, food festivals, brewery tours, ethnic restaurants, etc. Food tourism has become such a worldwide trend that Brand USA (a US destination-marketing programme) specifically promotes regional cuisines to draw visitors to the US.

Patronizing traditional and local-sourcing restaurants is a common way in which food tourists explore and experience a destination. The desire to visit local-sourcing restaurants is evidenced by the National Restaurant Association's 2015 Restaurant Industry Forecast, which reported that 70% of consumers were more likely to visit a restaurant offering locally sourced items. Additionally, the 'Top 5 2015 Menu Trends' included locally sourced proteins (meats, seafood, etc.) and locally grown produce as the top two trends (National Restaurant

Continued

CABI case study: continued.

Association, 2015). Schmit *et al.* (2010) found that restaurant patrons in New York strongly supported the sourcing of local food in restaurants and preferred to eat at those that prepare local foods. These studies demonstrate the benefits of sourcing local food for chefs and restaurant owners, given customer interest in local foods, especially while travelling.

Utah is a primary tourism destination for national park visitors, skiers and other outdoor enthusiasts, as well as those wishing to experience Mormon heritage. In 2013, Utah had 23.5 million visitors, including 4.2 million skier visits and 10.4 million state/national park visits. Tourism is a key industry for Utah, as total visitor spending in 2012 was $7.5 billion (Leaver, 2014). The cuisine offered in cities near key tourism destinations, such as Salt Lake City, Park City, Moab and Springdale, has become an important attraction for visitors and has resulted in the expansion of locally owned restaurants (Yang, 2014). Rural–urban linkages, in terms of connections between urban chefs and rural growers and ranchers, will be necessary to improve the tourist experience in Utah, especially for those visitors interested in food culture. The following case study will examine Utah Farm-Chef-Fork, a programme of Utah State University (USU) Extension, which focuses on fostering connections between growers, ranchers and chefs in Utah, and, ultimately, on increasing the volume of locally sourced restaurant ingredients in urban areas.

Local Food Sourcing Benefits to Growers and Communities

Utah experienced agricultural land losses of 301,300 acres (121,931 hectares) between 1982 and 2007 (Vilsack and Clark, 2009). Research has shown, however, that when farmers direct-market their products to local restaurants, farmer income is increased and farmland losses decrease due to increased farmer revenues (Adam *et al.*, 1999). As mentioned in a recent US Department of Agriculture (USDA) report, local food sourcing not only helps sustain small-scale farms but also supports a more diverse and wider variety of products, as opposed to monoculture farming normally associated with large-scale agriculture (Martinez *et al.*, 2010). Sourcing to restaurants provides direct benefits to farmers through expanded markets and improved pricing for their specialty crops. Additionally, farmers have more control over the production and processing methods they employ, as well as the opportunity to learn entrepreneurial business skills (Martinez *et al.*, 2010). These results are associated with longer-term economic impacts for rural communities in that 'a climate of entrepreneurship and risk-taking' is encouraged (Gale, 1997, p. 25). Overall, the key benefits of selling to chefs/restaurants for growers include increased farm sales (Schmit *et al.*, 2010), ability to develop a unique product brand and differentiate farm products (Curtis and Cowee, 2009), securing a market for products that may otherwise be lost due to excess supply in peak production seasons (Thilmany, 2004), and providing insight into current market trends and changing consumer demand (Pepinsky and Thilmany, 2004).

Local food sourcing has been linked to generating economic development in local communities, fostering public health outcomes related to food security, addressing food safety issues linked to the spread of disease, fostering an improved sense of community, and providing opportunities for both farmers and restaurants to promote environmental sustainability, leading to positive public perceptions (Pearson and Bailey, 2012). For example, studies in Iowa found that replacing imports with locally produced goods created jobs and boosted local retail returns in industries throughout Iowa (Swenson, 2010a,b). In Florida, local food purchases created 183,625 jobs and $10.47 billion in added value to the community (Hodges *et al.*, 2014).

Continued

The contribution of local food to total food sales varies substantially by region, primarily due to differences in the products or varieties grown, the proximity of consumers to farming areas, and population density. For example, between 1992 and 2007, local food sales grew three times faster in the Far West and Rocky Mountain regions than in other US regions (Low and Vogel, 2011). Fresh fruits and vegetables dominate local food sales and, thus, areas where growing conditions favour their production see strong sales. The value of local foods is highest in areas where farmers' markets and farms are near a large urban population centre. Overall, the value of local food sold is highest in the north-east and western US regions (Rushing, 2013).

Thus, the benefits associated with local food sourcing extend beyond the farmer to the community as a whole. This is demonstrated by Bachmann (2004), who states, 'selling to local chefs is among the alternatives that will help to build a diverse, stable regional food economy and a more sustainable agriculture' (p. 1). Other studies have shown that local food sourcing, or the reduction in food miles, may benefit the environment by reducing carbon emissions associated with traditional food supply systems (Pirog and Benjamin, 2003).

Barriers to Local Food Sourcing

Despite the documented benefits of direct-marketing local farm products to chefs, research shows that many barriers exist to fostering the required relationships. For example, Curtis *et al.* (2008) discovered via focus groups with growers in Nevada that nearly all would like to enter this type of market but that a lack of information was the biggest barrier to doing so. The growers were unsure of how to enter the market, saying they needed more information about what types of products and quantities chefs desire, as well as the timing and delivery methods preferred. In a study of restaurants in New York, the top three barriers listed by chefs in sourcing locally included lack of time to contact or communicate with farmers, lack of confidence in product consistency and lack of confidence in consistent product quality (Schmit *et al.*, 2010).

This is not surprising as restaurants typically rate product attributes, such as taste or quality, unique items and dependability, which includes receiving expected quantities and quality consistently, as most important in their purchasing decisions (Curtis and Cowee, 2009; Schmit *et al.*, 2010). In fact, studies find that chefs are not aware of high-quality local foods available and discuss the need for growers to provide samples to chefs along with seasonal availability information (Curtis *et al.*, 2008). Unfortunately, restaurant owners commonly voice frustration regarding the high transaction costs associated with local food purchases (Brimlow and Matson, 2015), including lack of information regarding product availability, inconvenient ordering processes, difficulty setting up and enforcing contracts, and poor grower communication.

Chefs of higher-end or gourmet restaurants, however, were open to adjusting menus to include seasonal fresh products, willing to take the best products, even in small quantities, and willing to provide input on the varieties desired prior to planting (Curtis *et al.*, 2008). These chefs were also the most interested in knowing the growers and their production methods; they saw the value in production methods such as organic. These chefs thus provide a prime market for smaller local growers using specialty production methods.

Continued

CABI case study: continued.

Utah Farm–Chef–Fork Programme Overview

The benefits and barriers to local-sourcing restaurants prompted the development of a state-wide programme aimed at connecting growers and chefs, called Utah Farm-Chef-Fork. Utah Farm-Chef-Fork was established in 2012 through a USDA Specialty Crop grant and is a collaborative project between Utah State University Extension and Slow Food Utah. The programme's primary goal is to 'enhance community vitality and reduce food miles by connecting Utah growers and restaurants' through workshops, mingles (meet-and-greets), farm and restaurant tours and other local-sourcing food events.

Farm-to-restaurant sourcing programmes – including New York's Columbia County Bounty, Home Grown Wisconsin, Red Tomato in the north-east US, Practical Farmers of Iowa and Colorado Crop to Cuisine – have been successfully launched in many other states. As a result, several 'how to' guides exist regarding direct marketing to restaurants developed by the USDA, Cooperative Extension and others (Pepinsky and Thilmany, 2004; Gregoire et al., 2005). These guides provide suggestions to growers for dealing with chefs, including product availability, brochures on farm history, mission and products, and providing chefs with free samples. Other tips include guidelines for establishing relationships and specifics on product handling. The existing research, programmes and associated curricula provided a foundation for developing the Utah Farm-Chef-Fork initiative.

Prior to programme delivery, a comprehensive needs assessment was conducted, including an in-depth literature review and web-based (SurveyMonkey) interest surveys conducted with growers and local chefs. The surveys were conducted state-wide in the spring of 2013 in an effort to understand perceived barriers and benefits to sourcing locally, and the types of information and interaction that would increase the incidence of local-food sourcing at Utah restaurants. The interest survey was completed by 20 chefs and 36 growers. Survey results were used to customize programme materials, delivery methods and activities to the needs of the target audience.

The initiative was launched with four major objectives to guide programming:

- Educate chefs/owners of locally owned restaurants on effective communication and outreach techniques to use with local growers via a series of state-wide workshops.
- Educate growers regarding effective communication, marketing and production planning via a series of state-wide workshops.
- Conduct mingles and farm and restaurant tours for growers and chefs to increase communication and understanding of each other's abilities, needs and requirements.

Organize farm dinners for the general public, with local chefs preparing the meal from products provided by host farms, to promote and educate residents and visitors on the cuisine and food culture of Utah.

Impacts on Local Food Sourcing

After the programme launch, the project team developed a programme logo, website and curricula for grower and chef workshops. To measure the impact of programme activities on decreasing barriers to local sourcing for growers and chefs, a comprehensive programme evaluation plan, including retrospective post-activity and annual follow-up surveys, was conducted.

Continued

CABI case study: continued.

Educational Workshops

From 2013 to 2015, nine grower workshops and chef workshops were held across Utah. Over 150 growers and 60 chefs participated in these workshops, representing 18 Utah counties and three surrounding states.

Workshop evaluations analysed through paired-sample t-tests indicated that, as a result of workshop attendance, the overall post-workshop score on growers' confidence in performing a selection of marketing activities was significantly higher (series average = 3.68, SE = 0.11) than the overall confidence score prior to the workshop (series average = 2.50, SE = 0.18). All grower participants also listed an increased intention to implement various marketing activities, such as developing a delivery plan and preparing a list of product prices, as a result of workshop attendance. Growers (80%) anticipated sale amounts to restaurants ranging from $50 to over $1000 per week. Also, over 88% of growers anticipated sourcing to between one and ten restaurants annually.

Chefs showed similar results following the one-day workshops, as paired-sample t-tests indicated that the overall post-workshop score on chefs' confidence in performing a series of activities was significantly higher (series average = 3.77, SE = 0.20) than the overall confidence score prior to the workshop (series average = 2.42, SE = 0.19). Additionally, 62% of chef participants said they would complete a number of marketing activities within six months of the workshop, including developing delivery and payment procedures; highlighting locally sourced products and their growers on table tents and restaurant windows; and developing food safety, insurance and/or production method (organic, grass-fed, etc.) requirements. Approximately 71% indicated that they would increase the percentage of their restaurant ingredients sourced locally as a result of the workshop.

The following quotes from two chefs who attended the workshops perhaps best illustrate the impact of the programme:

> The most critical hurdle to overcome in our effort towards building a sustainable infrastructure between local producers/artisans and chefs has, in my experience, been communication. As we have laboured to make those connections on our own, it has become apparent to our team that we needed more help. Someone who has a vested interest in strengthening the fabric of our food community but isn't directly involved with the day-to-day operations of running a farm or a restaurant. How lucky we now are to have the Farm-Chef-Fork programme and those at Utah State who are concerned about the same issues we are and are willing to help find solutions to the problems we are facing. I was honoured to represent my company this past week in sharing our experiences buying locally, supporting those in our community and the benefits that our company has seen as a result of this effort. I have no doubt that the Farm-Chef-Fork programme can go on to play a crucial role in bringing our community together, thereby allowing all of us to benefit from the shared efforts of each other. I look forward to continued support of this programme and the positive outcome I know it can bring.

> We are a food truck and catering company in Salt Lake City, Utah, and we specialize in seasonal handcrafted street food. UT Farm-Chef-Fork provides important communication channels between the farm and us (the chefs), and the consumer. Local food practices NEED to grow in order to sustain not only our community/ economy, but our Earth. This training was a great way to meet those farmers face-to-face and develop a level of understanding and trust, and build further the relationships

Continued

CABI case study: continued.

that will continue throughout time. We have placed local food as a staple and priority in our business plan, and will continue to reach out and obtain products from several farms within the area.

Workshop follow-up evaluations conducted with grower attendees online (SurveyMonkey) one year following the workshops found that 42% of the participants had increased the number and range of products grown as well as their local sales. Sixty-six per cent had expanded their customer base, 58% had increased their land use and 17% had increased the number of marketing outlets used. Almost half (50%) felt their operation was more economically viable, and 19% felt their operation was more efficient, while 62% and 83% felt their quality of life and their community had improved, respectively.

Grower attendees indicated their level of confidence with 12 of 18 skills related to marketing their locally grown produce to chefs or restaurants was relatively high (rated a 3 or higher on a five-point Likert scale, where 1 = not at all confident and 5 = completely confident). The highest ranked skills were 'knowing the best time of day to call on a new chef' (M = 3.5, SD = 1.06) and 'understanding what chefs need to know about their farm/business' (M = 3.5, SD = 0.74).

On the follow-up evaluations, growers were asked to describe what they felt to be the primary factors that contributed to the achievements made by them and others as a result of participating in the programme. Comments from various participants included:

I was able to get an agreed weekly delivery to one restaurant and occasional to four others; this is mostly a result of having lists of interested restaurants and learning ice-breaking techniques for approaching chefs.

I gained a better understanding of what chefs need and how to communicate with them.

The workshop opened my mind to many potential challenges and possibilities as I move forward building our farm.

I learned how to approach restaurants for the first time, learned about current Farm to Table operations in the area and what they charge or how they value their products, resource and networking from the programme that helped me with current ideas.

When asked to identify economic, social and environmental benefits that resulted from their participation in the workshops, comments from various participants included:

I am able to approach new marketing opportunities, chefs with confidence. I will be able to convert this skill into cash flow next season.

I think we will save a lot of money in the long run by being better prepared.

The income from restaurant sales far exceeds farmers' markets.

I have expanded the number and variety of crops that we are growing and used techniques that allow us to extend our growing season. It has definitely benefited our own family's table.

My increased knowledge of local food production and the exciting possibilities this presents.

Networking Mingles

The Utah Farm-Chef-Fork programme also hosted 'mingles' across Utah in conjunction with Slow Food Utah. The mingles provided an opportunity to connect growers and chefs at

Continued

CABI case study: continued.

private venues, where growers set up tables with samples and promotional materials and chefs/owners walked through and 'mingled' with the growers. Approximately 32 chefs and 48 growers participated in the six mingles held across Utah in 2013 and 2014, with some growers attending multiple events.

As a result of attending the mingles, 71% of the growers stated they believe their sales to local chefs will increase in the following year. The mingles provided a venue for starting conversations, making connections with chefs who care, and gaining a better idea of what products chefs/owners desire and in what seasons they need them.

The following quotes from two growers who attended the mingles illustrate the impact of the programme:

> We were able to make connections and leads with a local grocery that may lead to selling eggs through their store. Additionally, it was great to meet other producers and make additional connections for our network.

> I thought it was a great experience overall. As for how it has changed my business, I feel like I have a better idea of how to approach restaurants in our area and what the restaurant owners'/chefs' expectations are.

Almost all (96%) chefs/owners attending the mingles stated that they are showcasing local sourcing on their promotional materials, and 80% stated they will source a higher percentage of local food next year as a result of attending the mingles. Reasons given for increasing local food sourcing included knowing more farmers/vendors, access to farm produce and other resources they did not know were available, and the appeal to their clientele.

Future Directions

The Utah Farm–Chef–Fork programme is currently organizing farm and restaurant tours, as well as farm dinners for the general public. The tours provide educational opportunities for chefs and growers regarding farm practices, seasonal challenges, and restaurant needs and challenges, and continue to establish connections between the two groups. Farm dinners in a range of locations, from just outside Zion National Park to a county-owned experiential farm in Salt Lake City, will be the next step in the initiative. These dinners will provide local food opportunities for both residents and tourists to Utah. More information about the Utah Farm–Chef–Fork programme can be found at https://extensionsustainability.usu.edu/programs/ (accessed 18 November 2022).

Conclusions

The Utah Farm–Chef–Fork programme has clearly reduced barriers to sourcing local food and expanded the availability of locally produced foods at restaurants across Utah. The rural–urban linkages established through programme efforts have created additional economic opportunities for rural growers and urban chefs while also improving the tourist experience and enhancing Utah's overall destination image and, more specifically, its potential for food-and drink-related tourism. The number of Utah restaurants publicly sourcing locally rose by 140% from 2012 to 2016 (Utah's Own, 2016). While tourists may continue to be

Continued

CABI case study: continued.

initially drawn to Utah for its national parks and outdoor activities, they will now have more opportunities to enjoy the tastes of Utah as well.

References

Adam, K., Balasubrahmanyam, R. and Born, H. (1999) *Direct Marketing*. National Center for Appropriate Technology. Available at: https://attra.ncat.org/attra-pub/summaries/summary.php?pub=263 (accessed 15 April 2015).

Bachmann, J. (2004) *Selling to Restaurants: Business and Marketing*. National Center for Appropriate Technology. Available at: https://attra.ncat.org/attra-pub/viewhtml.php?id=266 (accessed 23 April 2015).

Brimlow, J. and Matson, J. (2015) Buying local? An exploratory analysis of barriers to local food sales from the perspective of intermediary buyers in California and North Carolina. Paper presented at the 2015 Annual Meeting of the Agricultural and Applied Economics Association, San Francisco, California, 26–28 July.

Curtis, K.R. and Cowee, M. (2009) Direct marketing local food to chefs: chef preferences and perceived obstacles. *Journal of Food Distribution Research* 40(2), 26–36.

Curtis, K.R., Cowee, M., Havercamp, M., Morris, R. and Gatzke, H. (2008) Marketing local foods to gourmet restaurants: a multi-method assessment. *Journal of Extension* 46(6).

Gale, F. (1997) Direct farm marketing as a rural development tool. *Rural Development Perspectives* 12(2), 19–25.

Gregoire, M.B., Arendt, S.W. and Strohbehn, C.H. (2005) Iowa producers' perceived benefits and obstacles in marketing to local restaurants and institutional food service operations. *Journal of Extension* 43(1).

Hodges, A., Stevens, T. and Wysocki, A. (2014) Local and regional food systems in Florida: values and economic impacts. *Journal of Agriculture and Applied Economics* 46(2), 285–298.

Leaver, J. (2014) The state of Utah's tourism, travel and recreation industry. *Utah Economic and Business Review* 73(4), 1–15.

Low, S.A. and Vogel, S. (2011) *Direct and Intermediated Marketing of Local Foods in the United States*. US Department of Agriculture Economic Research Service Economic Research Report ERR-128. Available at: http://www.ers.usda.gov/publications/44924/8276_err128_2_.pdf?v=41056 (accessed 23 April 2015).

Low, S.A., Adalja, A., Beaulieu, E., Key, N., Martinez, S. *et al.* (2015) *Trends in US Local and Regional Food Systems: A Report to Congress*. US Department of Agriculture Economic Research Service Administrative Publication AP-068. Available at: https://www.ers.usda.gov/webdocs/publications/42805/51173_ap068.pdf?v=1128.6 (accessed 27 April 2015).

Martinez, S., Hand, M., Da Pra, M., Pollack, S., Ralston, K. *et al.* (2010) *Local Food Systems: Concepts, Impacts and Issues*. US Department of Agriculture Economic Research Service Economic Research Report ERR-97. Available at: http://www.ers.usda.gov/publications/err-economic-research-report/err97.aspx (accessed 15 April 2015).

National Grocers Association (2014) SupermarketGuru Consumer Survey Report. Available at: http://origin.library.constantcontact.com/download/get/file/1102509927195-2152/ConsumerSurveyReport2014.pdf (accessed 23 April 2015).

Continued

CABI case study: continued.

National Restaurant Association (2015) Restaurant Industry Forecast. Available at: http://
www.restaurant.org/downloads/pdfs/research/whatshot/whatshot2015-results
(accessed 23 April 2015).

Pearson, D. and Bailey, A. (2012) Exploring the market potential of 'local' in food systems.
Locale: The Australasian-Pacific Journal of Regional Food Studies 2(2), 82–103.

Pepinsky, K. and Thilmany, D. (2004) *Direct Marketing Agricultural Products to Restaurants:
The Case of Colorado Crop to Cuisine* [AMR04-03]. Department of Agricultural and
Resource Economics, Colorado State University. Available at: http://hdl.handle.
net/10217/44603 (accessed 2 May 2015).

Pirog, R. and Benjamin, A. (2003) *Checking the Food Odometer: Comparing Food Miles
for Local Versus Conventional Produce Sales to Iowa Institutions*. Leopold Center for
Sustainable Agriculture, Iowa State University. Available at: http://www.leopold.iastate.
edu/pubs-and-papers/2003-07-food-odometer (accessed 15 April 2015).

Rushing, J. (2013) *Buying into the Local Food Movement*. A.T. Kearney. Available at:
http://www.atkearney.com/paper/-/asset_publisher/dVxv4Hz2h8bS/content/buyingin-
to-the-local-food-movement/10192 (accessed 20 June 2013).

Ryan, B. and Brown, L. (2011) *Evaluating Restaurant and Culinary Opportunities*. University
of Wisconsin – Extension. Available at: http://fyi.uwex.edu/downtown-market-analysis/
files/2011/02/Restaurant101211.pdf (accessed 23 April 2015).

Schmit, T.M., Lucke, A. and Hadcock, S. (2010) *The Effectiveness of Farm-to-chef Marketing
of Local Foods: An Empirical Assessment from Columbia County, NY.* Cornell University
Department of Applied Economics and Management. Available at: http://publications.
dyson.cornell.edu/outreach/extensionpdf/2010/Cornell_AEM_eb1003.pdf (accessed 3
May 2015).

Sohn, E. and Yuan, J. (2013) Who are the culinary tourists? An observation at a food and
wine festival. *International Journal of Culture, Tourism and Hospitality Research* 7(2),
118–131.

Swenson, D. (2010a) *Investigating the Potential Economic Impacts of Local Foods for
Southeast Iowa*. Leopold Center for Sustainable Agriculture, Iowa State University.
Available at: https://www.leopold.iastate.edu/pubs-and-papers/2010-01-local-foods-
southeast-iowa (accessed 3 May 2015).

Swenson, D. (2010b) *The Economic Impact of Fruit and Vegetable Production in Southwest
Iowa Considering Local and Nearby Metropolitan Markets*. Leopold Center for
Sustainable Agriculture, Iowa State University. Available at: https://www.leopold.iastate.
edu/pubs-and-papers/2010-01-fruit-and-vegetable-production-metro-markets (accessed
17 April 2015).

Thilmany, D.D. (2004) Colorado crop to cuisine. *Review of Agricultural Economics* 2(3),
404–416.

USDA-ERS (2008) Agricultural Resource Management Survey. Available at: http://www.
ers.usda.gov/data-products/arms-farm-financial-and-crop-production-practices/
(accessed 2 May 2015).

Utah's Own (2016) *Dining Guide*. Available at: http://www.utahsown.org/Dining (accessed
23 April 2015).

Vilsack, T. and Clark, C. (2009) *2007 Census of Agriculture*. US Department of Agriculture.
Available at: http://www.agcensus.usda.gov/Publications/2007/Full_Report/usv1.pdf
(accessed 23 April 2015).

Yang, B. (2014) *Setting the Table*. Devour Utah. Available at: http://www.cityweekly.net/utah/
setting-the-table/Content?oid=2562288 (accessed 3 May 2015).

Discussion Questions

1. Identify the types of business networks that have been established through the Utah Farm–Chef–Fork programme (e.g., associative networks, professional networks, etc.).
2. Categorize the type of benefits that have been derived from the business networks that have been established through the Utah Farm–Chef–Fork programme.
3. The case study highlights the benefits achieved through the networking of restaurant chefs with their suppliers. Discuss other potential networks that restaurant chefs can attempt to build, and the benefits that may eventuate from the networks you propose.

References

Adler, P.S. and Kwon, S.W. (2002) Social capital: prospects for a new concept. *Academy of Management Review* 27(1), 17–40. DOI: 10.2307/4134367.

Anderson, A.R. and Miller, C.J. (2003) 'Class matters': human and social capital in the entrepreneurial process. *The Journal of Socio-Economics* 32(1), 17–36. DOI: 10.1016/S1053-5357(03)00009-X.

Atterton, J. (2007) The 'strength of weak ties': social networking by business owners in the Highlands and Islands of Scotland. *Sociologia Ruralis* 47(3), 228–245. DOI: 10.1111/j.1467-9523.2007.00435.x.

BarNir, A. and Smith, K.A. (2002) Interfirm alliances in the small business: the role of social networks. *Journal of Small Business Management* 40(3), 219–232. DOI: 10.1111/1540-627X.00052.

Baym, N.K. (2010). *Personal Connections in the Digital Age*. Polity Press, Cambridge, UK.

Bosma, N., Van Praag, M., Thurik, R. and De Wit, G. (2004) The value of human and social capital investments for the business performance of start-ups. *Small Business Economics* 23(3), 227–236. DOI: 10.1023/B:SBEJ.0000032032.21192.72.

Burt, R.S. (1992) *Structural Holes: The Social Structure of Competition*, Harvard University Press, Cambridge, Massachusetts.

Burt, R.S. (2000) The network structure of social capital. *Research in Organizational Behavior* 22, 345–423. DOI: 10.1016/S0191-3085(00)22009-1.

Davidsson, P. and Honig, B. (2003) The role of social and human capital among nascent entrepreneurs. *Journal of Business Venturing* 18(3), 301–331. DOI: 10.1016/S0883-9026(02)00097-6.

Fischer, E. and Reuber, A.R. (2011) Social interaction via new social media: (how) can interactions on Twitter affect effectual thinking and behaviour? *Journal of Business Venturing* 26(1), 1–18. DOI: 10.1016/j.jbusvent.2010.09.002.

Foley, D. and O'Connor, A.J. (2013) Social capital and the networking practices of indigenous entrepreneurs. *Journal of Small Business Management* 51(2), 276–296. DOI: 10.1111/jsbm.12017.

Granovetter, M.S. (1973) The strength of weak ties. *American Journal of Sociology* 78(6), 1360–1380.

Greve, A. and Salaff, J.W. (2003) Social networks and entrepreneurship. *Entrepreneurship Theory & Practice* 28(2), 1–22. DOI: 10.1111/1540-8520.00029.

Hernández-Carrión, C., Camarero-Izquierdo, C. and Gutiérrez-Cillán, J. (2017) Entrepreneurs' social capital and the economic performance of small businesses: the moderating role of competitive intensity and entrepreneurs' experience. *Strategic Entrepreneurship Journal* 11(1), 61–89. DOI: 10.1002/sej.1228.

Honig, B. (1998) What determines success? Examining the human, financial, and social capital of Jamaican microentrepreneurs. *Journal of Business Venturing* 13(5), 371–394. DOI: 10.1016/S0883-9026(97)00036-0.

Hughes, M., Ireland, R.D. and Morgan, R.E. (2007) Stimulating dynamic value: social capital and business incubation as a pathway to competitive success. *Long Range Planning* 40(2), 154–177. DOI: 10.1016/j.lrp.2007.03.008.

Kristiansen, S. (2004) Social networks and business success: the role of subcultures in an African context. *American Journal of Economics and Sociology* 63(5), 1149–1171. DOI: 10.1111/j.1536-7150.2004.00339.x.

Quinton, S. and Wilson, D. (2016) Tensions and ties in social media networks: towards a model of understanding business relationship development and business performance enhancement through the use of LinkedIn. *Industrial Marketing Management* 54, 15–24. DOI: 10.1016/j.indmarman.2015.12.001.

Smith, C., Smith, J.B. and Shaw, E. (2017) Embracing digital networks: entrepreneurs' social capital online. *Journal of Business Venturing* 32(1), 18–34. DOI: 10.1016/j.jbusvent.2016.10.003.

Stam, W., Arzlanian, S. and Elfring, T. (2014) Social capital of entrepreneurs and small firm performance: a meta-analysis of contextual and methodological moderators. *Journal of Business Venturing* 29(1), 152–173. DOI: 10.1016/j.jbusvent.2013.01.002.

Zhou, L., Wu, W.P. and Luo, X. (2007) Internationalization and the performance of born-global SMEs: the mediating role of social networks. *Journal of International Business Studies* 38(4), 673–690. DOI: 10.1057/palgrave.jibs.8400282.

11 Crisis Management and Entrepreneurial Resilience

Introduction

Prior to the COVID-19 pandemic, travel and tourism contributed US$9.2 trillion to the global economy, representing 10.4% of global GDP, and accounted for 25% of all new jobs created in the world (World Travel and Tourism Council, 2021). The social, economic and health impacts of the pandemic have caused an unprecedented crisis for the travel and tourism sector with an estimated fall in international tourist arrivals of between 70% and 75% over the course of 2020, and an estimated loss of US$2 trillion to global GDP (United Nations World Tourism Organization, 2020). COVID-19 forced a temporary shutdown of the tourism industry and tourism firms. In 2021, the sector began to re-emerge due to easing of travel restrictions and the roll-out of vaccinations; however, the long-term consequences are likely to include profound social and economic shifts that will continue to impact the tourism sector (Sigala, 2020; Peco-Torres *et al.*, 2021).

Evidence shows that tourism and hospitality businesses are particularly exposed to the impacts of crisis events. This unique vulnerability is due to the vast majority of businesses being independently owned small and medium enterprises with significant resource constraints. The industry is also characterized by interdependencies and interacting activities leading to high exposure to disruptions. Moreover, demand for tourism and hospitality products is characterized by high elasticity – often considered as luxuries or non-essentials (Pappas and Brown 2021).

In recent decades, the tourism industry and tourism enterprises have battled through a wide range of crisis events including the oil shocks of the 1970s, military conflict in the Middle East, natural disasters ranging from wildfires and hurricanes to volcanic eruptions and tsunamis, the global financial crisis of 2007–2008, the SARS outbreak of 2003, the Ebola outbreak of 2014, etc,. (Hall, 2010; Pennington-Gray, 2018; Duan *et al.*., 2021). The fact that the industry continues to thrive despite all these challenges is testament to the resilience and

© Rob Hallak and Craig Lee 2023. *Managing Tourism Enterprises: Start-up, Growth and Resilience* (R. Hallak and C. Lee)
DOI: 10.1079/9781789249446.0011

adaptability of tourism businesses and their entrepreneurs. Looking forward, 'resilience' will continue to be the major focus as the effects of climate change, in terms of the increased frequency of natural disasters (Intergovernmental Panel on Climate Change, 2021) as a potential driver of widespread migration (Cattaneo *et al.*, 2019) and as a precursor to future conflict (Koubi, 2019), will continue to present substantial challenges to tourism. Thus, there is a need for tourism businesses to not only be responsive or reactive in the aftermath of disaster events but also to structure themselves in a way that strengthens their preparedness, resilience and agility (Prayag, 2018). This chapter focuses on crisis management in the tourism industry and presents insights into how tourism organizations can build resilience.

Learning Outcomes

After completing this chapter, you should have:

- Understood the concept of crisis management in tourism
- Learnt how tourism businesses can build resilience
- Understood the concept of entrepreneurial resilience
- Identified the factors that can drive resilience.

Crisis Management in Tourism

A crisis can be defined as 'an unpredictable event that threatens important expectancies of stakeholders related to health, safety, environmental and economic issues which can seriously impact an organization's performance and generate negative comments' (Coombs, 2019, p. 3). Crisis has a broad meaning and incorporates both human error and uncontrollable events, such as earthquakes or hurricanes. A crisis can occur at different levels, such as within an organization, within an industry, within a country, or globally. The extreme level of a crisis can be termed a 'disaster' event where the impact on stakeholders is determined to be catastrophic. Certain crisis events can be controlled by an organization – for example, minimizing food poisoning or cross-contamination in a restaurant, in contrast to natural disasters, which are deemed to be outside the control of organizations.

A crisis event can impact on the tourism and hospitality industry in different ways. For example, the Asian financial crisis and the global financial crisis impacted on people's spending power and disposable income. It also affected consumer confidence and willingness to spend on tourism and travel products. Paradoxically, an economic downturn in a destination, while it may impact on outbound tourism, may have a positive impact on inbound tourism if the local currency depreciates in value and the destination becomes better value for money.

Wu *et al.* (2021) in their meta-review of crisis management research in hospitality and tourism identify seven crisis types (Box 11.1).

Box 11.1. Crisis types.

- Political events (e.g, Occupy Central)
- Terrorism (9/11; Bali bombings)
- Health issues and disease outbreaks (Ebola; SARS, COVID)
- Financial crisis (global financial crisis)
- Natural disasters (tsunami, typhoons, wildfires)
- Political events (conflicts, war, refugee exodus)
- Human error (plane crash)

In addition, the tourism industry is susceptible to digital and technological crisis events such as data and security breaches, cyber-attacks, etc. These events have varying impacts on different tourism industry stakeholders including airlines, accommodation, tour operators, food and hospitality. Depending on the crisis and its impacts, the duration of the crisis and time for recovery can also vary significantly.

Tourism crisis management can be defined as 'an ongoing and extensive effort...that organizations put in place in an attempt to understand and prevent crises and to effectively manage those that occur, taking into account in each and every step of their planning and training activities, and the interest of their stakeholders' (Santana, 2004, p. 308). In the case of tourism and hospitality organizations, crisis management depends heavily on the attitudes and intentions of managers to establish crisis management practices (Ghaderi et al., 2022).

Crisis management is conceptualized as a cyclical process that includes (Figure 11.1):

- Risk assessment
- Prevention
- Preparedness
- Response
- Recovery
- Learning. (Pursiainen, 2018)

Risk assessment

Risk assessment provides the framework for identifying and mitigating crisis events, determining their likelihood and possible impacts on the tourism organization. Risk assessment identifies the known risks, but should also point toward risks that are yet unknown, where information is lacking and where further understanding is needed. In this sense, tourism business owners should incorporate risk assessment as integral to disaster management planning. Understanding the risks facing the tourism business, the extent to which these risks can create crisis, is the foundation for preparedness, response, and recovery planning. In assessing risk, tourism business owners should focus on three tasks: identification, analysis and evaluation.

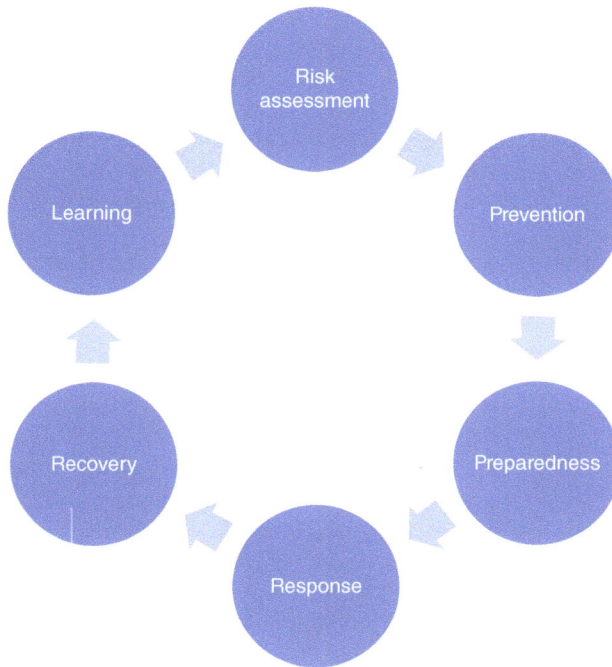

Figure 11.1. Crisis management cycle. (Source: adapted from the crisis management cycle; Pursiainen, 2018, p. 5.)

Risk identification is the screening exercise that lists all possible risks, including risks that the business owner can control or mitigate, and those that are outside the control of the organization. Thus, risk identification is about 'pinpointing, recognizing and describing risks' (Pursiainen, 2018, p. 16). This is where tourism entrepreneurs need to be both pragmatic but also imaginative, recognizing that while some risks are known, as they have occurred in the past, there may be new risks and events that can occur which have not been previously encountered.

Risk analysis: The second stage of risk assessment evaluates the risks identified from the first stage to rate and rank these risks in terms of the likelihood and impact on the tourism organization. Thus, tourism entrepreneurs, having listed the broad range of risks facing their organization, will now need to evaluate each risk to determine how likely this is to occur, and what is the impact on the tourism business if this risk did emerge. This can be presented as a function of: risk = likelihood × impact.

The likelihood of a risk can be estimated based on historical data and time series. Likelihood can then be categorized on a scale (e.g., 1= very low probability, to 10= very high probability), or can be categorized into classes such as 'very low', 'low', 'medium', 'high', 'very high'. The consequence or impacts of the risk can be assessed in terms of the financial or reputational impact on the organization, for example, loss in sales, loss in market share, changes in consumer perceptions. There may also be social and environmental impacts that affect the tourism industry, and by default affect the individual tourism business.

Risk evaluation considers the risks identified and their assessment (impact × likelihood) to determine whether the risks are tolerable. Organizations cannot eliminate all risks; thus, a certain risk appetite is needed to accept the risk and its occurrence, or to mitigate against it. Thus, as risks are highly subjective and contextual, tourism organizations need to establish their own criteria for risk tolerance.

Information from the risk identification and assessment can be presented in a risk matrix; this provides an evaluative tool to determine the risks facing the tourism organization, the likelihood of the event occurring, its impact on the business, the scale and type of impact, as well as the consequences (see Table 11.1).

Prevention

Following the assessment and analysis of risks, tourism business operators need to implement measures and strategies that mitigate, minimize or even eliminate potential risks. It is important to note that not all risks can be eliminated. This may be due to the impact or probability of the risk being considered to be too low or too costly to address. Thus, the business operator may accept the risk and be willing to absorb its consequences.

Underestimating certain risks can in itself pose financial risk to the organization, therefore tourism business operators, as part of their crisis management plans, should outline 'risk treatment', which can include:

- Risk avoidance
- Risk removal
- Diminishing the likelihood of the risk
- Preventing or mitigating the risk's consequences
- Risk sharing (Pursiainen, 2018, p. 44).

Entrepreneurship in its essence involves a degree of risk taking, as does innovation, which entails organizations experimenting with new ideas where success is not guaranteed. Thus, tourism entrepreneurs have a high tolerance for risk and are cognizant of external factors that can impact on their businesses. In regard to risk prevention, the tourism organization needs to look internally to assess what organizational, operational, legal or human resource risks

Table 11.1. Risk matrix table.

Risk item	Likelihood	Impact type	Impact scale	Risk response

Source: author developed.

can be prevented or mitigated. For example, a major risk for food service businesses in the tourism and hospitality sector is food poisoning; this is primarily caused by human error and improper food handling procedures. Proper staff training, supervision, hygiene practices, and health and safety procedures are implemented to diminish the risk of food poisoning from occurring.

As mentioned earlier in this chapter, there are certain risks that cannot be removed, or their removal would be too costly or create other risks (such as financial risks). One risk treatment option is to retain the risk by 'informed decision' (ISO, 2009, p. 18). Looking at the risks on a spectrum of their impact and likelihood identifies the high, low and medium risks for the organization (Figure 11.2).

The approach for risks categorized as 'low risk' would be to retain and absorb them, recognizing these risks may have a negligible impact on the organization. Risks that are considered to be 'high risk', where there is a high probability and impact, cannot be ignored and must be addressed – eliminated, reduced or mitigated. The middle ground of the inverse pyramid are the medium risks, where such 'medium risks' can range on scale from medium-to-low or medium-to-high, etc. Risks categorized in the middle ground can be addressed following the 'as low as reasonably practical' approach (ALARP) (Yoe, 2012; Pursiainen, 2018). Using a grading system to determine the scale of medium-level risks, ALARP categorizes these risks in terms of their tolerability. For example, risks at the higher end of the pyramid – medium- to high-level risks – can be tolerated only if reduction of this risk is deemed to be impractical or the cost to minimize them is highly disproportionate to any improvement gains. Thus the risk is accepted, considering that tolerating the risk is more practical than reducing or eliminating it. Similarly, medium risks that sit lower in the pyramid (i.e. medium-to-low) are tolerable if 'the cost of reduction would exceed the

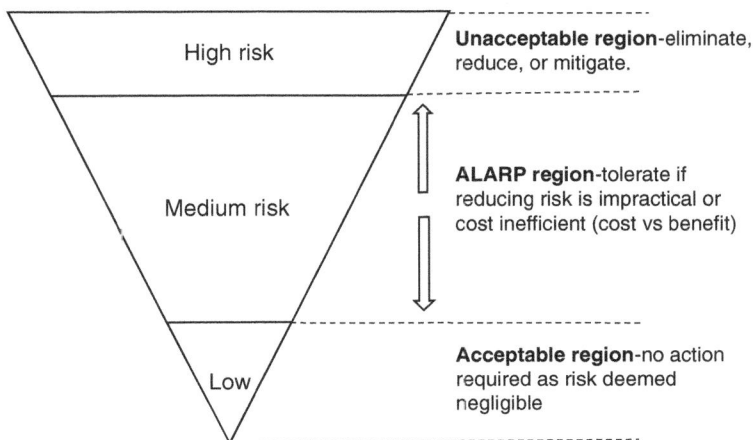

Figure 11.2. Risk pyramid. (Source: developed by authors.)

improvement gained' (Pursiainen, 2018, p. 60). Therefore, ALARP provides a pragmatic and practical approach to dealing with mid-level risks.

Preparedness

Following the identification, assessment, mitigation or prevention of risks, tourism business operators need to be prepared for those crisis events that cannot be prevented, which are often external to the organization and have major consequences for the tourism enterprise. Preparedness relates to anticipation of disruption and the readiness to effectively action a response. Preparedness also ties closely to resilience (discussed later in this chapter).

Preparedness involves planning the roles and responsibilities of key staff in the tourism organization required to action a response to unexpected events. It also involves building organizational capacity and capabilities. Resources need to be available and ready to deploy. A crisis event results in the tourism organization operating in a manner that is radically different to its daily operations and requires the availability of resources and capabilities to adapt to new operations. Staff need to be trained and become part of the tourism business's preparedness strategies. Leadership is also required to build human capital, resilience and staff empowerment. Social networks and social capital enable tourism enterprises to be engaged with and informed of what is happening in the industry, enabling access to information on early-warning signs and potential disruption.

Response

A crisis can be a sudden and pronounced event or it may stem from a gradual build-up of smaller events, also known as a 'creeping' crises (Pursiainen, 2018). Either way, recognition that the tourism enterprise is facing a crisis, or is in a crisis state, is needed in order to articulate and execute a response. Response involves a combination of crisis communication and decision making. Communications can include both internal, within the tourism enterprise to stakeholders, as well as external communication to suppliers, media, industry association, customers, etc. Communication and dissemination of information through effective channels is a critical response to manage the impacts of crises and advance the recovery. Conversely, failing to do so can exacerbate uncertainty and panic, and presents consequences for the tourism organization's trust and credibility (Barbe and Pennington-Gray, 2018). Situational crisis communication theory (Coombs, 2007) emphasizes that in times of crisis an organization needs a strategic and appropriate response to protect its 'reputational assets'. SCCT identifies three components of a crisis communication response:

1. Instructing information – this provides a factual explanation of the crisis to stakeholders.
2. Adjusting information – information that is designed to help stakeholders deal with the crisis.
3. Reputation management – the actual response and remedial actions undertaken by the organization to protects its reputation.

Increasingly, tourism businesses are turning to social media platforms as a channel for real-time crisis communication to guests/customers/general public due to its reach and accessibility (Sigala, 2011). In their study of how hotel businesses used social media to communicate during a crisis, Barbe and Pennington-Gray (2018) found that hotels' communication strategies focused heavily on protecting their own reputation, or to make explicit that they are not to blame or that they may be the victim of the crisis. While a tourism organization may not be directly responsible for a crisis, it is important that the firm plays an active role in communication of important information to external stakeholders, including visitors to a destination. Thus, a bolstering strategy of protecting its own image and reputation needs to be complemented with instructing and adjusting information regarding the event (Barbe and Pennington-Gray, 2018).

In addition to external communication, tourism entrepreneurs need to establish sound lines of communication within the organization for its internal stakeholders. Communication released to the media or external bodies can differ from internal communication, especially if the crisis is caused by human error within the tourism enterprise. Internal communication within a tourism enterprise should recognize the needs of the employees, ensuring that the organizational culture of the tourism enterprise is not compromised or that previously satisfied employees do not lose trust in and commitment to the organization. Failure in internal communication and not providing employees with the information that they need results in employees creating their own 'truth' based on their interpretation of the crisis, which may differ from that of the management (Pursiainen, 2018).

Recovery

The extent to which small and medium enterprises are able to recover from disaster events, and the factors that can support or hinder recovery has gained recent interest (Hall *et al.*, 2016; Stevenson *et al.* 2018). Post-crisis recovery is particularly complex for businesses in the tourism and hospitality industry as the crisis may have caused (1) loss of infrastructure and the inability of tourists to visit the destination where the business operates; (2) travel restrictions and government travel warnings; (3) booking cancellations; (4) inability of the business to restart operations caused by external factors, such as rescue activities or damage repairs; and (5) negative media reports about tourism or a destination that affect a business's ability to attract visitors. The ripple effects of COVID-19 and the variant outbreaks of Delta and Omicron presented significant challenges to the recovery of the tourism sector. For example, despite Australia reopening its borders and stimulating domestic and international travel in

November 2021, growing numbers of COVID cases and hospitalizations forced state governments such as the South Australian government to impose density restrictions on tourism and hospitality businesses. For example, restaurants, pubs and nightclubs were restricted to 25% capacity limits for indoor seated activities, as well as seated-only food and beverage consumption being mandatory. As a consequence of such restrictions many tourism and hospitality venues chose to cease operations, reporting that it was commercially unviable for them to open for business (ABC News, 2021).

In their study of post-disaster business recovery of hospitality businesses following the Canterbury earthquakes in New Zealand (2010–2011), Morrish and Jones (2020) argue that post-disaster recovery is multifaceted and dependent on a multiplicity of factors. Their proposals are given in Box 11.2.

Learning

The final stage of the crisis management process is organizational 'learning', where businesses review and assess their crisis management procedures and utilize this information to innovate and improve preparedness and crisis management capabilities for future events. Organizational learning is described as 'an evolutionary process in which organizations or their components adjust to changing settings by generating and adapting organizational routines' (Ghaderi et al., 2014, pp. 628–629). In this sense, learning can be considered as integral to the whole process rather than an individual component. Learning from crisis events should inform future risk assessment, preparation, prevention and response. Learning should illuminate any shortcomings and failures of the existing system, with the purpose of making improvements to the tourism businesses' ability to manage crisis events moving forward. Thus, crisis management is an iterative process that is informed by learning. In 2020, CPA Australia launched their 'Small Business COVID-19 Recovery Toolkit' that stipulated the need for business's to 'build on lessons' learned from COVID-19 in order to improve future business performance. Tourism business operators should adopt reflective practices to evaluate where improvements can be made across business operations (see Box 11.3).

Box 11.2. Post-disaster recovery. (Source: Morrish and Jones, 2020.)

1. Post-disaster recovery requires a comprehensive understanding of the micro and macro business environment.
2. An entrepreneur's decision to resume business operations is strongly influenced by their level of self-efficacy and ability to engage in effectual reasoning.
3. Entrepreneur action post-disaster requires immediate attention to relocating and securing premises, financial injection to trading operations and being flexible with new business configurations and with competition.
4. Post-disaster entrepreneurial marketing behaviour requires the entrepreneur to engage in speedy opportunity seeking, resource organizing, creating new customer value, and accepting higher levels of risk.

Box 11.3. Reflective practices. (Source: adapted from CPA Australia, 2020.)

- Are there lessons to be learned in how the business adopts new technologies, e.g. can finance processes be automated to free up time and improve efficiency in financial management?
- Can the business implement better streamlined invoicing processes, helping to manage cashflows and timely accounts receivables? This is important for the business operator to stay on top of what money is owed to the business.
- Is this business up to date in regard to IT infrastructure, including cybersecurity?
- Are there lessons learned and improvements necessary for building stronger relationships with customers, suppliers and employees to strengthen social capital and the business ecosystem resilience?
- Are there lessons to be learned in staffing and flexible working arrangements? How can this be improved for future operations?
- Finally, what have we learned from our crisis communication strategies to various stakeholders (employees, customers and potential customers, suppliers etc.)? Are there improvements needed to strengthen our crisis communication approach?

Research looking at how tourism enterprises learn from disasters, and consequently implement changes, actioning the lessons learned, highlights many of the challenges. For example, while larger oganizations such as hotel chains and airlines have well established crisis management plans informed through organizational learning, smaller tourism operators lack the skills or capabilities to develop crisis management plans, or to revise and adapt these plans through organizational learning from crisis events. Thus, organizational learning based on 'double-loop' learning where there is a process for deep and critical reflection, and a process for implementing change based on reflective knowledge, remains a critical challenge for tourism enterprises. These challenges are brought about due to a lack of a 'learning culture', undefined procedures for learning, and a rigid mindset that fails to challenge and 'unlearn' previous beliefs (Ghaderi *et al.*, 2014).

To effectively learn from crisis events, tourism enterprises should follow six main steps:

1. Knowledge acquisition
2. Knowledge diffusion
3. Knowledge utilization
4. Reflection
5. Organizational memory
6. Crisis and organizational change (Ghaderi *et al.*, 2014).

Knowledge acquisition: Tourism enterprises need to constantly monitor any external events, scanning the environment and doing their research to keep up to speed with important information that can affect their business, their risk, and crisis management plans.

Knowledge diffusion: Information and knowledge gathered from research needs to be distributed and shared among stakeholders. These stakeholders include employees of the organization but also suppliers and other businesses in the destination that may be affected by the crisis. Crisis management in tourism destinations requires collaborative knowledge.

Knowledge utilization: Knowledge gained needs to be utilized in planning, preparation and decision making. Knowledge is also critical for formulating business strategies.

Reflection: Reflection involves a critical and honest review of the business practices and decisions. It involves collecting feedback on what has worked and what needs to be improved.

Organizational memory: Tourism enterprises need mechanisms to store important knowledge gained from previous events for future utilization. Without a repository of learning, lessons learned from the past are forgotten and mistakes will be repeated.

Crisis and organizational change: Although crisis events can have significant impacts on tourism enterprises, recovery and learning from crises can provide an opportunity for businesses to implement positive changes to the organization. Disruptions in the tourism industry are to be expected; business can look at these disruptions as opportunities to adapt and innovate.

Entrepreneurial Resilience

The resilience of the tourism enterprise, as well as the resilience of the entrepreneur driving the tourism business, is an important predictor of the business's ability to withstand the shocks of a crisis and its ability to recover and 'bounce back'. From a psychological perspective, resilience has a number of key attributes. It is generally understood to mean an individual's capacity to adapt successfully and continue to function in response to adversity (Southwick et al., 2014). As a trait, resilience may refer to the relatively stable qualities, strengths and characteristics of an individual entrepreneur that allow them to continue to function after a crisis event (Fisher et al., 2016; Kuldas and Foody, 2021). Resilience may also include the processes through which an individual continually adapts to challenges and stressors, as well as how they harness and develop the resources necessary to maintain healthy functioning and wellbeing (Peco-Torres et al., 2021; Southwick et al., 2014). The American Psychological Association also introduces the idea of 'bouncing back' as a key element of resilience (APA, 2021). This leads to the idea that resilience might also involve the capacity to attain a better level of functioning following an adverse event (Joyce et al., 2018). In this sense, the psychological literature has begun to view resilience as existing on a continuum from low (poor ability to 'bounce back' in response to crisis) to very high (ability to 'bounce back better' than previous functioning) (Meichenbaum et al., 2006; Joyce et al., 2018).

'Entrepreneurial resilience' can be broadly defined as the ability of an entrepreneur to overcome challenges or withstand adversity while persisting in the entrepreneurial process (Awotoye and Singh, 2017). Additionally, it has been operationalized as a process of adaptation through which entrepreneurs are able to 'continue to look towards the future despite harsh market conditions, and despite the destabilizing events they must continually face' (Ayala and Manzano, 2014, p. 127). Entrepreneurial resilience is therefore distinct from resilience in the general population, in the sense that entrepreneurs face a range of very-high-impact challenges that are not present for most people (Awotoye and Singh, 2017).

At the level of the individual entrepreneur, traits such as optimism, perseverance, self-belief and a sense of self-efficacy have been associated with entrepreneurial resilience in response to crises (Hmieleski et al., 2015; Doern et al., 2018; Zhao and Wibowo, 2021). Further, the extent to which individual entrepreneurs display a 'venture creation mindset' in response to crises has been positively associated with better post-crisis performance compared to those who sought to simply recover losses (Williams and Shepherd, 2016).

Outcomes of Resilience for Business Operators

Evidence from the tourism and hospitality industry shows strong evidence that the resilience of the entrepreneur has positive outcomes for the tourism organization. A recent systematic review (Walsh and McCollum, 2020) investigating the impact of individual resilience on entrepreneurial success identified four key findings:

1. There exists a positive association between individual resilience and entrepreneurial success.
2. Experience as an entrepreneur may also nurture resilience at an individual level.
3. Internal locus of control is a fundamental element of resilience with regards to business success.
4. Resilience and self-efficacy are mutually reinforcing factors that affect entrepreneurial behaviour (Walsh and McCollum, 2020).

In addition to having a direct effect on performance, resilience is an important driver of creative self-efficacy and innovation (Hallak et al., 2018). For tourism enterprises, the psychological resilience of business owners has a positive effect on building employee resilience, which in turn contributes to strengthening the overall resilience of the enterprises. Resilience also has positive outcomes on the tourism entrepreneur's life satisfaction and wellbeing (Prayag et al. 2020).

How Can Tourism Entrepreneurs Build Their Resilience?

Recognizing the importance of entrepreneurial resilience for crisis management, innovation and tourism enterprise performance, the question remains as to how tourism entrepreneurs can strengthen their entrepreneurial and organizational resilience. Evidence suggests resilience is driven by psychological traits, as well as processes and resources. Psychological traits, including locus of control (the extent to which an individual believes they can control their surrounding environment), self-efficacy and willingness to learn from failures, can all contribute towards an entrepreneurial resilience (Zhao and Wibowo, 2021). Other factors include the entrepreneur's prior experience, their ability to focus on the positive, ability to manage stress and negative emotions, willingness to ask for help, persistence and determination; all are positively associated with building resilience (Doern, 2016, p. 295).

Tourism entrepreneurs can also build their resilience by focusing on human capital and social capital. Human capital, which includes education, training and experience, builds capabilities to manage and respond to crisis events. Professional development in areas such as ICT, customer service skills, digital marketing, negotiating and continuity planning are also vital to building resilience (Lindsay-Smith *et al.*, 2021). Entrepreneurs tend to 'learn by doing', and so their experiences of dealing with adverse events is a valuable way in which resilience is increased; experience of success and experience of failure both seem relevant in helping foster resilience (Duchek, 2018).

The tourism entrepreneur's social networks and professional and personal connections foster social capital, which in turn strengthens resilience. The interaction between the entrepreneur and their environment provides fertile ground for the development of resilience (Fisher *et al.*, 2016). Resilient entrepreneurs are known to draw on social capital in order to access information, support and resources in the aftermath of crisis events (Grube and Storr, 2018).

Conclusion

This chapter provided an overview of crisis management processes for tourism enterprises. It presented and described a system for crisis management that includes:

- Risk assessment
- Prevention
- Preparedness
- Response
- Recovery
- Learning.

Crisis management is a fluid and adaptive process where entrepreneurs need to learn from events, and implement this learning into adapting new processes. Essentially, making the same mistakes as before needs to be avoided. Organizational learning involves six main steps:

1. Knowledge acquisition
2. Knowledge diffusion
3. Knowledge utilization
4. Reflection
5. Organizational memory
6. Crisis and organizational change (Ghaderi *et al.*, 2014).

This chapter also introduced and discussed the concept of entrepreneurial resilience as a mechanism to manage, respond and bounce back from crises.

Entrepreneurial resilience is a catalyst for organizational resilience, and has positive outcomes on the business's recovery, as well as innovation and overall performance. The chapter emphasized the importance of human and social capital in helping to build resilience among tourism entrepreneurs.

Discussion Questions

1. Identify three recent (past 5 years) events that had a major impact on the tourism industry.
2. What was the impact on the tourism organizations as a result of these crisis events?
3. How did tourism organizations respond to the crisis and what was their recovery?
4. What are the ways in which entrepreneurs in tourism can build their entrepreneurial resilience?

CABI case study: How the Singapore Tourism Board confronted the 2002–2003 SARS crisis.

An interesting flashback to the first COVID outbreak and how it was successfully managed in Singapore, with an emphasis on the role of the tourist authorities.

Author: Joan Henderson

Origin: Adapted from Chapter 14 – International tourism and infectious diseases: managing the SARS crisis in Singapore. In: Laws, E., Prideaux, B. and Chon, K. (eds) *Crisis Management in Tourism*. CAB International, Wallingford, UK, pp. 186–199.

© CAB International 2007

Background and Context

SARS is a type of contagious pneumonia which first appeared in the southern Chinese province of Guandong in late 2002, subsequently infiltrating other parts of Asia and beyond. Research is continuing into the coronavirus, which has been found to have a mortality rate of 14–15%, and lack of knowledge about it originally intensified public dread. There is no known cure and a vaccine has still to be developed, making it imperative to identify and isolate victims. A total of 8096 cases in 29 countries and 774 deaths had been recorded by July 2003 when the epidemic was over. Most of these were in Asia and especially mainland China. The first victims in Singapore were diagnosed in February, numbers rising steadily thereafter to reach final figures of 238 cases and 33 fatalities. There were later incidences, provoking worries about a second wave of infection and scientific agreement that it might never be totally eradicated. Several new cases were reported in China in mid-2004, raising concerns that SARS could again cross borders, but fortunately these cases were contained.

   A deadly disease about which little was understood and the unprecedented speed of its advance became a serious matter worldwide, generating extensive media publicity. There

Continued

CABI case study: continued.

was a tendency amongst some reporters to dramatize events and overstate risks, given the comparatively small percentage of those who succumbed, provoking unnecessary agitation. The resulting crisis was multidimensional and reverberated through economies and societies, but was exceptionally acute for the international tourism industries of those states most severely hit. The virus was carried abroad by travellers, and air transport came to be perceived as particularly dangerous, together with visits to any afflicted areas, prompting a sharp downturn in demand.

The Evolution of the SARS Crisis in Singapore

The stages of the SARS crisis

SARS, as both a public health and a tourism crisis, arrived and unfolded at great speed with little warning and few detectable signals. Preparation and prevention by the tourism industry were not realistic options so crisis management essentially began at containment and damage limitation as described here, where the conventional pre-crisis stages have been compressed into a single onset of crisis period. The evolution of the crisis was closely tied to the progress of the epidemic which informed responses, optimism rising as the daily number of SARS cases fell and travel warnings being revised and ultimately revoked. Learning was ongoing and formed a series of feedback loops into the system of decision making.

Another striking feature of the SARS crisis was its scope and the numerous parties from which action was demanded, extending from managers and staff of single enterprises to intergovernmental organizations.

Stages 1 and 2: The onset of crisis, containment and damage limitation

The medical significance of SARS and its ramifications were not immediately obvious and the crisis for tourism commenced when this became apparent and there was no chance of evasion. Stage 1 was very brief and the crisis quickly moved to stage 2. Decisions on Singapore's response were based on information from a number of sources including government and non-government agencies.

The WHO distributed information about SARS and details of countries with local transmission, including Singapore, warning against visits and proposing health screening for departing international passengers. Instructions were prepared about how to handle possible infected air and surface transport passengers and those with whom they had come into contact when in transit. The thorough disinfection of aircraft and other vehicles was also advised.

Intergovernmental meetings of Asian tourism officials were held on a bilateral and multilateral basis in parallel with those attended by senior politicians and health ministers. The need for cooperation and coordination was accepted with regard to sharing data on SARS victims and their movements, and health checks on international departures, especially by air. Progress was made towards achieving these goals by the Association of South East Asian Nations (ASEAN), for example, although it was observed that an absence of

Continued

CABI case study: continued.

resources could restrict implementation for some members. Officials from the APEC (Asia Pacific Economic Cooperation) grouping drew up an action plan which also sought to standardize approaches to the health screening of air passengers and information exchange.

Regional trade organizations expressed their concerns and support for the industry. The Pacific Asia Travel Association (PATA) claimed that it was endeavouring to educate the travel trade through its SARS information kit and help the public make properly informed choices. Press releases reminded audiences that the WHO had not blamed the tourism industry for the diffusion of SARS and that it was generally safe to visit the region. PATA representatives met with others from the APEC Tourism Working Group and World Travel and Tourism Council (WTTC), calling for the wider circulation of data and asserting the importance of keeping the media fully up to date. In addition, research studies into the longer-term impact of SARS were conducted.

While the analysis here focuses on SARS as a disaster for states such as Singapore, where it was spreading amongst the community, its relationship with inbound and outbound tourist flows could not be ignored by other governments and tourism industries. It was thus a crisis for generating markets and authorities of destinations where those who might be carriers of the virus were arriving, albeit one of lesser magnitude. Nations such as Australia, the USA and the UK cautioned their nationals about non-essential travel to places on the WHO list, while many tour operators, travel agents and MICE (Meetings, Incentives, Conferences and Exhibitions) organizers were reluctant to send customers there. Several international companies and organizations prohibited employees from journeying to SARS-affected locations and some insurance companies withdrew their cover. More stringent health checks on inbound passengers were also introduced in certain instances in a bid to avert the importation of the virus.

In the relatively small city state of Singapore, where there is not the same distinction between national and local institutions found elsewhere, the STB was one of the major official actors. Representing both government and the industry, it sought to maintain Singapore's credibility as a tourist destination by the provision of up-to-date information for markets and the industry at home and abroad. Favourable news stories of tourists continuing to visit and enjoying their stay were given prominence. However, there was an interruption in conventional marketing due to a sense that doubts about the means by which SARS was transmitted and negative global publicity would probably render this ineffective.

A Director of Emergency Planning and a 'Cool Team' task force were appointed, and steps were taken to safeguard the health of visitors and minimize the chances of infection. Practical schemes were initiated such as the COOL Singapore programme, which granted COOL awards to hotels, shops and other sites that complied with eight-point certification criteria. Tools employed were mass temperature taking of staff and visitors, fever being an easily observable symptom of the virus, and regular cleaning and disinfection of premises, with machinery for contact tracing should a SARS suspect be discovered to have visited a particular location. Ministry of Health instructions and complementary STB guidelines were also drawn up and adhered to.

The Board was supported in its efforts by the government which pledged to aid the tourism industry, unveiling a S$230- (US$131) million relief package to tide the hardest hit businesses over the crisis. A major portion was allocated to hotels and constituted various forms of tax relief, bridging loans for small and medium enterprises and training grants. The first priority of government was, nevertheless, to bring SARS under control, and nearly every department was expected to contribute. Pursuit of this aim led to constant health screening and schemes to enhance hygiene, which impacted on the lives of both visitors to Singapore

Continued

CABI case study: continued.

and residents. The regime meant that all air and sea international travellers were scanned thermally by machines capable of detecting those with a high temperature. Singapore is connected to Malaysia by a causeway, and those crossing by public transport or on foot were also scanned, with motorists subject to random testing with ear thermometers.

Sectoral agencies such as the Singapore Hotel Association (SHA), Association of Singapore Attractions (ASA) and National Association of Travel Agents of Singapore (NATAS) were a forum for discussion and voiced industry forebodings. Their members and other businesses adopted policies of cost savings (especially regarding labour), reductions in capacity and lobbying for official aid. Prices were cut to stimulate demand and attempts made to retain the goodwill of customers choosing to cancel or postpone bookings. Much marketing was directed at Singaporeans in a move to enlarge the domestic market, formerly of little commercial interest. Infection control meant that great stress was placed on hygiene standards, with continuous cleaning, and staff and customer temperature checks.

Stage 3: Resolution and recovery

Singapore was eventually declared free of local transmission of SARS by the WHO at the end of May, an occasion which was a clearly defined turning point and allowed the crisis to enter recovery and resolution mode. Delisting by the WHO was a cause of great rejoicing, celebrated by the Singapore industry in a party which was publicized around the world. The focus of national and international parties then shifted from defensive and reactive to offensive and proactive tactics, especially those of intensive advertising and special promotions which had an underlying theme of reassurance.

A statement issued by the WTO at an assembly devoted to recovery argued that it was safe to resume travel in Asia, except to Beijing, which was still under a WHO advisory, and a marketing plan for Asia and the Pacific region was launched. PATA similarly urged a resumption of travel and revealed its global 'welcome back' campaign entitled Project Phoenix. Goals were to restore confidence and business and establish a common Asian voice, making use of the power of the media to deliver consistent messages containing balanced information. While displaying good intentions, some industry observers were sceptical about the efficacy of such proposals given the comparatively small size of their budgets, short-term timeframe, widespread geographical coverage and competitive rivalries. Investment by national tourism organizations in the PATA scheme indicates limits to their commitment, with US$250,000 raised by July compared with US$50 million and US$115 million spent by Hong Kong and Singapore, respectively, on independent marketing.

The STB's own 'global recovery programme' comprised testimonial advertising, worldwide marketing, the promotion of packages devised jointly with industry, and the hosting of travel trade and media personnel. A parallel project administered by the Civil Aviation Authority of Singapore disbursed financial inducements totalling S$10 (US$5.7) million amongst airlines, which raised their passenger volumes into Singapore. Renewed and aggressive marketing by sectoral bodies and individual companies was also conducted, with several examples of collaboration. The Singapore Association of Convention and Exhibition Organizers and Suppliers (SACEOS) commenced a S$10.2 (US$5.7) million public relations and promotion exercise, and the SHA and ASA partnered Singapore Airlines in selling 'Fabulous Offers' to overseas markets. Domestic tourists were not forgotten, with special hotel packages on sale during the school holiday period.

Continued

CABI case study: continued.

Improvements in international arrivals from June onwards indicated progress towards recovery; this was further evidenced by rising hotel occupancies, the restoration of cancelled airline services and attendances at attractions. Partial resolution was thus achieved, although fears of a return of SARS lingered, accompanied by an acknowledgement that the tourism industry was very much at its mercy. However, there was also a feeling that health authorities were strongly positioned to contain any more outbreaks after the measures conceived and executed during the first which were said to have been acclaimed worldwide.

The tourism industry also professed to have learnt from SARS. While learning is continuous throughout a crisis, resolution permits reflection and creates opportunities to make longer-term changes with a view to being more ready and equipped for eventualities ahead. At the WTO meeting referred to above, participants vowed to unite in deriving lessons from SARS, be better prepared in the future and work closely with the media in an honest and transparent manner. In Singapore, the STB established a new Emergency Planning Division headed by the Director of Emergency Planning for SARS. Hoteliers spoke of SARS as an educational experience, leading to amendments to existing crisis management plans or the creation of new ones.

Finally, the challenges of 2003 disclosed the benefits of close relationships and the construction of alliances within and between the government and private sectors. The 'Cool Team' task force was accordingly transformed into a Tourism Consultative Council (TCC) of 25 members from 11 associations, four government agencies and seven individuals from the tourism and non-tourism industries elected by the STB. The TCC is intended to yield intelligence about and insights into critical issues facing the industry and assist in the pursuit of new strategic directions.

Implications of SARS

Locations such as China, Hong Kong, Taiwan and Vietnam faced falls of over 50% in inbound tourism in the early months of 2003, and heavy damage to Canadian tourism was predicted due to the presence of the virus in Toronto. Table 11.2 depicts the negative growth in Singapore's tourist arrivals from March onwards, with a drop of over 70% in May compared with the previous year. There were signs of recovery as time passed, but 2003 saw an annual reduction of 19.1%. Major generators performed differently, and the Japanese market contracted by 40% in contrast to that of Indonesia which had a 3.7% drop, raising interesting questions about the reasons for such variations. However, the decline in the first quarter was sudden and extreme across all origin countries, with repercussions for every component of the industry.

The International Labour Organization anticipated that countries experiencing an epidemic could lose a third of their travel and tourism employment, while those on the perimeter might register losses of 15%.

Hotel occupancies demonstrate the extent of the problem, with five-star hotels in Singapore having average occupancies of 15% in April 2003. Numbers were worse for some properties where rates below 10% persisted until June. Singapore's south-east Asian neighbours were not exempt, and occupancies in Bangkok hotels were eroded by 20–30% in April, even though Thailand had only nine SARS cases and two deaths. The costs of lost business were heavy and estimated to be in excess of S$23 (US$13) million for Singapore's hoteliers. Airlines serving Singapore were also forced to rationalize and abandon flights, and attendance at attractions plummeted, alongside retail spending. The pattern of an industry

Continued

CABI case study: continued.

Table 11.2. Monthly international arrivals in Singapre, 2002 and 2003.

Month	2002	2003	Year-on-year change (%)
January	596,069	641,159	+7.6
February	597,415	612,897	+2.6
March	654,710	559,289	−4.6
April	621,957	203,282	−67.3
May	605,532	177,543	−70.7
June	601,599	315,878	−47.5
July	679,198	540,373	−20.4
August	671,154	601,819	−10.3
September	597,115	556,263	−6.8
October	638,237	586,016	−8.2
November	588,141	635,213	+8.0
December	709,143	690.671	−2.6
Total	6,560,270	6,120,493	−19.0

Source: Singapore Tourism Board Monthly Factsheets, 2002–2003.

descending into crisis was repeated elsewhere, notably in Hong Kong, which was to record 5327 SARS cases and 299 deaths.

Conclusions

The outbreak of SARS in Singapore and its repercussions reveals international tourism's vulnerability to the actual and perceived dangers of infectious disease. A study of the case suggests some conformity to conventional crisis dynamics, although the opening phase was of limited duration and precluded preventive action with an immediate onset of crisis representing the first stage. The pace of the crisis was then dictated by the unfolding of the epidemic which was beyond the authority of tourism industry managers, such a loss of control imposing significant constraints which do not always prevail in situations of crisis.

Stage 2 of containment and damage limitation within Singapore sought to restrain the havoc being wreaked by the virus. The third and final stage of resolution and recovery comprised programmes centred on promotional campaigns. There was also time for review and the application of knowledge gained, reforms being introduced to ensure preparedness for a return of SARS or a similar virus. Communication was a vital function throughout, with many different audiences to address. The messages conveyed changed as the crisis evolved, but the circulation of accurate information and management of fear were core objectives.

It is clear that virulent infections do not respect territorial boundaries, and SARS became an international as well as a national problem, warranting official and commercial involvement. International actions were also determined by the phase of the crisis and the interests and agendas of the stakeholders, but tended to mirror those undertaken in the national sphere. While aspects of preferred solutions and the characteristics of the crisis demanded a coordinated approach, this may have been frustrated by the multiplicity of agents with a part to play and some conflicts of interest.

Continued

CABI case study: continued.

Nevertheless, it would seem that appreciation of the risks to tourism from known and undiscovered viruses have been heightened in Singapore and more generally, with a greater willingness to engage in cooperation at a domestic and transnational level. Detection of warning signals of any future threats is likely to occur earlier than in 2003 because of the learning which accompanied the experience of the SARS crisis that year. This is suggested by the prompt recognition of the potential damage to tourism posed by avian influenza and the second Chinese outbreak of SARS in 2004, already made reference to, and the rapid assumption of a state of alert which could be seen as the adoption of a pre-crisis position.

References

Asia Pacific Economic Cooperation (2003) *Tourism Risk Management for the Asia Pacific Region*. APEC International Centre for Sustainable Tourism, Griffith University, Queensland Australia.

Aziz, H. (1995) Understanding attacks on tourists in Egypt. *Tourism Management* 16, 91–95.

Barton, L. (1994) Crisis management: preparing for and managing disasters. *Cornell Hotel and Restaurant Association Quarterly*, April, pp. 59–65.

Blake, A. and Sinclair, T. (2003) Tourism crisis management: UK response to September 11. *Annals of Tourism Research* 30, 813–832.

Bland, M. (1998) *Communicating Out of a Crisis*. Macmillan Business, Basingstoke, UK.

Canadian Tourism Commission (2003) *SARS: The Potential Impact on the Domestic and Selected International Markets to Canada*. Executive Summary, Canadian Tourism Commission, Ottowa.

Caribbean Tourist Organization (2003) Tourism sector responsiveness to health crises. Caribbean Tourist Organisation. Available at: http://www.onecaribbean.org (accessed 20 December 2003).

Carter, S. (1998) Tourists' and travellers' social construction of Africa and Asia as risky locations. *Tourism Management* 19, 349–358.

Cassedy, K. (1991) *Crisis Management Planning in the Travel and Tourism Industry: A Study of Three Destination Cases and a Crisis Management Planning Manual*. Pacific Asia Travel Association, San Francisco, California.

Centres for Disease Control and Prevention (2003) Vessel Sanitation Program. CDC website. Available at: http://www.cdc.gov (accessed 20 December 2003).

Chien, G. and Law, R. (2003) The impact of severe acute respiratory syndrome on hotels: a case study of Hong Kong. *International Journal of Hospitality Management* 22, 327–332.

Clift, S. and Page, S.J. (eds) (1996) *Health and the International Tourist*. Routledge, London.

de Sausmarez, N. (2003) Malaysia's response to the Asian financial crisis: implications for tourism and sectoral crisis management. *Journal of Travel and Tourism Marketing* 15, 217–231.

Drabek, T.E. (1995) Disaster responses within the tourism industry. *International Journal of Mass Emergencies and Disasters* 13, 7–23.

Durocher, J. (1994) Recovery marketing: what to do after a natural disaster. *Cornell Hotel and Restaurant Association Quarterly*, April, pp. 66–71.

Continued

CABI case study: continued.

Faulkner, B. (2001) Towards a framework for tourism disaster management. *Tourism Management* 22, 135–147.

Faulkner, B. and Vikulov, S. (2001) Katherine, washed out one day, back on track the next: a post-mortem on a tourism disaster. *Tourism Management* 22, 331–344.

Fink, S. (1986) *Crisis Management*. American Association of Management, New York.

Gonzalez-Herrero, A. and Pratt, C.B. (1998) Marketing crises in tourism: communication strategies in the USA and Spain. *Public Relations Review* 24, 83–97.

Henderson, J.C. (2003a) Communicating in a crisis: flight 006. *Tourism Management* 24, 279–287.

Henderson, J.C. (2003b) Managing a health-related crisis: SARS in Singapore. *Journal of Vacation Marketing* 10, 67–78.

Huang, J.H. and Min, J.C. (2002) Earthquake devastation and recovery in tourism: the Taiwan case. *Tourism Management* 23, 145–154.

International Labour Organization (2003) Press release, 14 May.

Lepp, A. and Gibson, H. (2003) Tourist roles, perceived risk and international tourism. *Annals of Tourism Research* 30, 606–624.

National Center for Biotechnology Information (2003). Welcome to NCBI. National Library of Medicine. Available at: http://www.ncbi.nlm.nih.gov (accessed 20 December 2003).

Ng, X.Y. (2004) Crisis management in the travel industry: the impact and management of SARS in the Singapore hotel industry. Unpublished dissertation, Nanyang Technological University, Singapore.

Pacific Asia Travel Association (2003) People should be travelling: World Health Organization. Press Release, 2 May.

Pine, R. and McKercher, B. (2004) The impact of SARS on Hong Kong's tourism industry. *International Journal of Contemporary Hospitality Management* 16, 139–143.

Pizam, A. (2002) Tourism and terrorism. *International Journal of Hospitality Management* 21, 1–3.

Pottorff, S.M. and Neal, D.M. (1994) Marketing implications for post-disaster tourism destinations. *Journal of Travel and Tourism Marketing* 3, 115–122.

Prideaux, B. (1999) Tourism perspectives of the Asian financial crisis: lessons for the future. *Current Issues in Tourism* 2, 279–293.

Prideaux, B. (2003) The need to use disaster planning frameworks to respond to major tourism disasters: analysis of Australia's response to tourism disasters in 2001. Journal *of Travel and Tourism Marketing* 15, 281–298.

Prideaux, B., Laws, E. and Faulkner, B. (2003) Events in Indonesia: exploring the limits to formal tourism trends forecasting methods in complex crisis situations. *Tourism Management* 24, 475–487.

Ray, S. (1999) *Strategic Communication in Crisis Management: Lessons from the Airline Industry*. Quorum Books, Westport, Connecticut.

Regester, M. and Larkin, J. (1998) *Risk Issues and Crisis Management: A Casebook of Best Practice*. Kogan Page, London.

Richter, L.K. (1992) Political instability and tourism in Third World countries. In: Harrison, D. (ed.) *Tourism and the Less Developed Countries*. Belhaven Press, London, pp. 35–46.

Richter, L.K. and Waugh, W.L. (1986) Terrorism and tourism as logical companions. *Tourism Management* 7, 230–238.

Ritchie, B.W. (2004) Chaos, crises and disasters: a strategic approach to crisis management in the tourism industry. *Tourism Management* 25, 669–683.

Continued

CABI case study: continued.

Rudkin, B. and Hall, C.M. (1996) Off the beaten track: the health implications of the development of special interest tourism activities in South East Asia and the South Pacific. In: Clift, S. and Page S.J. (eds) *Health and the International Tourist*. Routledge, London, pp. 89–107.

Santana, G. (2003) Crisis management and tourism: beyond the rhetoric. *Journal of Travel and Tourism Marketing* 15, 299–321.

Scott, R. (1988) Managing a crisis in tourism: a case study of Fiji. *Travel and Tourism Analyst* 6, 57–71.

Sharpley, R., Sharpley, J. and Adams, J. (1996) Travel advice or trade embargo? The impacts and implications of official travel advice. *Tourism Management* 17, 1–7.

Singapore Hotel Association (2003) *Hotelierclick* 2(7).

Singapore Ministry of Health (2003) Press releases, March–June. Available at: http://app. moh.gov.sg (accessed 6 June 2003).

Singapore Tourism Board (2003a) Media release, 29 April.

Singapore Tourism Board (2003b) Media release, 24 April.

Singapore Tourism Board (2003c) Media release, 4 June.

Sonmez, S.F., Apostolopoulos, Y. and Tarlow, P. (1999) Tourism in crisis: managing the effects of terrorism. *Journal of Travel Research* 38, 13–18.

The Straits Times (2003a) It's not looking good. *The Straits Times*, 8 April.

The Straits Times (2003b) Drive to get Changi Airport humming again. *The Straits Times*, 3 June.

The Straits Times (2003c) Calling for Singaporeans. *The Straits Times*, 14 May.

The Straits Times (2003d) Singapore's approach earns foreigners' trust. *The Straits Times*, 25 April.

The Straits Times (2003e) SARS-free, now to fine-tune crisis-handling. The Straits Times, 1 June.

ten Berg, D. (1990) *The First 24 Hours: A Comprehensive Guide to Successful Crisis Communications*. Basil Blackwell, Oxford UK.

Travel Business Analyst (2003) July.

TTG Daily News (2003) 10 July.

Turner, B.A. (1976) The organizational and inter-organizational development of disasters. *Administrative Science Quarterly* 21, 378–397.

World Health Organization (2002) *International Travel and Health*. WHO Geneva Switzerland.

World Health Organization (2003) WHO SARS website. Available at: http://www.who.int/csr/ sars (accessed 6 June 2003).

World Tourism Organization (1991) Recommended measures for tourism safety. WHO. Available at: http://www.world-tourism.org (accessed 20 December 2003).

World Tourism Organization (1996) *Tourist Safety and Security: Practical Measures for Destinations*. WHO, Madrid.

World Tourism Organization (1998) *Handbook on Natural Disaster Reduction in Tourist Areas*. WHO, Madrid.

World Tourism Organization (2002) *Tourism after 11 September 2001: Analysis, Remedial Actions and Prospects*. WHO, Madrid.

World Tourism Organization (2003) *Findings of the WTO Secretariat Survey on the Effects and Management of the SARS Epidemic in the Field of Tourism*. Available at: http:// www.unwto.org (accessed 4 August 2003).

World Travel and Tourism Council (2003) *SARS Reports on China, Hong Kong, Singapore and Vietnam*. Available at: http://www.wttc.org (accessed 13 June 2003).

References

ABC News (2021) COVID-19 restrictions hit businesses hard ahead of New Year's Eve as SA battles spread of Omicron. Available at: https://www.abc.net.au/news/2021-12-27/business-sa-compensation-call-amid-omicron-covid-restrictions/100726648

APA (2021) Building your resilience. Available at: https://www.apa.org/topics/resilience (accessed 20 November 2022).

Awotoye, Y. and Singh, R. (2017) Entrepreneurial resilience, high impact challenges, and firm performance. *Journal of Management Policy and Practice* 18(2), 28–37.

Ayala, J.C. and Manzano, G. (2014) The resilience of the entrepreneur. Influence on the success of the business: a longitudinal analysis. *Journal of Economic Psychology* 42, 126–135.

Barbe, D. and Pennington-Gray, L. (2018) Using situational crisis communication theory to understand Orlando Hotels: Twitter response to three crises in the summer of 2016. *Journal of Hospitality and Tourism Insights* 1(3) 258–275.

Bulmash, B. (2016) Entrepreneurial resilience: locus of control and well-being of entrepreneurs. *Journal of Entrepreneurship and Organization Management* 5(1). Available at: https://doi.org/10.4172/2169-026X.1000171 (accessed 20 November 2022).

Cattaneo, C., Beine, M., Frohlich, C., Kniveton, D., Martinez-Zarzoso, I. *et al.* (2019) Human migration in the era of climate change. *Review of Environmental Economics and Policy* 13(2), 189–206.

Coombes, W.T. (2007) Protecting organization reputations during a crisis: the development and application of situational crisis communication theory. *Corporate Reputation Review* 10(3), 163–176.

Coombes, W.T. (2019) *Ongoing Crisis Communication* (5th edn). Sage Publications Inc., Thousand Oaks, California.

CPA Australia (2020) Small business COVID-19 recovery toolkit. Available at: https://www.cpaaustralia.com.au (accessed 20 November 2022).

Crick, J. and Crick, D. (2016) Developing entrepreneurial resilience in the UK tourism sector. *Strategic Change: Briefings in Entrepreneurial Finance* 25, 315–325.

Doern, R. (2016) Entrepreneurship and crisis management: the experiences of small businesses during the London 2011 riots. *International Small Business Journal* 34(3), 276–302.

Doern, R., Williams, N. and Vorley, T. (2018) Special issue on entrepreneurship and crises: Business as usual? An introduction and review of the literature. *Entrepreneurship & Regional Development* 31(5–6), 400–412. Available at: https://doi.org/10.1080/08985626.2018.1541590 (accessed 20 November 2022).

Duan, J., Xie, C. and Morrison, A. (2021) Tourism crises and impacts on destinations: A systematic review of the tourism and hospitality literature. *Journal of Hospitality & Tourism Research* 20(5), 1–29. https://doi.org/DOI: 10.1177/1096348021994194

Duchek, S. (2018) Entrepreneurial resilience: a biographical analysis of successful entrepreneurs. *International Entrepreneurship and Management Journal* 14, 429–455.

Fisher, R., Maritz, A. and Lobo, A. (2016) Does individual resilience influence entrepreneurial success. *Academy of Entrepreneurship Journal* 22(2), 39–53.

Ghaderi, Z., King, B. and Hall, C.M. (2022) Crisis preparedness of hospitality managers: evidence from Malaysia. *Journal of Hospitality and Tourism Insights* 5(2), 292–310. DOI: 10.1108/JHTI-10-2020-0199.

Ghaderi, Z., Som, A.P.M. and Wang, J. (2014) Organizational learning in tourism crisis management: an experience from Malaysia. *Journal of Travel and Tourism Marketing* 31(5), 627–648.

Grube, L. and Storr, V. (2018) Embedded entrepreneurs and post-disaster community recovery. *Entrepreneurship & Regional Development* 30(7), 800–821.

Hall, C. (2010) Crisis events in tourism: subjects of crisis in tourism. *Current Issues in Tourism* 13(5), 401–417.

Hall, C.M., Malinen, S., Vosslamber, R. and Wordsworth, R. (2016) Introduction: the business, organisational and destination impacts of natural disasters – the Christchurch earthquakes 2010–2011. In: C.M. Hall, S. Malinen, R. Vosslamber, and R.Wordsworth (eds.) *Business and Post-disaster Management: Business, Organisational and Consumer Resilience and the Christchurch Earthquakes*. Routledge, London & New York, pp. 3–20.

Hallak, R., Assaker, G., O'Connor, P. and Lee, C. (2018) Firm performance in the upscale restaurant sector: the effects of resilience, creative self-efficacy, innovation and industry experience. *Journal of Retailing and Consumer Services* 40, 229–240.

Hmieleski, K., Carr, J. and Baron, R. (2015) Integrating discovery and creation perspectives of entrepreneurial action: the relative roles of founding CEO human capital, social capital, and psychological capital in contexts of risk versus uncertainty. *Strategic Entrepreneurship Journal* 94(4), 289–312.

Intergovernmental Panel on Climate Change (2021) Climate change widespread, rapid, and intensifying. Available at: https://www.ipcc.ch/2021/08/09/ar6-wg1-20210809-pr/ (accessed 21 November 2022).

ISO (2009) *Risk Management – Principles and Guidelines*. ISO 31000.

Joyce, S., Shand, F., Tighe, J., Laurent, S., Bryant, R. and Harvey, S. (2018) Road to resilience: a systematic review and meta-analysis of resilience training programmes and interventions. *BMJ Open* 8. Available at: https://doi.org/doi:10.1136/bmjopen-2017-017858.

Koubi, V. (2019) Climate change and conflict. *Annual Review of Political Science* 22, 343–360.

Kuldas, S. and Foody, M. (2021) Neither resiliency-trait nor resilience-state: transactional resiliency. *Youth & Society*. Available at: https://doi.org/10.1177/0044118X211029309 (accessed 21 November 2022).

Lindsay-Smith, G., Pyke, J., Nguyen, V., Shaikh, S., Gamage, A. and de Lacy, T. (2021) *Building the Resilience of Tourism Destinations to Disasters: the 2020 Victorian Bushfires and COVID-19 Pandemic*. Victoria University. Available at: https://www.vu.edu.au/sites/default/files/tourism-resilience-report.pdf> (accessed 21 November 2022).

Meichenbaum, D., Calhoun, L.G. and Tedeschi, R.G. (2006) *Handbook of Posttraumatic Growth: Research and Practice*. Lawrence Erlbaum Mahwah, New Jersey.

Morrish S.C. and Jones, R. (2020) Post-disaster business recovery: an entrepreneurial marketing perspective. *Journal of Business Research* 113, 83–92.

Pappas, N. and Brown, A.E. (2021) Entrepreneurial decisions in tourism and hospitality during crisis. *Management Decision* 59(5), 1025–1042.

Peco-Torres, F., Polo-Pena, A. and Frías-Jamilena, D. (2021) The effect of COVID-19 on tourists' intention to resume hotel consumption: the role of resilience. *International Journal of Hospitality Management* 99(103075).

Pennington-Gray, L. (2018) Reflections to move forward: where destination crisis management research needs to go. *Tourism Management Perspectives* 25, 136–139.

Prayag, G. (2018) Symbiotic relationship or not? Understanding resilience and crisis management in tourism. *Tourism Management Perspectives* 25, 133–135.

Prayag, G. (2020) Time for reset? Covid-19 and tourism resilience. *Tourism Review International* 24(2–3), 179–184.

Pursiainen, C. (2018) *The Crisis Management Cycle*. Routledge, Oxford, UK.

Rotter, J. (1966) Generalized expectancies for internal versus external control of reinforcement. *Psychological Monographs* 80, 1–28.

Santana, G. (2004) Crisis management and tourism. *Journal of Travel & Tourism Marketing* 15(4), 299–321. DOI:10.1300/J073v15n04_05.

Sigala, M. (2011) Social media and crisis management in tourism: applications and implications for research. *Information Technology & Tourism* 13(4), 269–283.

Sigala, M. (2020) Tourism and COVID-19: impacts and implications for advancing and resetting industry and research. *Journal of Business Research* 117, 312–321.

Southwick, S., Bonanno, G., Masten, A., Panter-Brick, C. and Yehuda, R. (2014) Resilience definitions, theory, and challenges: interdisciplinary perspectives. *European Journal of Psychotraumatology* 5. Available at: https://doi.org/10.3402/ejpt.v5.25338 (accessed 21 November 2022).

Stevenson, J.R., Brown, C., Seville, E. and Vargo, J. (2018) Business recovery: an assessment framework. *Disasters* 42(3), 519–540.

United Nations World Tourism Organization (2020) Impact assessment of the COVID-19 outbreak on international tourism. Available at: https://www.unwto.org/impact-assessment-of-the-covid-19-outbreak-on-international-tourism (accessed 21 November 2022).

Walsh, C. and McCollum, W. (2020) Exploring the impact of individual resilience on entrepreneurial success. *Journal of Entrepreneurship & Organization Management* 9(5), 1–6.

Williams, T.A. and Shepherd, D.A. (2016) Victim entrepreneurs doing well by doing good: venture creation and well-being in the aftermath of a resource shock. *Journal of Business Venturing* 31(4), 365–387. Available at: https://doi.org/10.1016/j.jbusvent.2016.04.002 (accessed 21 November 2022).

World Travel and Tourism Council (2021) *Economic Impact Reports*.

Wu, T., Xu, J. and Wong, S. (2021) Crisis management research (1985–2020) in the hospitality and tourism industry: a review and research agenda. *Tourism Management* 85.

Yoe, C. (2012) *Primer on Risk Analysis: Decision Making Under Uncertainty*. CRC Press, Boca Raton, Florida.

Zhao, H. and Wibowo, A. (2021) Entrepreneurship resilience: Can psychological traits of entrepreneurial intention support overcoming entrepreneurial failure? *Frontiers in Psychology* 12(3753). Available at: https://doi.org/10.3389/fpsyg.2021.707803 (accessed 21 November 2022).

12 Digital Disruption and New Business Models

The accelerating and synergistic interaction between technology and tourism in recent times has brought fundamental changes in the industry and on our perceptions of its nature. The significance of crossing the new information threshold of universal, ubiquitous communications access has brought the entire tourism industry to the new levels of interactivity, propelling management by wire. (Buhalis and Law, 2008, p. 609)

Introduction

The business environment of the tourism industry is dynamic and constantly shifting due to a variety of factors such as changes in geopolitics, technology, consumer behaviour, and the economy. Many enterprises across the tourism service chain have seen their usual way of doing business challenged by these shifts in the marketplace. Thus, it is imperative for tourism enterprises to update and consider how they can better create, capture and disseminate value for their long-term viability and survival.

The business model is a core concept that helps enterprises to understand existing ways to do business and how to change these ways to benefit the tourism sector (Reinhold *et al.*, 2017). The concept comprehensively describes how tourism enterprises can create and capture value following a procedural input, throughput and output logic (Reinhold *et al.*, 2017).

In recent years, technology has played a major role in altering the business model of many tourism enterprises. Many tourism enterprises have had to redesign their business models to benefit from advancement in information technology (IT). When technology causes a paradigm shift in the way tourism enterprises do business, this is called a 'digital disruption'. This chapter will discuss the concept of business models and digital disruption, and explain recent technological advances that have caused digital disruption in tourism.

© Rob Hallak and Craig Lee 2023. *Managing Tourism Enterprises: Start-up, Growth and Resilience* (R. Hallak and C. Lee)
DOI: 10.1079/9781789249446.0012

Learning Outcomes

After completing this chapter, you should be able to:

- Define what a business model is and how it creates and captures value for tourism enterprises
- Understand the dynamic nature of business models
- Define what digital disruption is in the context of tourism
- Identify the recent technological advancements causing digital disruption in the tourism industry

What Is a Business Model?

A business model is a multifaceted concept that, at its core, seeks to provide a comprehensive understanding of ways of doing business and how value is captured from business activities (Reinhold *et al.*, 2017). While multiple definitions exist as to what a business model can be, most research tends to converge on a set of core principles coined in the strategy and entrepreneurship domain (Lecocq *et al.*, 2010; Martins *et al.*, 2015). According to Teece (2010, p. 172), a business model is a template for how an 'enterprise delivers value to customers, entices customers to pay for value, and converts those payments to profit'. Zott and Amit (2010) and Zott *et al.* (2011) refer to a business model as an interdependent system of activities that explains how an individual or collective actor creates and captures value.

An integrative consideration of activities to create and capture value is at the core of business model research. With a focus on activity systems, researchers pay equal attention to the value a customer derives from an offering and the value stakeholders on the supply side can capture by means of their capabilities and different revenue streams (Johnson *et al.*, 2008; Zott *et al.*, 2011). Thus, customer value, customer equity and shareholder value are considered alongside public value intentionally shared or unintentionally diffused to a general public or special interest groups (Meynhardt, 2009; Svejenova *et al.*, 2010; Demil and Lecocq, 2015).

Business models can be specified at different levels of analysis for individual or collective actors, although activity systems are frequently specified within a focal organization. The conceptualization of business models as systems of interdependent activities allows researchers to model value creation across these different levels and include diverse stakeholders that contribute in various ways. This is particularly important for many tourism enterprises as they co-produce value with customers and their actors coordinate multiple virtual co-production networks in ways that are not accounted for in traditional value chains (Beritelli *et al.*, 2014).

Enterprises might pursue more than one business model (Markides, 2013). Organizations are frequently made up of portfolios of business models (Sabatier *et al.*, 2010). Complex organizations may employ multiple business models for particular divisions and/or product lines depending on organizational structures and/or contexts at different moments (Benson-Rea *et al.*, 2013).

Business Models Change Over Time

Business models are not static templates. As business environments change, so business models change and innovate over time (Teece, 2010; Afuah, 2014). To respond to contemporary market forces, enterprises may update, switch, or evolve their business model(s) to reflect current strategic imperatives (Rauter *et al.*, 2015). Over time, new business models will emerge, successful business models will persist, while poor business models will be phased out (Coles *et al.*, 2017). Throughout such evolutionary cycles, the relative emphasis for value creation may vary, reflecting market conditions both experienced and anticipated when they are formulated (Afuah, 2014; Rauter *et al.*, 2015).

Digital Disruption and Tourism

Technology has played a significant role in revolutionizing the tourism industry and acts as a catalyst for new developments and increased competitiveness in tourism (Buhalis, 2000). Many tourism enterprises have had to redesign their business models to benefit from advancement in information technology (IT). When technology causes a paradigm shift in the way tourism enterprises do business, this is called a digital disruption. Some of the more recent technological advances that have caused digital disruption in tourism are the rise of online travel agencies (OTAs), online social networks (OSNs) and peer-to-peer systems.

Online travel agencies

Online travel agencies emerged from the growth and application of the internet and e-commerce. OTAs, or third-party booking websites, have transformed the tourism industry in terms of its distribution channels (Buhalis and Law, 2008). An OTA refers to a travel agency that primarily exists on digital channels (i.e. no physical location), such as a website, enabling customers to search, compare and book travel independently without the assistance of an agent.

Before and during the early days of the internet, when booking tourism products and services customers would have to engage in the services of a bricks-and-mortar travel agent (that typically charges a service fee) or book directly with the tourism enterprise (e.g., by telephone or the tourism enterprise's website). This meant a customer's choice was bound by how much knowledge the travel agent possessed, or customers would have to expend an inordinate amount of time and energy visiting multiple travel agents or calling multiple tourism enterprises to compare features and prices to find the best travel deal.

OTAs entered the market at a time when the internet was largely accessible to most of the world's population. Bolstered by the rapid uptake of smartphones, this confluence of technological factors offered customers the convenience and freedom to access information regarding tourism products and services without restrictions of time or geography. The popularity of OTAs is now evident in their dominant position within tourism's distribution channels. Statistics show that the Expedia Group and Booking Holdings (formerly Priceline) account for nearly two-thirds of OTA global gross bookings and have captured a 90% share of the US online travel market (Quinby, 2017). In Asia Pacific, OTAs have captured 70% of the overall online hotel-booking market (Hutchison, 2018).

To consolidate their dominant positions, Expedia and Booking spent a combined $10 billion in advertising in 2018 (HotelTechReport, 2021). This strong position has created high barriers to entry for new entrants as well as contributing to the demise of traditional bricks-and-mortar travel agencies. For example, Thomas Cook, known as one of the world's oldest travel agencies, collapsed in 2019. While there were several reasons for its demise, a contributing factor was the reduced necessity and relevance of travel agents to consumers during the internet age. The rise of OTAs shifted power in the industry where more informed customers no longer had to rely on the expertise of travel agencies to plan their travel (Martinez and Bunyan, 2019).

Online social networks

Online social networks (OSNs) refer to popular sites such as Facebook, Instagram, Twitter and LinkedIn, while also encompassing blogs, wikis, message boards, podcasts and vlogs (Thevenot, 2007). OSNs have substantially impacted the tourism industry, as travellers increasingly forgo traditional information sources (e.g., websites, travel agents and traditional advertising) and instead use OSNs to acquire travel-related information and share their personal experiences, comments, reviews, vacation suggestions and travel packages (Nusair et al., 2013). Consumers increasingly turn to OSNs as trusted sources of information because of several benefits: (i) it is easier to access up-to-date information through OSNs; (ii) information about tourism products and services is more substantial and incorporates different viewpoints; and (iii) there is usually the ability to find end-user evaluation metrics (e.g., ratings, aggregate scores, etc.) (Dedeoğlu et al., 2020).

One of the essential ways travellers use OSNs is the sharing of travel experiences. Posting texts, images and selfies from a destination during and after a trip is increasingly the norm. This information can shape the experiences of new travellers because they are able to use this information to plan their journeys. Ultimately, this practice influences a traveller's decision about which destination to go to and which tourism products and services to use while there (Chilembwe and Mweiwa, 2020).

From a tourism enterprise perspective, scanning user-generated content and managing/using OSNs has become a part of doing business. A deeper understanding of the factors that underline travel experience-sharing behaviour and how this information shapes decision making will assist tourism enterprises in making strategic decisions in using OSNs for marketing (Hawk *et al.*, 2019). Sites such as Tripadvisor and Booking.com allow consumers to write reviews, which enables a tourism enterprise to measure performance and respond to negative reviews as a service-recovery mechanism. Using social media sites such as Twitter, Facebook and Instagram are key tools tourism enterprises can use to develop e-word-of-mouth through posts, tweets and sharing pictures of products, services and experiences. Video sharing services such as YouTube offer alternative avenues for tourism enterprises to upload video content in a cost-effective way. OSN capabilities engage customers in collaborative conversations. Through OSN platforms, customers can be converted to 'fans', who tend to be more loyal and committed to the company and more willing to trust corporate advertising (Della Corte *et al.*, 2020).

Peer-to peer-systems

The 'sharing economy' phenomenon is now well established in the tourism marketplace. Information and communication technology has enabled the creation and sustenance of online peer communities (i.e. OSNs), and this increased connectivity allows people to share access to products among themselves (Tussyadiah and Pesonen, 2018). This phenomenon is known as 'collaborative consumption', where people coordinate the acquisition or distribution of resources for a fee or other compensation among themselves. Companies that have leveraged the sharing economy in their business model (such as Airbnb and Uber) have flourished in the marketplace. These companies developed scalable platforms allowing individuals to distribute and share excess capacity of accommodation and transportation with one another, bringing consumers together to better link supply and demand in hospitality and tourism (Tussyadiah and Pesonen, 2018).

Airbnb is arguably the most recognized facilitator of paid online peer-to-peer accommodation trading (Dolnicar, 2019). On one hand, the value proposition of Airbnb's business model for hosts includes identifying suitable guests, managing payment, marketing, inventory, risk and opportunities to socialize with guests and other hosts. On the other hand, the value proposition to guests is in identifying suitable accommodation spaces, reducing risk, and offering value-added accommodation experiences. Airbnb captures value by charging the host and guest a commission for facilitating each transaction between each other for use of the accommodation space (Dolnicar, 2019).

The rise of Airbnb has disrupted the traditional accommodation industry. Established short-term accommodation businesses now face a different kind of competition (Dolnicar, 2019). Paid online peer-to-peer accommodation can substitute some types of established commercial accommodation (Zervas *et al.*, 2017). For example, hotels in the lower price range are affected by Airbnb the most, especially if they cater to the leisure segment and offer limited services (Zervas *et al.*, 2017). Studies have shown that tourists feel that the risk that paid online peer-to-peer accommodation will replace hotels at the bottom of the star ranking is the highest, while luxury accommodation will be the least affected (Hajibaba and Dolnicar, 2017).

The success of the paid online peer-to-peer accommodation trading business model is starting to diffuse into other sectors of tourism. Airbnb has branched out to include paid online peer-to-peer tours as an extension of its business model, offering customers the opportunity to meet ordinary locals who act as local tour guides (airbnb.co.nz/s/experiences, accessed 21 November 2022). Eatwith provides paid peer-to-peer dining, allowing customers to book dining experiences with local hosts in their private homes or exclusive venues (eatwith.com). RVshare provides paid peer-to-peer motor-home renting, allowing customers to rent RVs from private owners who may have their own RVs sitting unused at home (rvshare.com). These new platforms thus have the potential to disrupt the food service, tour and transportation sectors, respectively.

Summary

This chapter has reviewed the business model concept and the role technology plays in revolutionizing the tourism industry through digital disruption. A business model refers to an interdependent system of activities that explains how an individual or collective actor creates and captures value. Business models are not static and evolve over time. New business models emerge, successful business models persist and become the industry norm, while poor business models will phase out. Technology has played significant roles in revolutionizing the tourism industry, causing enterprises to redesign their business models to benefit from advancements in IT. Some of the recent technological advances bringing about digital disruption in tourism are online travel agencies, online social networks and peer-to-peer systems.

Review Questions

1. Do some research and identify what the business models are for enterprises in different sectors of tourism (e.g., tour operators, accommodation providers, food service businesses, attractions, etc.).
2. What are some other examples of companies that have caused digital disruption in the tourism industry? How do these new companies create and capture value?
3. What technological changes in the industry do you think will cause digital disruption in the tourism industry in the future?

CABI case study: Solar technology lowers the noise level in the waters surrounding Bora Bora.

In island destinations such as Bora Bora, conventional motorized craft can be disturbing for visitors and destructive of the marine ecology. Solar power may be the way forward.

Authors: Silvia Marinescu, Julien Andre, Aurelie Lods, Yini Jiang and Jiatong Liu

Affiliation: Skema Business School

Origin: Written on the basis of material provided by David Czap, founder of Soel Yachts company.

© CAB International 2021

Background

In island destinations such as French Polynesia, boat transportation has a significant role to play in the way people and goods circulate. In many ways, it is as important as that of cars and planes. This is particularly the case on and around smaller islands.

The problem of conventional boat traffic

Bora Bora in French Polynesia is famous for its lagoon and coral reef. It is hugely attractive to tourists and the site of a number of luxury hotel complexes, including the Le Bora Bora resort. Boat traffic around the island is heavy, starting early in the morning. More than 50 outboard and diesel-powered excursion and shuttle boats operate around the island, consuming more than two million litres of imported fuel per year.

For an island that is chosen as a remote get away spot, the pollution caused by boats is an issue negatively impacting the image and the visitor experience. The biggest problem is noise. Guests in luxury accommodation can be woken by the roar of passing boats and, instead of fresh sea air, the smell of fuel. In Bora Bora, primary tourist activities are snorkelling and scuba diving for the discovery of marine life, and the island's reputation depends on its clear, untroubled water.

The impact on this marine life is considerable. Underwater noise created by motorized boat traffic is seriously damaging to ocean ecosystems. It can alter the behaviour of fish and other marine animals, reducing their ability to feed or to avoid predators and even to reproduce. Indirectly, this ecological damage is also a threat to humans: degrading the natural resources that many local communities depend on – in particular for fishing – and, in the longer term, impoverishing the biodiversity that is essential to their survival.

Fossil-fuel powered engines are also emitters of carbon dioxide (CO_2). Although emission levels from these islands are low compared with those of other nations, they are of huge symbolic importance. Climate change has a destructive impact on coral reefs and on the very survival of low-lying islands in the South Pacific. These island nations would be the first to benefit from effective action on CO_2 emissions and should therefore be setting the example.

Profile of Naval DC and Soel Yachts

The Dutch company Naval DC is a designer of propulsion systems and its sister-company Soel Yachts builds and commercializes solar-electric catamarans and yachts, fully energy-

Continued

CABI case study: continued.

autonomous and silent on the water. Soel Yachts was founded in 2011 by David Czap and Joep Koster, convinced from the outset that small, solar-powered electric boats – for personal or business use – could be better designed and could represent a significant share of the market.

The company offers a range of boats for different environments and purposes. This case study features, in particular, the SoelCat-12, suitable for high-end tourism destinations such as the island of Bora Bora.

The Story

The Okeanos Foundation and the Vaka Project

The Okeanos Foundation for the Sea is a non-governmental organization that defends the culture and rights of Pacific Islands and islanders, focusing in particular on their navigational heritage. By the early 2000s, the foundation was designing and starting construction of a large sailing catamaran of a design similar to that of the craft traditionally used by islanders on long journeys across the sea: the *Vaka Moana* (Boat of the Ocean). The foundation was keen to avoid any dependence on fossil fuels and approached Naval DC to design a solar propulsion system that could be used to complement the sails and, for example, for precise manoeuvres.

By 2011 and 2012, seven such catamarans had been built and the foundation organized an epic journey to cross and re-cross the Pacific, from New Zealand to Hawaii via the historic island nations of the Pacific. Labelled 'Te Mana o Te Moana' (Spirit of the Ocean), the aim of the project was to 'connect the Pacific islands with their traditions, their ocean and themselves', in the words of Dieter Paulmann of the Foundation. following the Vaka Moana project came the *Vaka Motu* (Boat for the Island) suitable for transport between nearby islands.

Soel Yachts then proposed the idea of a '*Vaka Hapua*' (Boat for the Lagoon) – a working title for the boat that was to be become the *SoelCat-12*. The Okeanos Foundation liked the concept, provided initial funding and worked with Naval DC and Soel Yachts to design and develop it.

The *SoelCat-12*: a new departure

In relation to the foundation's two 'Vakas', the *SoelCat-12* was a new departure. Like the *Vaka Moana* and *Vaka Motu*, it was to be autonomous in terms of propulsion and energy usage. However, the voyaging Vakas both used traditionally made sails supplemented by solar power – with panels on the deck. The *SoelCat-12*, on the other hand, would have no sail and would be propelled entirely by energy produced by its solar panels installed on the roof of the cabin.

The purpose and ambition would therefore be different. For the *Moana* and the *Motu*, the overriding goal was to show that 20th-century modes of ocean transport could be replaced by vessels using principles similar to those of the historic catamarans of the ocean travellers of the past. The *SoelCat-12*, on the other hand, would look forward in terms of technology. It would also be a passenger transport vessel with a much more evident commercial application than any of the voyaging Vakas.

Continued

CABI case study: continued.

As David Czap puts it:

... the frequent inner lagoon excursions and the transfers to and from water-bound resorts require a much more developed and high-tech solution to work. The vessel may take many trips a day, a decent speed is important and it would have to be a purely motor-powered vessel: sails as means of propulsion do not make sense for transfers within the lagoon. The operational profile requirements were therefore much more challenging than those of the voyaging catamarans.

Implementation at Bora Bora

A commercial partner was needed as a proof of practice. The Le Bora Bora resort, a high-end Tahitian hotel operator, expressed great interest and the first contract for delivery of *SoelCat-12*s was signed. The resort could see the interest in offering their guests responsible, noiseless transport – whether on arrival from the airport or on silent cruises and excursions within the lagoon. Infrastructure was added to the Le Bora Bora's jetty, in the form of higher-power AC outlets, so that the boats could be charged from the grid.

For the resort, a primary requirement is to use the *SoelCat-12* catamarans for excursions, such as for private charters, sunset cruises or special outings within the lagoon. These excursions are vastly more attractive if conducted on boats without the engine noise and exhaust smells of conventionally powered vessels.

A benefit of the *SoelCat 12* is that it can be easily beached anywhere. The boat continues to collect and store power through its large PV roof; and can therefore be used as an electric power source, whether out on the water or when the vessel is beached. As David puts it, the *SoelCat 12* 'can support an entire beach concert, in terms of electricity. The vessel can provide 15kVA of inverter power, so it acts as your noiseless generator, providing AC power via the inverters from the large propulsion battery banks.'

The other requirement is to transport guests to the airport or to other destinations, for example to other islands. The Le Bora Bora would be the only one to offer its guests a zero-emission shuttle service. As David says, 'airport transfers to the resort and back happen several times a day, the fuel and cost-saving potential is therefore huge when using Soel Yachts' electric vessels.'

At the time of writing, the resort has one *SoelCat 12* excursion vessel in operation and two *Soel Shuttle 14*'s as electric airport ferries – the latter in the process of delivery.

Initial feedback from guests has been extremely positive, but it is too early to fully assess the results of implementation in Bora Bora, as activity at the resort effectively ceased during the COVID pandemic. It would be interesting to produce a follow-up case study in a couple of years' time.

The Innovation

The *SoelCat-12* can travel long distances at speeds of up to 15 knots (28 km/hour), in full autonomy, i.e. not requiring any additional (motorized) means of propulsion. In explaining Soel Yachts innovations, David compares them to those of Tesla design in automobiles and says that they apply some of the same principles. In an electric boat, 'resorts want the equivalent of

Continued

what they already have using fossil-fuel power,' says David. This means that Soel Yachts need to constantly improve the speed and range of their boats, to match those of conventional craft.

An advantage of solar-powered propulsion systems is that the motor is, for the user, a single unit that can simply be replaced, which makes the maintenance of boats very quick and easy. In general, the yearly cost of ownership is only 20%, much lower than that of a conventionally ICE-powered vessel.

Soel Yachts vessels are equipped with smart technology for an integrated monitoring, alarm and control system and can be technically supported by a remote-assistance service.

The company has been nominated for several awards such as Connect4Climate Award, is acclaimed with the Solar Impulse Efficient Solution Label, and was a finalist of the Tourism for Tomorrow awards, run by the World Travel & Tourism Council.

Soel Yachts' products line

The five standard models available for sale today cover a large range of water tourism and transportation needs. Most are designed as solar electric yachts for commercial shuttle applications. All vessels come with high-quality furnishing and finish and the company offers service 'anywhere and whenever in the world, if support is needed with your boat'.

Most Soel Yachts products are available with solar electric, pure electric or hybrid electric propulsion systems, adaptable according to the use of each specific customer. The company can also make custom models for their clients, for those looking for something more specific.

Future Perspectives

The Le Bora Bora implementation can be seen as a pilot project and as a proof of value: a door that opens up other possibilities. The resort's holding company, Pearl Resorts of Tahiti, is considering extending the use of solar-powered crafts to other properties; and other resort chains are showing interest.

The project has also been followed with close interest by the government of French Polynesia. Institutional partners in French Polynesia have expressed interest in extending solar-powered transport to other locations and for other purposes, including public transport, if investment can be found.

It is likely that pressure will increase on governments and on the private sector, throughout the world, to afford greater protection to the fragile marine ecosystems along their coastlines and to act to limit the damage caused by vessels and small craft powered by fossil fuels. Boats like the *SoelCat 12* are currently designed for a limited, high-end market, but the technology will progress, costs will come down and versions for wider usage will most certainly become available.

References

Animals, U. (2021) Boat noise is distracting, confusing, and lethal to aquatic animals. *Undark Magazine*. Available at: <https://undark.org/2018/04/12/underwater-noise-pollution-aquatic-animals/> (accessed 1 April 2021).

Paulmann, D. (2021) The Okeanos Project. Available at: https://www.sprep.org/attachments/VirLib/Regional/okeanos-project-3.pdf (accessed 1 April 2021).

Soel Yachts (2021) Homepage. Available at: https://soelyachts.com/ (accessed 28 March 2021).

Soel Yachts (2021) *Soel Yachts Solar Electric Boats*. Soel Yachts.

Discussion Questions

1. Discuss how the potential future widespread adoption of solar-powered watercrafts may cause digital disruption for island destinations and island resorts.

2. What are the potential benefits that marine-based tourism enterprises can realize by adopting solar-powered watercraft technology?

3. Consider the barriers that may prevent tourism enterprises from adopting solar-powered watercraft technology.

References

Afuah, A. (2014) *Business Model Innovation: Concepts, Analysis, and Cases.* Routledge, New York.

Benson-Rea, M., Brodie, R. and Sima, H. (2013) The plurality of co-existing business models: investigating the complexity of value drivers. *Industrial Marketing Management* 42, 717–729. DOI: 10.1016/j.indmarman.2013.05.011.

Beritelli, P., Bieger, T. and Laesser, C. (2014) The new frontiers of destination management applying variable geometry as a function-based approach. *Journal of Travel Research* 53(4), 403–417. DOI: 10.1177/0047287513506298.

Buhalis, D. (2000) Information technology in tourism: past, present and future. *Tourism Recreation Research* 25(1), 41–58. DOI: 10.1080/02508281.2000.11014899.

Buhalis, D. and Law, R. (2008) Progress in information technology and tourism management: 20 years on and 10 years after the Internet – the state of eTourism research. *Tourism Management* 29(4), 609–623. DOI: 10.1016/j.tourman.2008.01.005.

Chilembwe, J.M. and Mweiwa, V.R. (2020) Peer influence mechanism behind travel experience sharing on social network sites. In: Ramos, C., Almeida, C. and Fernandes, P. (eds) *Handbook of Research on Social Media Applications for the Tourism and Hospitality Sector.* IGI Global, Hershey, Pennsylvania, pp. 17–35.

Coles, T., Warren, N., Borden, D.S. and Dinan, C. (2017) Business models among SMTEs: identifying attitudes to environmental costs and their implications for sustainable tourism. *Journal of Sustainable Tourism* 25(4), 471–488. DOI: 10.1080/09669582.2016.1221414.

Dedeoğlu B.B., Taheri B., Okumus F. and Gannon M. (2020) Understanding the importance that consumers attach to social media sharing (ISMS): scale development and validation. *Tourism Management* 76, 103954. DOI: 10.1016/j.tourman.2019.103954.

Della Corte, V., Umachandran, K., Sepe, F., Nevola, G. and Periasamy, A. (2020) Impacts of social media on business value and performance. In: Ramos, C., Almeida, C. and Fernandes, P. (eds) *Handbook of Research on Social Media Applications for the Tourism and Hospitality Sector.* IGI Global, Hershey, Pennsylvania, pp. 82–101.

Demil, B. and Lecocq, X. (2015) *Crafting an Innovative Business Model in an Established Company: The Role of Artifacts, Business Models and Modelling* (Advances in Strategic Management, Vol. 33). Emerald Group Publishing Limited, Bingley, UK, pp. 31–58. DOI: 10.1108/S0742-332220150000033003.

Dolnicar, S. (2019) A review of research into paid online peer-to-peer accommodation: launching the *Annals of Tourism Research* Curated Collection on peer-to-peer accommodation. *Annals of Tourism Research* 75, 248–264. DOI 10.1016/j.annals.2019.02.003.

Hajibaba, H. and Dolnicar, S. (2017) Substitutable by peer-to-peer accommodation networks? *Annals of Tourism Research* 666, 185–188. DOI: 10.1016/j.annals.2017.05.013.

Hawk, A.T., van den Eijnden, R.J.J.M., van Lissa, C.J. and ter Bogt, T.F.M. (2019) Narcissistic adolescents' attention-seeking following social rejection: links with social media disclosure, problematic social media use, and smartphone stress. *Computers in Human Behavior* 92, 65–75. DOI: 10.1016/j.chb.2018.10.032.

HotelTechReport (2021) *The Evolution of OTAs in the Hotel Industry*. Available at: https:// hoteltechreport.com/news/otas-problems (accessed 22 November 2021).

Hutchison, C. (2018) Spotlight on: Direct Bookings in Asia-Pacific. Available at: https://www. 4hoteliers.com/features/article/10992/ (accessed 22 November 2021).

Johnson, M.W., Christensen, C.M. and Kagermann, H. (2008) Reinventing your business model. *Harvard Business Review* 86(12), 50–59.

Lecocq, X., Demil, B. and Ventura, J. (2010) Business models as a research program in strategic management: an appraisal based on Lakatos. *Management* 13(4), 214–225. DOI: 10.3917/mana.134.0214.

Markides, C.C. (2013) Business model innovation: What can the ambidexterity literature teach us? *The Academy of Management Perspectives* 27(4), 313–323. DOI: 10.5465/ amp.2012.0172.

Martinez, G. and Bunyan, R. (2019) This American said he had to pay $2,400 to get home after travel company Thomas Cook collapsed. Available at: https://time.com/5683934/thomas-cook-travel-collapse/ (accessed 22 November 2021).

Martins, L.L., Rindova, V.P. and Greenbaum, B.E. (2015) Unlocking the hidden value of concepts: a cognitive approach to business model innovation. *Strategic Entrepreneurship Journal* 9(1), 99–117. DOI: 10.1002/sej.1191.

Meynhardt, T. (2009) Public value inside: What is public value creation? *International Journal of Public Administration* 32(3/4), 192–219. DOI: 10.1080/01900690902732632.

Nusair, K., Bilgihan, A., Okumus, F. and Cobanoglu, C. (2013) Generation Y travelers' commitment to online social network websites. *Tourism Management* 35, 13–22. DOI: 10.1016/j. tourman.2012.05.005.

Quinby, D. (2017) Hotels vs. the (OTA) world: what's really at stake as hotels take on distributors. Available at: https://www.phocuswright.com/Travel-Research/Research-Updates/2017/ Hotelsvs-the-OTA-World/ (accessed 22 November 2021).

Rauter, R., Jonker, J. and Baumgartner, R. (2015) Going one's own way: drivers in developing business models for sustainability. *Journal of Cleaner Production* 140, 144–154. DOI: 10.1016/j.jclepro.2015.04.104.

Reinhold, S., Zach, F.J. and Krizaj, D. (2017) Business models in tourism: a review and research agenda. *Tourism Review* 72(4), 462–482. DOI: 10.1108/TR-05-2017-0094.

Sabatier, V., Mangematin, V. and Rousselle, T. (2010) From recipe to dinner: business model portfolios in the European biopharmaceutical industry. *Long Range Planning* 43(2/3), 431–447. DOI: 10.1016/j.lrp.2010.02.001.

Svejenova, S., Planellas, M. and Vives, L. (2010) An individual business model in the making: a chef's quest for creative freedom. *Long Range Planning* 43(2/3), 408–430. DOI: 10.1016/j. lrp.2010.02.002.

Thevenot, G. (2007) Blogging as a social media. *Tourism and Hospitality Research* 7(3), 287–289. DOI: 10.1057/palgrave.thr.6050062.

Teece, D.J. (2010) Business models, business strategy and innovation. *Long Range Planning* 43(2/3), 172–194. DOI: 10.1016/j.lrp.2009.07.003.

Tussyadiah, I.P. and Pesonen, J. (2018) Drivers and barriers of peer-to-peer accommodation stay – an exploratory study with American and Finnish travellers. *Current Issues in Tourism* 21(6), 703–720. DOI: 10.1080/13683500.2016.1141180.

Zervas, G., Proserpio, D. and Byers, J.W. (2017) The rise of the sharing economy: estimating the impact of Airbnb on the hotel industry. *Journal of Marketing Research* 54(5), 687–705. DOI: 10.1509/jmr.15.0204.

Zott, C. and Amit, R. (2010) Business model design: an activity system perspective. *Long Range Planning* 43(2/3), 216–226. DOI: 10.1016/j.lrp.2009.07.004.

Zott, C., Amit, R. and Massa, L. (2011) The business model: recent developments and future research. *Journal of Management* 37(4), 1019–1042. DOI: 10.1177/0149206311406265.

13 Template 1: Marketing Planning and Strategy

Introduction

A marketing plan functions to identify the most promising business opportunities for an enterprise to penetrate, capture and maintain market share in the markets they operate in. It is a tool to ensure that the enterprise's marketing mix is aligned in a coordinated manner to achieve the enterprise's goals. A marketing plan generally consists of three sections. First, managers need to understand their own business and the business's goals. This includes their organization's vision and mission, products and services, current market share and demand, and the organization's strengths and weaknesses. Second, managers need to understand the market they are in or are seeking to capture. Third, managers need to be aware of competing businesses within the same market to understand how their enterprise is differentiated from the rest. Fourth, managers must determine the goals they wish to achieve from their enterprise's marketing activities. Finally, to put the marketing plan into action, managers must identify the strategy that will be used to achieve the marketing goals and draw up a marketing budget that will fund the marketing activities. This chapter provides a marketing plan template to help readers work their way through developing a marketing plan for their tourism enterprise.

About our Business

Business name:

Date registered:

State/country registered in:

Business structure:

© Rob Hallak and Craig Lee 2023. *Managing Tourism Enterprises: Start-up, Growth and Resilience* (R. Hallak and C. Lee)
DOI: 10.1079/9781789249446.0013

Contact details

Name:	
Phone:	
Email:	
Address:	

Online and social media details

Site	Address (URL)
Website	
Social media (*e.g., Facebook, etc.*)	
[*Insert type*]	
[*Insert type*]	

Marketing plan executive summary

(Complete this at the very end to summarize your marketing plan)

What the business does:

The target market:

The unique selling point:

The business's goals:

Vision

Think about what you want your business to accomplish in the long term. What are the ultimate goals? Use language that is passionate, emotive, and inspiring.

```
┌─────────────────────────────────────────────────────────┐
│                                                           │
│                                                           │
│                                                           │
│                                                           │
│                                                           │
└─────────────────────────────────────────────────────────┘
```

Mission

Think about the purpose of the business and what it does for your customers. Describe what you want to do, how you will do it, and why you do it.

```
┌─────────────────────────────────────────────────────────┐
│                                                           │
│                                                           │
│                                                           │
│                                                           │
│                                                           │
└─────────────────────────────────────────────────────────┘
```

Products and services

Describe what the business sells.

```
┌─────────────────────────────────────────────────────────┐
│                                                           │
│                                                           │
│                                                           │
│                                                           │
│                                                           │
└─────────────────────────────────────────────────────────┘
```

Expected demand

Estimate the number of products and services customers are expected to buy over the next year.

```
┌─────────────────────────────────────────────────────────┐
│                                                           │
│                                                           │
│                                                           │
│                                                           │
│                                                           │
└─────────────────────────────────────────────────────────┘
```

SWOT analysis

Strengths [*What's good about your business?*]	Weaknesses [*What's not so good about your business?*]

Opportunities
[*What external factors can you take
    advantage of?*]
	Threats
	[*What external factors can cause problems
	    for you?*]

Response to weaknesses and threats

How will you deal with your weaknesses and external threats?

About the Market

Current market research

What research have you done about the market you are selling to? What do you know about the market you are selling to?

The market problem

What is (are) the market problem(s) that you aim to solve for customers?

Our solution

How will your business solve the market problem? What is the unique selling point that will help you succeed in the market?

Our target market

Who are the customers you want to sell your products to? What are their defining characteristics?

The sales targets

How much of your products and services do you plan to sell over the next year?

Competitors

Describe the main competitors who are operating in your desired market. List as many as relevant or necessary.

Business name	Strengths	Weaknesses	How we'll be different

Goals, Actions and Responsibilities

Goals for next year

	Actions to achieve goal	Due date for completion	Person(s) responsible
Goal 1 – [Enter goal here]	[Action] [Action] [Action] [Action]		
Goal 2 – [Enter goal here]			
Goal 3 – [Enter goal here]			
Goal 4 – [Enter goal here]			

Goals for next [X] years

	Actions to achieve goal	Due date for completion	Person(s) responsible
Goal 1 – [Enter goal here]	[Action] [Action] [Action] [Action]		
Goal 2 – [Enter goal here]			
Goal 3 – [Enter goal here]			
Goal 4 – [Enter goal here]			

Marketing Strategy

Product or service

Product/service	Description	Unique selling point

Price

Product/service	Price	Price structure

Place: distribution channels

Channel	Used for	Details

Promotion and advertising

Activity	Channel	Details	Estimated cost	Dates

People

List existing or required sales and marketing staff

Job title	Name	Responsibilities

Marketing budget

Item	Jan	Feb	Mar	Apr	May	Jun	Jul	Aug	Sep	Oct	Nov	Dec
Marketing/ promotion												
Marketing agency												
Television												
Radio												
Print												
Online												
Social media												

Continued

Continued.

Item	Jan	Feb	Mar	Apr	May	Jun	Jul	Aug	Sep	Oct	Nov	Dec
Search engine optimization												
Branding and artwork												
[*Add lines as necessary*]												
Marketing/ promotion TOTAL												

Administration

	Jan	Feb	Mar	Apr	May	Jun	Jul	Aug	Sep	Oct	Nov	Dec
Research												
Travel												
Postage												
Administration												
Incidentals												
[*Add lines as necessary*]												
Administration TOTAL												

Marketing costs TOTAL												

14 Template 2: Feasibility Analysis

Feasibility Analysis

A feasibility analysis is a tool used for assessing the viability and feasibility of a business idea, and if it is in fact an opportunity that is worth pursuing. By evaluating organizational capabilities, assessing the market needs and financial viability, and identifying potential pitfalls, entrepreneurs can make informed decision's based on the forecasted success of the business project (Box 14.1). A feasibility analysis is developed through data and information about the opportunity and the organization. It is often used as the precursor to the business plan.

A feasibility analysis allows a business to address where and how it will operate, its competition, possible hurdles, and the funding needed to begin. Figure 14.1 shows four major components of a feasibility analysis. A feasibility analysis should be conducted at the early stages of business startup.

Market Feasibility

With a market feasibility analysis, a company can define its competitors and quantify target customers by analysing their interest in the product or service

---

Box 14.1. Benefits of a feasibility analysis.

- Assessing the potential of a proposed business idea
- Determining the potential market for the proposed product or service
- Evaluating demand for the product or service
- Assessing the financial viability of the proposed product or service
- Understanding characteristics of potential customers such as spending patterns, demographics
- Determining potential competitors.

© Rob Hallak and Craig Lee 2023. *Managing Tourism Enterprises: Start-up, Growth and Resilience* (R. Hallak and C. Lee)
DOI: 10.1079/9781789249446.0014

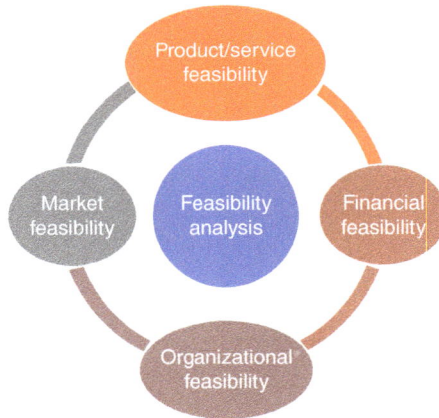

Figure 14.1. Components of a feasibility analysis. (Source: developed by the authors.)

offered to the target market. A market can be defined in terms of structure, size, trends, growth and sales potential. This information allows the entrepreneur to better position their business in competing for market share.

Financial feasibility analysis

Financial feasibility analysis evaluates the revenues and costs of a project, and its cashflow projections. The financial analysis may typically include:

- A 12-month profit-and-loss projection
- A three- or four-year profit-and-loss projection
- A cashflow projection
- A projected balance sheet
- A break-even calculation.

The financial analysis should estimate the sales revenue and expenditure that a business expects to generate and incur. A number of different formulas and methods are available for calculating sales estimates (see Chapter 9). You can use industry or association data to estimate the sales of your potential new business.

Product/service feasibility

Product feasibility assesses the viability of the proposed product or service. It should include an evaluation of costs to be incurred in product/service development and a description of the product's benefits to the customers.

Organizational feasibility analysis

Organizational feasibility aims to evaluate the management's ability and sufficiency of resources to develop an idea to product development and to the market. The company should consider management team interests and execution capability. Typical measures of management ability include assessing their entrepreneurial passion for the idea along with the required skills, expertise, educational background and professional experience. Small-business managers should be honest in their self-assessment when ranking these areas.

How to Write a Feasibility Analysis Report

A basic feasibility analysis report is highlighted below.

A: Executive summary

Here, describe basic business information and summarize the information relating to the business concept that is to be considered. Provide a general idea about the business, product, customers and market trends.

B: Management structure

List key management personnel, their positions and prior experience. (Is the management team's prior experience adequate for success in the company and the industry?)

Management personnel	Position	Prior experience

C: Feasibility analysis

Product analysis

Describe the products or services offered and how they fit into a target market (attractiveness, desirability and potential).

[ ]

Does the product solve a problem or fill a market gap?

[ ]

Market feasibility analysis

This section should include an evaluation of the proposed marketing plan (see Chapter 13).
Does the marketing plan include information on market attractiveness?

[ ]

Does the marketing plan include information on the industry that the company is competing in?

[ ]

Does the plan describe the timetable for implementation of the marketing plan?

```



```

Are the necessary resources available to implement it?

```



```

Does the plan state why the company's marketing efforts are unique or different from competitors' efforts?

```



```

Does the plan include a competitive analysis (perform a SWOT analysis in comparison with your competitors)?

Strength [what you do best]	Opportunity [potential opportunities in the industry]
• • • •	
Weakness [challenges within your business]	Threats [potential threats in the industry]
• • •	

Financial feasibility analysis

This section should include an evaluation of the projected financial plan.

What sources of financing will be considered (debt versus equity)? Perform a cost–benefit analysis.

Source	Benefits	Costs
Equity (e.g., share capital)		
Debt (e.g., loan, hire purchase)		

Prepare monthly (or annual) cashflow projection statement listing key assumptions.

Company name: Cashflow statement for the month ending:	
Cashflow from operating activities • Sales revenue • Salary and wages • Rent • Utilities	
Cashflow from investing activities • Purchase of equipment	
Cashflow from financing activities • Loans • Share capital	

Prepare projected financial statements (income statement; balance sheet).

An income statement summarizes the income and expenses of the business as shown below:

Company name: Income statement for the period ending:	
Sales revenue	XXX
Cost of goods sold (COGS)	(XX)
Gross profit	**XXX**
Expenses	
Rent	(XX)

Continued

Continued.

Salaries/wages	(XX)
Utilities	(XX)
Operating profit (before interest)	**XXX**
Interest expense	(XX)
Net Profit	**XXX**

A balance sheet shows a business's financial position at a specified date.

Company name: Balance sheet at:	
ASSETS	
Cash at bank	
Trade debtors	
Equipment	
Inventory	
Total assets	
Liabilities	
Loans	
Owner's equity	
Retained earnings	
Total liabilities & equity	

Organizational capabilities analysis

This section should include an evaluation of the organization's capabilities: Is the proposed business concept strategically relevant?

Are there sufficient financial and non-financial resources to pursue the proposed idea?

Is it a sole entrepreneur or team that has the business idea (management's capabilities)?

```
┌──────────────────────────────────────────────────────────────┐
│                                                                │
│                                                                │
│                                                                │
└──────────────────────────────────────────────────────────────┘
```

Does the entrepreneur or team understand the market in which the company operates?

```
┌──────────────────────────────────────────────────────────────┐
│                                                                │
│                                                                │
│                                                                │
└──────────────────────────────────────────────────────────────┘
```

D: Conclusion

```
┌──────────────────────────────────────────────────────────────┐
│                                                                │
│                                                                │
│                                                                │
└──────────────────────────────────────────────────────────────┘
```

E: Appendix

Source:adaptedfromhttps://www.smallbusiness.wa.gov.au/templates-tools-guides; https://www.dlgsc.wa.gov.au/department/publications/publication/feasibility-study-guide (accessed 22 November 2022).

Index

CABI – who we are and what we do

This book is published by CABI, an international not-for-profit organisation that improves people's lives worldwide by providing information and applying scientific expertise to solve problems in agriculture and the environment

CABI is also a global publisher producing key scientific publications, including world renowned databases, as well as compendia, books, ebooks and full text electronic resources. We publish content in a wide range of subject areas including: agriculture and crop science / animal and veterinary sciences / ecology and conservation / environmental science / horticulture and plant sciences / human health, food science and nutrition / international development / leisure and tourism

The profits from CABI's publishing activities enable us to work with farming communities around the world, supporting them as they battle with poor soil, invasive species and pests and diseases, to improve their livelihoods and help provide food for an ever growing population.

CABI is an international intergovernmental organisation, and we gratefully acknowledge the core financial support from our member countries (and lead agencies) including:

Discover more

To read more about CABI's work, please visit: www.cabi.org

Browse our books at: www.cabi.org/bookshop,
or explore our online products at: www.cabi.org/publishing-products

Interested in writing for CABI? Find our author guidelines here:
www.cabi.org/publishing-products/information-for-authors/

www.ingramcontent.com/pod-product-compliance
Lightning Source LLC
Chambersburg PA
CBHW050105220326
41598CB00043B/7391